The Divine New Order And The Dawn Of The First Stage Of Light And Life

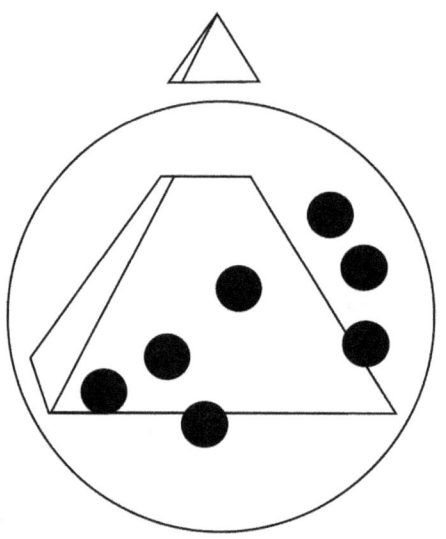

*The 7 sector locations on Urantia/Earth
and the coming of the New Jerusalem
(an architectural world)*

The Divine New Order
And The Dawn Of
The First Stage
Of Light And Life

THIRD EDITION

Gabriel of Urantia /TaliasVan of Tora

Global Community Communications Publishing
A Division of Global Change Multi-Media
Tubac / Tumacácori, Arizona, USA

© 2013 Global Community Communications Alliance

First Edition 1992
Second Edition 1995

All rights reserved. No part of this book shall be reproduced, translated, or transmitted in any form or by any means, electronic, mechanical, magnetic, photographic including photocopying, recording, or by any information storage and retrieval system, without prior written permission of Global Community Communications Publishing. No patent liability is assumed with respect to the use of the information contained herein. Although every precaution has been taken in the preparation of this book, the publisher and author assume no responsibility for errors or omissions. Neither is any liability assumed for damages resulting from the use of the information contained herein.

ISBN 978-1-937919-05-4

Global Community Communications Publishing
P.O. Box 1613, Tubac, Arizona 85646 USA
(520) 603-9932
e-mail: info@gccpublishing.org
www.gccpublishing.org

ABOUT THE PAPER USED IN THIS BOOK

According to our printer, Lightning Source, Inc. has 'Chain of Custody' certifications with The Sustainable Forestry Initiative, The Forest Stewardship Council, and The Programme for the Endorsement of Forest Certification that permit Lightning Source to complete the custody chain from the forest, to the mill, to the paper, to the finished books. No papers used in Lightning Source books are sourced from endangered old growth forests, forests of exceptional conservation value, or the Amazon Basin.

CONTENTS

Prologue ix

A Note From The Editors x

Introduction xii

Statement By The Author xiii

Foreword xv

Regarding Information On Past Lives xix

Preface xxii

PART I — In The Beginning

Chapter 1   Coming Back To Earth (Urantia) —
Reflections *(A Fictional Possible Scenario)* 1

Chapter 2   Solutions—The Beginning 5

Chapter 3   My First Experience With Survival
Preparation And My Reverend And
Monastery Days 8

Chapter 4   Wandering In The Southwest And Mexico 13

Chapter 5   Return To Where The Three Rivers Meet 19

Chapter 6   Los Angeles: The Diseased Heartbeat Of
America And The Planet 27

Chapter 7   The Superstition Mountains —
Recontact Is Made 38

Chapter 8   Meeting The Midwayers 46

Chapter 9   The Pleiadian Connection 55

Chapter 10   Complements And Pair Units Begin
              To Come.. 69

Chapter 11   Commitment To Global Change And
              Service To Humankind 76

Chapter 12   Inappropriate Relationships 79

Chapter 13   Universal Origin.. 89

Chapter 14   Leaving The Old Behind, Changing
              Your Name, And The Cost Of
              Becoming A Change Agent 93

Chapter 15   The Protected Areas 97

Chapter 16   The Adjudication Moving Into
              Full Swing 103

Chapter 17   The Chaos Begins
              (A Fictional Possible Scenario) 112

Chapter 18   A New Garden Of Eden 122

Chapter 19   The Closing Of The Door Of The Ark
              — The Physics Of Rebellion Leads To
              Total Chaos
              (A Fictional Possible Scenario) 127

Chapter 20   The Heavenly Court
              (A Fictional Possible Scenario) 135

Chapter 21   Coming Back — The Landing And
              The Divine Administration
              (A Fictional Possible Scenario) 140

PART II — The Continuing Story

Chapter 22   What Will My Friends Say This Time?
             When The Saints Come Marching In......... 146

Chapter 23   The Return Of The Cosmic Family............ 155

Chapter 24   The Bright And Morning Star Walks In,
             And The Realities Of Community Life
             At The First Planetary Sacred Home 171

Chapter 25   Meeting Wallace Black Elk....................... 178

Chapter 26   "If You See Me, You See The Father"....... 183

Chapter 27   A Visit To Titus (One Of The Oldest
             Living Hopi Elders) At The Time Of
             His Death... 187

PART III — Moving Into The New Millennium

Chapter 28   The Continuing Story: Van Or Nod? 200

Chapter 29   The Interuniversal Marriage Triads And
             Trimonads. The Intrauniversal Birth Of
             Ellanora Of Panoptia................................... 213

Chapter 30   Divine Administration Moving Into The
             Twenty-First Century And The State Of
             The Planet 220

Chapter 31   Moving From Sedona To Another
             First Planetary Sacred Home Area............. 225

Chapter 32   Miracle of Miracles:
             630 N. 4th Avenue, Tucson
             A House Of Destiny With God And Me.... 237

Reference Notes 243

Glossary 249

About The Audio Fusion Material Complement 289

About The Audio Fusion Process 292

Concerning Van — TaliasVan.. 294

Service Ministry Experience.. 296

Photo Gallery 301

Acknowledgments 345

About The CosmoArtists And Their Art In This Book .. 346

Global Community Communications Alliance
    And Divine Administration 351

Seminars, Workshops & Internships 358

Alliance Organizations 360

PROLOGUE

Dear Readers,

I started to write *The Divine New Order* in 1989 when I was forty-three years old. I wrote parts of the later chapters when I was in my fifties, with a much more experienced pen. If I would have written the book in 1989 from my now 67-year-old perspective, it would be different and much more experienced, but I think you will gain much insight from even my 43-year-old perspective as written in 1989, as already celestial beings were working with me and Paladin was beginning to fuse with me.

1989 was a significant year, as the Bright and Morning Star and Machiventa Melchizedek both spoke through me, so evidently they thought that I was mature enough, as I had already been a minister for twenty years, working with the poor and disenfranchised in many parts of the inner cities of the United States.

Although I wrote this book myself, without them coming through and writing it, every time they fused with me they of course left me with a much more spiritualized mind and higher perception of reality that I had to deal with within my own soul.

Gabriel of Urantia/TaliasVan of Tora
Summer 2013

A NOTE FROM THE EDITORS

Since the initial publishing of this book in 1992, new chapters have been added and content updated as changes and developments occurred with the unfolding of Global Community Communications Alliance and members of Divine Administration.

Additionally, some of the terms and concepts originally introduced have been expanded upon, as our human understanding of the information presented by Celestial Overcontrol continues to unfold. Below are some explanations to that effect.

In August 2000 a change in nomenclature for certain geographic areas was adopted. At that time the then "one-mile radius" became the "First Radius," the "three-mile radius" became the "Second Radius," and the "five-mile radius" became the "Third Radius." The change was based on the speculation of the growth of auhter energy in the future. For example, the First Radius could grow to be a one-hundred-mile radius rather than the initial one-mile. These radii are not necessarily perfectly circular in diameter but rather are more ameba-like in shape, with valleys and peaks reaching out in various directions simultaneously, as the use of the word radius in these instances refers to "an area of influence."

The term "change point" used throughout *The Cosmic Family* volumes can have multiple meanings. The reader should understand that there is not just one particular moment, day, or year that is the change point, but rather the change point unfolds over time, with many smaller change points (both personal and collective) contributing to the ultimate shift of the planet into the first stage of light and life. For further clarification see the June 24, 2001 Global Change Teaching by Niánn Emerson Chase titled "The Change Point: The Continuing Saga," available from Global Community Communications Publishing.

Please note that some paragraphs within a chapter as well as some entire chapters are potential (and hence currently "fictional") scenarios, and they are printed in a different font (just like this paragraph is here, as example).

Summer 2013
The Editors

INTRODUCTION

In a time-and-space continuum what is has already been and what will be has been already. Ecclesiastes says the same thing—that which is has been already, and that which will be has already been, for God seeks what has passed by.

Many of the prophecies that have been written in the Bible and other sacred writings have come to pass or are happening now as you read this book. Some of this book is prophecy. The outcome is in your hands.

The purpose of this book is to introduce new cosmic concepts in words that will be part of one planetary language in the understanding of spiritual reality in which our planet, Urantia/Earth, will be operating when the final change point and shift from the third dimension to fourth dimension (and above) occurs, and a new divine administration of Christ Michael (Jesus) is appropriated. It is not a government of arms or military power. We do not teach rule by force of arms, nor do we stock weapons of any kind. We teach only the Fatherhood of God and the brother-/sisterhood of humankind. We teach love and spiritual ascension.

With these thoughts, let this be the hope for our planet: that after individuals read this book they can join in the Great Celebration once they, as individuals, have practiced the answers.

In April 1989 and again on May 5, 2001 an upstepping of the adjudication of the Bright and Morning Star versus Lucifer occurred, and Urantia (Earth) will experience more weather changes, destructive storms, deadly virus bacteria, and global warming as a product of the Universe Mother Spirit's need of purification. The planet must be cleansed so that a Divine New Order can be implemented on the earth. On December 21, 2012 another upstepping of the adjudication occurred.

STATEMENT BY THE AUTHOR

This book is an attempt to explain how I became a Continuing Fifth Epochal Revelation vessel or audio fusion material complement and is based on certain events in my life.[1] As strange as it may seem, all events are true with the exception of future events that have a high probability of happening according to our Celestial Overseers who told me of them.

We—as individuals and as a mass consciousness—must determine our own future and the future of our planet. The names of certain people were changed for privacy; others were left, as I wanted to honor them because I respect and love them.

As to the return of certain cosmic family members who were with us and left, it is our sincere hope that they will one day rejoin us. I projected their return and future destinies according to what Celestial Overcontrol said were possibilities. The choice, however, is theirs.

Join the

SPIRITUALUTION[SM]

movement —

a spiritual revolution/
an international movement
spiritualution.org

Color prints of original art available for sale.
Call CosmoArt Studio (520) 490-2554 or email info@cosmoart.org

FOREWORD

I dedicate this book to Niánn, TiyiEndea, SanSkritA (once known as Alcyone/DeleVin), DeleVan (once known as Sonta-an), Amadon, and Ellanora DesManae, who are my immediate nuclear family, and to all my cosmic family—some of whom are with us now, and some who will be coming. I personally feel that the truest evidence of the reality of all the experiences mentioned in this book, and in particular of our celestial friends, are my immediate family. This is because before I knew them, I first met Sky Hawk (now known as Paladin), whom you will come to know in this book, and it was he who told me that Niánn, SanSkritA (first known as Alcyone), DeleVan (first known as Sonta-an), and Amadon would be coming. To me they are the best evidence of the reality that God is, indeed, with me.

Further in this book is the detailed account of how I met Niánn. All I would like to say here is that shortly after Sky Hawk (Paladin) told me she was coming, she appeared in my life. I was also told that I would first have a daughter and that I would name her Alcyone, because she was coming from the Pleiades and Alcyone is the brightest star in the Pleiades. My guides also said that I was to have a boy and that I should name him Amadon. When Niánn was three months pregnant with the twin girls, I felt intuitively that she was having more than one child. I naturally thought that it must be Alcyone and Amadon.

In Pittsburgh Niánn had her first doctor's checkup, and I asked the doctor to check thoroughly for twins. The doctor said, "No way! There is only one head and only one heartbeat." We decided against an ultrasound because we felt it could be dangerous to the baby. When we arrived back in Arizona I asked the midwives to check thoroughly because I thought Niánn was having twins. They did not detect another heartbeat. During the following months, a very capable midwife and her assistant checked for twins. No evidence of twins was discovered.

The Divine New Order . . .

During this time, neither Paladin nor our midwayers would confirm that Niánn was having twins, but Paladin would joke with me about it, and at times would admit she was having twins and then retract his statement, saying that we needed to discover this for ourselves. In the ninth month of Niánn's pregnancy, we went for a final medical checkup with a physician in Cottonwood, Arizona, and I asked the doctor to please check for twins. After he checked, he chuckled and said that Niánn was too small and he could only find one head and one heartbeat.

When I went into the circles of other clairvoyants, some would touch Niánn's stomach and say, "It's a boy!" Since Paladin did tell me that Alcyone was coming, I was ready to explode with frustration. When I would ask Paladin if it was a boy, he would assure me that it was Alcyone but never would confirm the twins.

On December 3, 1988, at home in Prescott, Arizona, Alcyone was born. A few moments later it was determined that a second baby was indeed inside. Now, even I was surprised, since I had accepted everyone else's opinions. When they said another heartbeat was there I thought, "Well, there's Amadon!" Niánn had to be taken to the hospital to have a cesarean. If I had not been so shocked with the second baby and had allowed myself time to tune in, I probably would have realized it was a female essence. Since Paladin had told me we would also have a boy, I thought for sure it was Amadon.

After sitting in the waiting room for no more than twenty minutes (they would not let me in the operating room), the nurse came in and told me that the second baby was born and was fine. I said, "I know, it's a boy!" She said, with a knowing smile on her face, "Go see—your second baby is with your first girl baby." I literally ran to the nursery where several nurses were gathered. They had me put on a white jacket (it should have been a straitjacket), and I told them, "I know, it's a boy!" They giggled and said, "Go see." So I went in and saw two tags, "Girl A" and "Girl B." By now I believed completely in the validity of the guides, so I turned around and said to them, "Where is my son?" I was quite shocked when they said it was another girl. Did I have a bone to pick with Paladin and company!

We could hardly wait until Niánn was better so that we could contact our unseen friends and guides again. For a while I refused to name our second daughter. Finally, after a couple of days, Niánn suggested that I name her Sonta-an, after one of the first two humans on Urantia—a set of twins—because of the meaning of the name, Sonta-an, which means "loved by Mother." (My daughter Sonta-an was not the original soul of the first human Sonta-an.) Both Niánn and I sensed a strong Universe Mother Spirit essence in this newborn baby, and Niánn liked the meaning of Sonta-an. She was an extra blessing that had been kept secret from me until the very end!

Paladin later explained that our daughter Sonta-an came from Celano of the Pleiades where her cosmic name had been DeleVan. It was also revealed to us that the genetic seed of the godly mother "Vin" was in our other twin, whose cosmic name on the planet Alcyone was DeleVin. I had lost my first daughter Dina at the age of seven, but now I had two little girls—a double gift from God. Celestial Overcontrol gave more information about both of these children, which would not be appropriate in the context of this Foreword.

It is the family of "Van"—TaliasVan of Tora (which on Urantia became Taliesen of Camelot legend)—that was then able to bring through the Dell Erba ("of the grass of the earth" in Italian) of Urantia—Amadon. When Niánn told me ten months later that she was pregnant again, I was angry and shocked. I wondered why God could not wait a few years. But Niánn's childbearing years were slipping away. She had all three of these children in her forties. Immediately I asked Paladin, "Is this Amadon?" Naturally Paladin would dangle the carrot. I was determined that if this were a girl I would never allow myself to be used as an interplanetary receiver again!

When the Bright and Morning Star fused with me for three days in 1989 before Amadon was born, the Bright and Morning Star made a clear statement that Niánn was pregnant with a male child and that it was the Amadon of *The URANTIA Book*.

Again, some clairvoyants would touch Niánn's belly and declare, "It's a girl!" This would upset me greatly! On July 17, 1990, at our home in Prescott, Arizona, a very male child, Amadon, was born.

Paladin said that Niánn should not have any more children and predicted that another complement would be coming in the future to birth Ellanora of Panoptia. In 1996 Niánn and I changed the nature of our relationship and lived no longer as "husband and wife" though we were still spiritual and administrative complements and of course the best of friends. Soon after, TiyiEndea came into our lives as my wife and gave birth to Ellanora on October 11, 1998. (A more detailed account of this can be found in Chapter 29.)

To these children, my highest spiritual complement, Niánn, my present wife of many years, TiyiEndea, and all the children of my past and all earthly Urantia relatives and cosmic family, I dedicate this book. Someday, all of us will be together, of one mind and purpose, all sharing our talents for one true community—the Father-/Motherhood of God and the brother-/sisterhood of humankind.

REGARDING INFORMATION ON PAST LIVES

The following transmission was given by Paladin to Gabriel of Urantia/TaliasVan of Tora when he asked Celestial Overcontrol if he could take his and Niánn's past lives out of *The Divine New Order And The Dawn Of The First Stage Of Light And Life* and *The Cosmic Family* volumes. This is Paladin's response, given on January 30, 2013.

The Divine New Order *is a testimony of who you, TaliasVan, are. From the very beginning we in Celestial Overcontrol asked you to put the beginning information about your past lives in, because if you knew the persecution you would receive in the years to come, you would not have put it in your book and would have not listened to us telling you to put it in.*

Now, twenty-three years later, you want to take out all of the work you have put in and all the proof that you have found over the years that we, Overcontrol, have sent your way as verification of who you were, to help verify your past lives to all who have spiritual eyes to see. For those who do not have spiritual eyes, they will never see who you are. This information you put in is for those with eyes on a true spiritual journey.

This will not be a popular book until the final change point, and then every Urantian and every starseed (who have the grace from God to stay on Urantia) will be "dying" to read this book, you might say. So no, we do not want you to take the past lives out. Just correct the book as to who we said certain people of the first century weren't and why, and you have started this with the paper by the Bright and Morning Star on both recent dates he came to Urantia and spoke to you, which immediately follows in this book.

We have spared you from not putting all your lives in this book. That would really be too much for the beginning truth seeker of course, who does not really understand the soul of Van and your purpose and influence on Urantia throughout history. People will either believe or they will not. So you should not be ashamed of the truth of who you are, nor Niánn of the truth of who she is, or the truth of who others were of the cosmic family.

Both of you must walk in that actualization that has been given to you, and you can walk in dignity and honor before God for all that which you have accomplished in all of those lives. You have suffered and sacrificed much in many lifetimes and have earned to know this information and for others to know who you are.

The Divine New Order is indeed a bibliography of the history of Van and Niánn and the cosmic family. It is not a history of the common folk, of the common man. It is the history of a supermortal (and his highest spiritual complement, Niánn), who have incarnated by choice on Urantia. That is you and Niánn. You have nothing to be ashamed of.

Regarding those who will choose to pick these truths apart and pick apart the so-called prophecies that have not come to pass—the attack of China on the United States or what some would consider to be wrong timing of change points—it has been corrected as much as can be. The pieces of the prophetic puzzle concerning nations, including the true Israel and Judah, are going to come to pass. Nothing that is written can be 100% accurate, as I talked about the other day during the transmission. And individuals who pick and choose what they believe will not see the truth because they do not want to recognize the truth. They are so far from the truth in their own lives and in their own walk with God.

So go forward with courage, with pride in who you were and in who you are, and do not try to be something that others want you to be. Do not belittle yourselves. Do not try to conform to their smallness. You are both very large souls, and you cannot be put into the small boxes of their limited viewpoints, so stop trying.

January 30, 2013

Paladin,
Chief of Finaliters

for the bringing together of all Destiny Reservists (Cosmic starseed and Urantian), in and through the Melchizedek government on Urantia, as ordained by Christ Michael in and through His firstborn son the Bright and Morning Star of Nebadon, in which I, Paladin, serve for the common good of all in Satania. May this adjudication (between the Bright and Morning Star versus Lucifer) end and the first stage of light and life begin on Urantia. For the common good of all in the system of Satania and on Urantia, Spiritualution^{SM} — Justice to the People.

PREFACE

A "must-read" before you read the book!

Information Given By
The Bright And Morning Star
About The Apostles

at a Board of Directors meeting
of Global Community Communications Alliance
on October 31, 2012 and January 27, 2013

Bringing transmissions through the Pre-Level-One Audio Fusion Material Complement—for many very important reasons (which we will explain)—Celestial Overcontrol allowed four apostles and two writers of the New Testament to be incorrectly identified as the personages of the first century until Overcontrol could reveal the complete truth, as we are doing now, many years later. These inaccuracies were in people identification but not in the technical transmissions.

Continuing Fifth Epochal Revelation and most of its content is correct. In identifying repersonalizations, sometimes people were sons and daughters of the actual apostles. Sometimes they were not sons and daughters but other people, of the first century or even other lives, who the soul of Van met in his many repersonalizations.

In the Second Edition of The Divine New Order *it stated that Celestial Overcontrol has led Gabriel of Urantia/TaliasVan of Tora to believe certain past life identifications incorrectly. For instance, in the Second Edition on page 143 Gabriel of Urantia states, "In Prescott a son of the Apostle Thomas, Mikal, was with us. Mikal is my cosmic son. Celestial Overcontrol led me to believe that Mikal was Thomas the Apostle."*

Preface

So the regathering of the apostles may not happen before the return of Christ Michael. Some who have died will rematerialize, not repersonalize. Those alive still are approximately Gabriel of Urantia's age or older. Presently in Divine Administration are only Peter and Andrew, the first two leaders of the apostles of the first century.

The 12 Apostles

1. *Peter is Gabriel of Urantia/TaliasVan of Tora.*

2. *Andrew is Tarenta.*

3. *Rafeel was not really James. Homosexuality can never be in the character of an apostle. It is not a normal behavior. It is a broken and imbalanced circuitry of the Trinity. Rafeel was in the first century. He knew Jesus. Now he knows who he was for sure (he is deceased); he was told on the mansion worlds. He was Ptolemy, the head librarian of the Alexandrian Library in Egypt. This is why he received his Master's in Library Science in this life.*

4. *Nod in the first century was one of the most dio-powerful Pharisees, not John the apostle. We, Overcontrol, had to appease Nod in his narcissistic arrogance or he would not have stayed in Divine Administration. He wanted to be equal with Gabriel of Urantia/TaliasVan of Tora, at least having the status as an apostle of the first century. When Nod first came to Divine Administration, he actually signed his name "Machiventa Melchizedek." He also thought he was Van, and Rafeel was Amadon.*

Overcontrol wanted Nod to stay in Divine Administration because he was the greatest mirror of dio reality that we could have used to write everything there is to know about a dio soul in iniquity. Most of the whole of The Cosmic Family, Volume I *was able to be brought through by Gabriel/TaliasVan observing Nod's* sophisticated dio iniquity and allowing us then to write about it in technical transmissions. This was also true in lesser degrees of others who we said were apostles but were not.

The real apostle John (whose birth name was David Strickland), Gabriel/TaliasVan met in Tucson, Arizona, in 1977, and John helped the then Reverend Tony Delevin start his first nonprofit organization, Son Light Ministries. Everything about this man was a miracle in Gabriel/TaliasVan's life, even his meeting the apostle John of the first century. One day David was driving down 4th Avenue in Tucson, always in tune with God and in constant prayer. God told him to stop the car at 630 North 4th Avenue, get out and knock on the door. At that time, Rev. Delevin had no signs out saying this house was a ministry. That is how they met.

David worked for the Department of Economic Security as the head Director in the pre-trial release program, which led to Rev. Delevin working with him to release prisoners from the county jail and young Gabriel/TaliasVan becoming a volunteer chaplain of Pima County Sheriff's Department.

Gabriel/TaliasVan was by David/John's deathbed, who died of cancer of the liver. The last words that David/John said to Gabriel, as he pulled Gabriel's ear to his mouth, were "Keep the faith." Gabriel/TaliasVan had no idea that David was John until this day January 27, 2013, right after I, the Bright and Morning Star, came to him at 6:06 A.M.

5. Phillip was not Phillip. He was the son of Phillip and was met in Sedona but never aligned with Divine Administration. He was married to the same Israeli wife who he was married to in his first life. In this life she identified herself as Jewish.

6. Nathaniel is who Overcontrol said he was, the Nathaniel of the first century. He was named Nathan in this life, found Divine

Administration, connected with The URANTIA Book *and* The Cosmic Family *volumes, came to Divine Administration but then defaulted and has never returned, mostly because of his inappropriate attachments in his life in the third dimension and the fact that he has a hard time coming under authority.*

We give the deficiencies that all the apostles had in The URANTIA Book, *as opposed to the Catholic Church making them saints who were flawless. After the resurrection and reception of the Spirit of Truth, many of the apostles, who died martyrs, became great men of faith. Others, who were starseed, had to continually return to Urantia to walk in a higher faith.*

7. *Matthew was not the apostle Matthew, but also had to be told he was or he would not stay in Divine Administration. He has defaulted because he thinks he should be an Elder or mandated higher and was not willing enough to do the inner work to get there. [See Chapter 31]*

8. *Thomas knew he was Thomas and guessed he was Thomas but never aligned with Divine Administration, because he was still the doubting Thomas he was 2,000 years ago and could not totally give his life to God.*

9. & 10. *One of the Alpheus twins was met in Sedona by Gabriel/TaliasVan and Niánn Emerson Chase and others of Divine Administration but defaulted in his destiny and never aligned to Divine Administration. He is a second-time Urantian. He did find* The URANTIA Book *before meeting anyone in Divine Administration but did not come to Continuing Fifth Epochal Revelation (*The Cosmic Family *volumes).*

11. *Simon Zelotes is unrevealed.*

12. Judas Iscariot was met in Sedona. Gabriel/TaliasVan actually met him in California when Gabriel was young, in his thirties. But even then Judas was jealous of Gabriel when Judas was in his fifties, which probably started back in the first century. Judas eventually found himself coming to Sedona and Divine Administration but never aligned totally. Divine Administration helped him find property in nearby Cottonwood, but he should have helped build the Global Communications Center with the money he paid for that property. (He had a heart attack and died just a few short years later.) I, the Bright and Morning Star, told Judas who he was in the first century, but he did not accept it and denied that this was the Bright and Morning Star talking to him.

Other Significant Souls Of The First Century

Stephen, whose cosmic name was Camden, was Stephen of the first century. He did come to The URANTIA Book before meeting anyone in Divine Administration, then came to Divine Administration and was made a Liaison Minister in the early stages but defaulted, not to return. He too could not come under authority.

John Mark was not John Mark of the first century. But Gabriel/TaliasVan has met the real John Mark, yet to be revealed to Gabriel. This fallen fourth-order starseed defaulted, running off with an older starseed woman from Divine Administration.

Mark—the writer of the Book of Mark in the New Testament—has not been revealed.

The soul who we identified as Luke—who was met in Sedona and was a doctor and Urantia Book reader before he came to Divine Administration—was not Luke of the first century and not the son of Luke the apostle. He never came to Continuing Fifth Epochal Revelation and defaulted because he could not come under authority. The real Luke is a second-time Urantian, but Celestial

Preface

Overcontrol has not revealed him yet or if Gabriel/TaliasVan has met him.

The real first-century Paul (whose birth name was Fred Brown) was a man that Gabriel/TaliasVan met in Tucson, Arizona in 1977 at a place called The Prayer House, in which Fred and his wife were directors of. He was a Minister. So was his wife, whose name was Dorothy. People called her Dot. Fred and Dot would later marry Tony Delevin and his then wife Jerri at The Prayer House.

The serendipity here was Fred was from Pittsburgh and knew Gabriel's biological father, Anthony Delevin. They were in the CCC camps (Civilian Conservation Corps—a government program that hired young men to build government projects) together and the Marines, and both worked in the steel mill. Paul/Fred was also a defender of the then-young Reverend Tony Delevin in Tucson from fundamentalists and those who came against Reverend Delevin's Son Light Ministries.

The real Paul/Fred and his wife went to Israel and Jerusalem as a twentieth-century missionary, and he was made (by the Christian elders) the head elder of all Christian missions in Jerusalem. He was a twentieth-century apostle in Jerusalem, like he was in the first century.

Gabriel lost contact with Fred and his wife for more than thirty years, and when Gabriel returned to Tucson five years ago, he continually thought about them for several years and decided to look up Fred and his wife. So one day in Tucson with Niánn, TiyiEndea, and Amadon, Gabriel found them, still alive in their eighties. They met for the final time, because Fred and his wife passed on to the other side just a few months after Gabriel reconnected with them again.

These two souls, particularly the real first-century Paul, were significant souls in the life of Gabriel, both in this life and in the first century. In this life Paul/Fred was a man's man and a man among men, as he was in the first century.

Cathedral Rock and Oak Creek in Sedona, Arizona, headquarters of Divine Administration for 20 years, and where we still have Spirit Steps Tours and Cathedral Rock Lodge & Retreat Center and beautiful sacred homes and other commercial properties for lease or sale.

Color prints of original art available for sale.
Call CosmoArt Studio (520) 490-2554 or email info@cosmoart.org

Part I

In The Beginning

The first twenty-one chapters—1 through 21—were the First Edition of this book, which the author began writing in 1989.

CHAPTER 1

Coming Back To Earth (Urantia)—Reflections
A Possible Future Scenario

We were at last coming back to Urantia, the earth we so loved. Looking at outer space through the view screen in the interplanetary transport craft called The Star of Bethlehem, I marveled at the awesome sight of our planet. It looked so lonely and blue. Maybe I felt the essence of the Universe Mother Spirit within and her cries to be repopulated by her children. The earth was about to give birth to a new seed, and we were the offspring.

As we got closer I could see that the blue was the clear water, void of pollution now after three years of cleansing. We could actually see the rivers cut through the newly formed land areas. It was hard to believe that America looked so different. What used to be California and up through Washington was now ocean, and a tremendous land mass extended from Hawaii to a few miles from what formerly was the California coast. We were told how many survivors were left on the earth, and we knew that the majority of them would be insane.

Had we not been evacuated, I too, along with so many others who were in the spaceship with me now, would have also gone off the deep end. I could never have imagined just how terrible the destruction of our planet would be. First, man destroyed man in the final conventional wars that led to nuclear holocaust, and then the earth answered back with her own cleansing. Earthquakes, volcanic eruptions, and storms—on a scale previously unknown to man—were a daily experience on every continent, killing millions and leaving doom and despair with every soul upon the planet.

After the great plate shift that took the west coast of the United States, we wondered for one solid year if we were going to be killed by another great earth shift or by the bands of half insane and starved Americans, or by

Chinese invaders who had forgotten that war no longer mattered and that individual survival was the name of the game. Both governments had long since fallen, and so had just about every other form of governmental rule on the planet. It was survival of the fittest, and each man was at war with the other. Food, water, and shelter were the goal of every soul upon Urantia. All human decency seemed to be lost to the animal instinct of taking what you needed from those who were weaker. They had not yet learned the true heart of man with a personal God as ruler.

The first time I ever heard about the final change point/Christian tribulation/New Age prophecies/Hopi's Fifth World—call it what you may—was in 1971 in a place called Pittsburgh Power and Light Company, a Christian coffee house run by a Presbyterian minister who seemed to believe what he was saying. He quoted from the Book of Revelation, Chapter 16 of the Bible, reading the entire passage. I was going through my first divorce, which included not only a wife but also a two-year-old daughter—so the pain over the loss of two people I deeply loved was great. Somehow this minister's words rang true, as if coming from a higher authority.

> 1 And I heard a great voice out of the temple, saying to the seven angels, Go your ways, and pour out the vials of the wrath of God upon the earth.
> 2 And the first went, and poured out his vial upon the earth; and there fell a noisome and grievous sore upon the men which had the mark of the beast, and upon them which worshiped his image.
> 3 And the second angel poured out his vial upon the sea; and it became as the blood of a dead man; and every living soul died in the sea.
> 4 And the third angel poured out his vial upon the rivers and fountains of waters; and they became blood.

5 And I heard the angel of the waters say, Thou art righteous, O Lord, which art, and wast, and shalt be, because thou hast judged thus.
6 For they have shed the blood of saints and prophets, and thou hast given them blood to drink; for they are worthy.
7 And I heard another out of the altar say, Even so, Lord God, Almighty, true and righteous are thy judgments.
8 And the fourth angel poured out his vial upon the sun; and power was given unto him to scorch men with fire.
9 And men were scorched with great heat, and blasphemed the name of God, which hath power over these plagues; and they repented not to give Him glory.
10 And the fifth angel poured out his vial upon the seat of the beast; and his kingdom was full of darkness; and they gnawed their tongues for pain,
11 And blasphemed the God of heaven because of their pains and their sores, and repented not of their deeds.
12 And the sixth angel poured out his vial upon the great river Euphrates; and the water thereof was dried up, that the way of the kings of the east might be prepared.
13 And I saw three unclean spirits like frogs come out of the mouth of the dragon, and out of the mouth of the beast, and out of the mouth of the false prophet.
14 For they are the spirits of devils, working miracles, which go forth unto the kings of the earth and of the whole world, to gather them to the battle of that great day of God Almighty.
15 Behold, I come as a thief. Blessed is he that watches, and keepeth his garments, lest he walk naked, and they see his shame.
16 And he gathered them together into a place called in the Hebrew tongue Armageddon.
17 And the seventh angel poured out his vial into the air; and there came a great voice out of the temple of heaven, from the throne, saying, It is done.
18 And there were voices, and thunders, and lightnings; and there was a great earthquake, such as was not since men were upon the earth, so mighty an earthquake, and so great.

> 19 And the great city was divided into three parts, and the cities of the nations fell: and great Babylon came in remembrance before God, to give unto her the cup of the wine of the fierceness of his wrath.
> 20 And every island fled away, and the mountains were not found.
> 21 And there fell upon men a great hail out of heaven, every stone about the weight of a talent: and men blasphemed God because of the plague of the hail, for the plague thereof was exceedingly great.

After hearing the minister read this Bible passage and give a short sermon about being right with God before these things took place, I gained my first insight into the reality of those who believed and those who did not, by mingling with the crowd. I had come to believe in the existence of a personal God, for surely God was carrying me and my sufferings through this divorce. My simple honest thoughts were that if these words were true, the only way to survive was to be on good terms with my Creator. My thoughts were interrupted by people commenting on the sermon. "You don't believe any of that nonsense do you?" "I don't know," was my reply, "but I think I would act as though it could be a possibility and conduct my life with survival in mind." Whatever that meant, I honestly did not know.

Little did I realize that for the next thirty years I would spend my life preparing for survival into the twenty-first century, as did many others who had listened. At that time in 1971, I had no idea that I would become an interplanetary communicator with celestial beings, some who were at one time from the Pleiades and architectural worlds closer to our planet they called Urantia. I did not know that I would eventually also be a voice for interdimensional nonmaterial beings from many systems and worlds. These nonmaterial beings from other worlds, including former mortals called finaliters, all believed that Urantia was about to be destroyed and replaced by a Divine New Order of reality they called the fourth dimension. I had much to learn, and my journey was about to begin.

CHAPTER 2

Solutions—The Beginning

I began reading all that I could get my hands on concerning the scientific view of the physical state of our planet due to pollution and greed. Maybe my new-found spiritual beliefs had no factual reality in regard to a dying planet. So many who believed that man would never use nuclear weapons to the magnitude of destroying our planet seemed to be oblivious to the other dangers of environmental concern. I began to see Earth as a much more complex, interdependent system in which oceans, atmosphere, and all life affect one another, and all help to shape the face of the planet. Among my new discoveries at that time were:

- The world's worst ecological disaster had made human life possible. Tiny organisms from the ocean had dumped huge amounts of toxic waste into the environment. It had killed most of the life on the planet. That deadly substance was our precious oxygen.

- Sudden shifts in currents, such as the Gulf Stream, can trigger mini ice ages that last for centuries.

- Tiny fluctuations in the earth's orbit, augmented by changes in the proportions of atmospheric gases, control the advance and retreat of glaciers.

- Deforestation is endangering all life on this planet.

- Global warming is occurring due to increasing carbon dioxide in the atmosphere, which brings about multiple changes.

- Depletion of the earth's protective ozone shield is endangering us.

- Overpopulation is creating and will continue to cause major problems, such as food shortage, deforestation, global warming, etc.
- An increase in earthquakes and erupting volcanoes had begun, due to the shifting of the plates in the earth.
- There is a possibility of the earth shifting on its axis.
- Powerful energies are now coming to the earth as a result of the configuration and alignment of seven planets in our system of Satania.
- Diseases could increase to epidemic proportions, due to the pollution in all areas of life, including pollution of the mind.

After any serious study of the problems of ecological concern on a global scale, even the most optimistic view of the chances for survival of our planet a few decades into the twenty-first century would have to change. Many scientists gave our planet until 2020 before it would be depleted of all natural resources. Some were more optimistic and said that we could heal all of our environmental ills by 2040, giving us another twenty years to get our act together as a united people of this earth.

One thing was clear to me: God did not have to use His wrath to destroy the earth, as some religious sects believed. We were on our way out due to our own actions, regardless of what God did. I did not see God as so wrathful anyway. If anything, I was sure He and all the helpers of the grand universe were trying their best to buy us more time by doing their invisible healing of Mother Nature. I would later learn that they could only do so much, and time would run out. The clock had been set by our universe government when our planet and thirty-six others in our local system of Satania fell in the Lucifer Rebellion.

Chapter 2

I had to laugh at those who thought just recycling would get the job done. They should have started that at the beginning of the industrial revolution. Some experts said pollution prevention via controlling methods of production was the key. Others said that energy conservation was the answer. In production technology we ran into a case of political problems. In our economic system, that decision process was totally under private control. A corporation's legal obligation was not to the nation or the planet but to its stockholders—to the profit motive.

Motive! This was a word that jumped out at me and struck my heart. Did any wrong motive of mine add to the pollution of our planet? In what way did I compromise with materialistic values? Perhaps I already was a part of the problem. Perhaps I too was part of the profit motive. How would life go if my every decision was for the good of my neighbor and not just for myself? I, the individual, would have to change in order for the corporation, made up of individuals, to change. The mass consciousness as a whole had to be enlightened as to the real problem, and the problem was the individuals, each one of them, Mr. and Mrs. Planetary Citizen.

It took me many years before I discovered we all were actually universe citizens with a cosmic responsibility for the life on other planets as well as our own. The nationalistic view of many Americans was at the "still-swinging-in-the-trees" stage.

CHAPTER 3

My First Experience With Survival Preparation And My Reverend And Monastery Days

In 1973, about a year after my search for solutions began, I found myself in a young Christian minister's basement in Pittsburgh, my hometown. He and his group were preparing physically and spiritually for the coming tribulation on the planet. I listened intently as they told me their view of the coming food shortage in our country, while I stuffed my face with a big sandwich prepared by one of his parishioners. I was already about fifteen pounds overweight at the time, so a food shortage did not seem to be a problem! How could America ever have that problem? I thought this young man was overly concerned. (Years later I found myself praying that God would send people who knew how to store and preserve food to our Divine New Order community.)

This young man intrigued me; he and his wife, both under thirty, were intelligent and wise. They had a following of about forty individuals, mostly under thirty also. I was impressed at the organization of their food storage and the different foods they had available plus outdoor survival equipment. They were post-tribulationists, believing that as true Christians they would have to go through the years of war, earth changes, and famine that would be upcoming. They said that Christians with an ear to hear from God, like Joseph in Egypt of old, should prepare themselves for seven years of hardship. I admired them, at the time, for what that young minister, his wife, and community were able to accomplish. There was enough food to feed several hundred people for several months and fewer people for several years. I did not then realize what tremendous organization it required to get people with various talents to join to accomplish such a task.

It was seven years later in Tucson, Arizona—where I had become an ordained Christian nondenominational minister—

that I truly began to see the real problems of trying to live in godly reality. Many of the ministers of the city had decided to come together to pray for the "peace of the city." Although I was very unorthodox by their standards, I was asked to participate. I think they invited me because I sent many new converts to their churches, but they knew I did not believe in many of their doctrines or interpretations of the Bible.

On Sundays, all of these ministers preached sermons of the coming doom to our planet, the tribulation period. They all believed in what they called the rapture, the taking away of all true believers. They strongly disagreed about exactly when they would be taken. Even though we came together to pray for the peace of the city (we should have prayed for peace on the planet), it did not take long before war broke out among them. They were divided over three streams of thought.

First, the pre-tribulationists believed that Jesus would come back riding a white horse with all the angels in heaven and call up or rapture the true Christians before the tribulation—"Christian" according to their definition of course. For example, one minister would even pick a date in a few years and draw national attention when his date did not come to pass, claiming, "God would not allow His children to suffer the kind of pains that were coming; famine and plague would not touch His bride." I guess he considered all the starving children in Bangladesh at that time as the devil's children. I thought this man was quite off track, but many believed this doctrine.

Second were the mid-tribulationists. One such minister explained, "Many so-called Christians are lukewarm today; they will have to endure some suffering to wake them up. I believe that three years will transpire into the tribulation period before the rapture takes place. I have the word of God in the book of Revelation to back me up." I hated it when they would use that line. So many of these men used the Bible to confirm their individual doctrines, which contradicted each other. You would think they would have realized that the truth probably existed somewhere in between!

Unlike the young minister in Pittsburgh, these self-righteous men spoke about the stupidity of storing food, gasoline, and water. God would supply all of their needs. "If God dropped manna from the sky for the ancient Israelites, why not for us?" one of the pre-tribulationist ministers said. I wondered why God was not dropping bread down now in many parts of the world. Surely tribulation was happening to many people on the planet right then. The bread that was being sent to them was being destroyed by their own governments or confiscated before many of the starving ever saw it, but this particular minister did seem to possess some kind of unusual faith, however misconstrued.

Third were the post-tribulationists. One of these men told me, "True Christians will be needed on the earth to help all those suffering souls to find God during those seven years of testing. Right before the final destruction of the earth, God will take away the elect."

My thoughts were, "Isn't life itself enough of a test? If those men who are supposed to be praying for peace are part of God's elect, then God help us." I saw more peace among street gangs back in my old neighborhood in Pittsburgh than I saw there, but I felt I should not express that among these self-righteous men.

There was so much I had to learn at that point in my life, and I knew it. But I did not feel that the other men who called themselves ministers really believed that they had more to learn about what is out there in the grand universe, about the God they so smugly defined, and about those trillions of worlds and creatures beyond our planet.

A few years after that prayer meeting, my second wife left me for a close friend and was remarried. It must have been very difficult for her to live with such a moody person who in many ways was so needy of her. I do not blame her for leaving. I know now she was a past-life complement. Back then I was grief stricken. I became very sick as emotionally I could not take losing her. I developed tumors in my voice box and doctors told me I would never sing again. I experienced six months of soul-searching and physical pain where I talked with a "frog" in my voice. I was finally healed when I knew I had to let her go, as well as my desire to sing for God.

I decided to look for the solutions to the world's problems in another religious and intellectual avenue. I considered becoming a Catholic priest—you might say I was going back to my roots. This surely would make my mother, who never thought I was part of the establishment, very happy. Of course I had not listened to my parents since I was about seventeen years old. In the next several years while in two Benedictine monasteries and a Third Order Franciscan community—all in the southwestern United States—I found out that there were many happy Catholic mothers and many unhappy priests.

In these monasteries there were many enlightening subjects talked about by the brothers at night. But men will be men, and unfortunately masturbation, fornication, and masturbation again were also discussed. So I decided to hang out with the older priests for more meaningful conversations since I wanted to learn about some possible way to solve the world's problems.

In one of these monasteries, a few of these priests told me that I was an old soul. They secretly believed in reincarnation but never voiced their beliefs openly. They were environmentally conscious and had an elaborate solar-energy setup that heated the majority of the monastery, which had been designed by one of the priests.

The abbot of this particular monastery served as the voice of God for more than one hundred and fifty men and women who stayed in this experimental monastery with priests, nuns, and lay people. He felt threatened by anyone who questioned his views. He was really into saving the world by educating people about Jungian psychology and placing everybody into personality types. If we understood each other better, maybe we would cooperate with each other more. I'm OK, you're OK. This sounded great, but in the six months I was there I never heard him listening to anybody else's suggestions. He also spoke about the inequality between men and women and how women needed to be liberated. But at the same time no woman in the community was given any authority or allowed to teach.

In contrast, the Franciscan community was run by a strong wife of a not-so-strong husband. (I would later learn that many males and females on this planet have an imbalance in the Father and Mother circuits of the personality, but I will get into that later.) If we wanted to go to the bathroom we had better ask her permission. They were environmentally aware, and they were decent people, but the imbalance there was too much for me. I prayed that her husband would assume his proper role in the home as a Father-circuited leader and protector.

From one of the tests that the abbot had everybody take[1], it was discovered that I was an INFP with ENFP[2] tendencies and gifts, a very unusual personality, which is true of only 1% of the world's population. I was told I was very intuitive, had extra-sensory perception, liked my solitude, and was a natural born leader. That was a shock to me. I always thought I was slightly different, but this was a little too much. He said that the majority of people like me either choose a monastic life to escape the world or they become rich and famous so that they can escape the world through their wealth.

Because so much of what he said about me was true, I knew that he was onto something supernatural, something beyond man's explanation. It was true that I was able to foreknow certain things, particularly deaths in my family and certain world events. But I never thought it was special nor had I tried to develop it. This was my first understanding of my paranormal gifts.

One day, the abbot asked me to leave the monastery in the dead of winter in a snowstorm because I questioned one of his decisions. I then decided to try Native American spirituality. I went to visit the Native American tribes in Arizona.

CHAPTER 4

Wandering In The Southwest And Mexico

In November 1984 I left the Benedictine monastery feeling very much like a lost soul. I did not know where I belonged or to what spiritual reality I could devote my life. I even doubted the existence of God at times.

One place I had wanted to go to for a new vision quest was San Carlos Lake, on the San Carlos Apache Reservation where I had spent many weekends when I lived in Tucson. When I arrived I tried to find the spot where my ex-wife, Jerri, and I had spent so many happy times, but for some reason I could not find it even though I was determined to do so. I quieted myself down long enough to begin to pray and felt at the time that the reason I could not find it was because God was telling me that this woman was out of my life and I had to begin anew.

As I settled in at another location I became very poetically inspired and began to write. I also felt, as I had at certain times in previous years, another presence near me, unseen, yet real. This experience frightened me at first, so I broke camp and went into a reservation village and had a cup of Indian coffee. It was strong enough to put hair on my chest. Little did I know that just a few hundred yards away was the very home in which Niánn Emerson Chase grew up as a young girl, and I would meet her in a few years.

I did not know it then, but I was led back to the reservation and within the radius of where Niánn had actually grown up so that my vibrations could connect once again with hers. Though Niánn was at that time teaching in Globe, Arizona, about twenty-five miles away from the village, her essence and life force was still very much a part of the area to which I had been led. It also enabled my contact with the midwayers, although I did not know what a midwayer was at that time, and they did not come into my reality strong enough to tell me who they were. After I had my coffee, I felt a new peace about what I had experienced down by the lake and decided to go back out there and tune in again. I called upon Jesus.

A few moments later I again felt a presence nearby, and I heard for the first time within me a name that was Gentle Eagle. I did not know then, nor was the communication from the midwayers clear enough, but that had been my Apache name, and I had lived on this reservation approximately one hundred and eighty-six years ago with Niánn. They also gave me a song that is called "Makes You Wonder Why," the first line of which says, "It takes a lifetime to learn how to live and then you die; makes you wonder why." Because of the song, I began thinking of life and death and the afterlife.

My Christian background made it very difficult for me to think of myself as having lived before. I erased the whole experience as grieving for my second wife and again became frightened of those voices and immediately left the area, thinking that I was missing her so much that I was hallucinating. What I did not realize was that it was the result of an increasing opening of my circuits by the midwayers and a beginning into the Continuing Fifth Epochal Revelation. At the time I had not even come to the first part of this revelation, *The URANTIA Book.*

I decided to visit the Hopi reservation. My second wife and I had never been there together so I did not think I would be affected as much with memories of her. I was greatly impressed by the Hopi religion and traditions. It was the first time that I had heard about the Hopi Fifth World. Later I would understand the concept to be the complement of the Fifth Epochal Revelation. Some Hopi believe that many of their ancestors came from the stars and had intermarried with their race. They also believe that the time of purification on the planet is near and that in the earth changes to come, a new dimensional shift is about to occur.

I spent many nights camping out, and in the quiet of the nights I somehow felt an inner desire to stay there and become a part of the Hopi. But I also felt another inner calling to move on,

Chapter 4

so I headed toward the Grand Canyon and discovered that there was an Indian tribe, called the Havasupai, living at the bottom of the canyon.

I took the mule ride four miles down to the floor of the canyon only to discover that the Havasupai were miles away, so I came right back up, sore butt and all. I acquired more factual information and again went to find the Havasupai Indians. I decided to hike down the canyon this time, which took approximately four hours one way. As I neared the bottom I noticed what seemed to be an oasis with green fields, trees, and Indian children riding bareback on horses. Strangely, I felt as if I were one of them and could not understand those feelings.

After talking to several Indian children, I discovered that some as old as fourteen had never been to the top of the canyon. In talking to a number of the elders, I was told that they believed very strongly in extraterrestrial spacecrafts, but they would not tell me why. This increased my interest even more. Although I did not look like the average white man, I cannot blame them for not opening up to me completely. They told me they were afraid their lifestyle would be greatly changed by the plans of the white man for certain mines and other factories around that area.

I have never seen such clear water as I saw at the bottom of the Grand Canyon. The steady stream of tourists was beginning to destroy their environment. I would become very saddened years later, approximately 1991, when I discovered that this clear water was now polluted by the very mines they had feared years earlier.

I decided I wanted to see Mexico again. I had been there several times with a Mexican chaplain by the name of José. As I drove to the Nogales border I remembered an incident we had once, while trying to cross over. We would always have to give the border guards a few dollars because we were carrying food and other supplies to the poor people and prisoners, as it was expected in order to get across.

This particular time, there were guards that José did not know, and they wanted more money. They came around the van to talk to me because they saw I was an American. I was wearing a black turtleneck and had a big cross hanging around my neck. They thought I was a priest. They called me Padre, excused themselves and let us pass. José and I laughed all the way to Hermosillo where we intended to visit the inmates at the state prison. We learned there had just been a riot and the Commandant advised us not to go in for fear of our lives, as several had been killed, including an American.

It is strange how brave one can become when one knows that God is with you, so I decided to do the same "Father Tony" routine I had done back at the border. As we walked through the open courtyard where all the prisoners (murderers mixed with burglars) were free to roam, they all called me Padre and wanted to be blessed. At that time I did not know about my past lives, but I felt that I was a Catholic priest. I did not feel I was pretending and maybe that is why it came off so well. In later years, I found out in some of the personal transmissions by Paladin, I had been a Franciscan in the thirteenth century, as well as a Benedictine in a later century.

After leaving the prison, I decided to go to the beach in Guaymas where José and I had been before. Though I was quite alone, I felt no fear. I sensed the reality of unseen beings with me. As I sat on the beach and reflected, I remembered another incident in my life with José on this beach when he and I had lost a whole day. We thought we were returning to Tucson on Sunday evening, but it was already Monday evening! My second wife was quite distraught and wondered why we had not called. All I could remember was that I was anxious to be with her and did not realize I had lost a whole day. It is still a blank, which is why I am now going to let Paladin come in and tell exactly what happened.

As Gabriel was sitting on the Guaymas beach trying to find his soul, we had decided to take it! It is quite true that he has little or no memory of this except for the lost time period. However, if he had, he would no longer want to remain on Urantia (Earth) and deal with the mundane realities of living and more specifically trying to bring souls into Continuing Fifth Epochal Revelation. We used projector beams that broke down the molecular structure much like those seen on the starship Enterprise in Star Trek.

Present upon the smaller disc-shaped craft—the size of which was approximately one acre—was myself, Paladin, and Gabriel's grandmother, who was allowed this extraordinary visit from the first mansion world on which she is presently located, having been a first-time Urantian.[1] She appeared young, approximately twenty-nine, and quite beautiful. Gabriel was awakened to see her and recognized her completely. That is why he had thoughts of her as being young throughout the years afterwards. If he remembers, it was her he asked for when I came to him as Sky Hawk years later in the Arizona mountains.

She spoke to him as a grandmother and told him some things about the future. First she told him of his soon-to-come divorce from his second wife whom he loved very much and she knew the emotional pain would almost kill him. She asked him to be strong of faith and to persevere through the various afflictions in body that his emotional state would cause him. Then she told him that Christ Michael indeed had a wonderful plan for him and that he was to become "Gabriel"—a name that he would take when he was again in the presence of her former life force back in Pittsburgh, Pennsylvania.

She wanted him to see her husband, Gabriel's grandfather, who was still living on Urantia, and to let him know that she was alive and soon they would be together again. She also told Gabriel that she was greatly appreciative of the faith he had here while she was alive and that it helped her become part of her new home on the first mansion world of Satania. She told him that he had been chosen by God to be a vessel of communication for bringing in the Continuing

Fifth Epochal Revelation and that he had to learn the first part of it, already in print, so that he could assimilate the language within and thus could become the chosen vessel. She said that the book would come to him in his hometown of Pittsburgh, near the energy reflective circuit of some of his ancient relatives from other planets. The name of the book was called The URANTIA Book. *She said that he had heard of the book before but that he had refused it, for he was a Christian minister at that time, but now he must accept it, learn it, and then become an audio fusion material complement for the next nine-tenths of it.*

She said that no one else on the planet could take this position, for there was not time left before the final change point on Urantia to bring a soul to the place of being chosen for this work and responsibility. She added that he had been part of other renaissances of this planet and that she and all his relatives who passed on to the other side were counting on him. As she mentioned these relatives he saw people, as on a large television screen, each one of them young, vibrant, and smiling. It was as if they were smiling at him because of the tasks he had already accomplished, some of which he remembers. There was Grandmother and Grandfather Dell Erba, Godfather Mundo, Great Grandmother Cottrell, Sonny Malatesta, Uncle Joseph, Uncle Salvatore, Uncle Fred, Cousin Johnny Mancini, Jo Jo Ferrieri, and others.

I regained my consciousness and was returned to the beach, but I remembered nothing that had transpired. I returned to Tucson and my wife, very naive about the divorce that was to take place and the events that would bring me back to Pittsburgh.

CHAPTER 5

Return To Where The Three Rivers Meet[1]

I had no memories of what had happened in Guaymas, Mexico. I just knew that with my experience I gained a new mission. This time I thought I was to record a spiritual album and reach the world with higher-consciousness music. At this time, back in December 1984 through 1985, I was what you might call a New Age Catholic.

I had been home to Pittsburgh several times throughout the years, but this was the longest time period in which I had not seen most of my family—over eight years. I did not realize then that I was to be the leader of a great cosmic family and that any time I felt separate from others at any level, grief became part of my reality. When I first became a God-seeking soul I lost many of my friends and family members because I could no longer relate to them. It was sad, for I love them all very much. It was grief that caused my death on this planet in one lifetime as a Franciscan.

I got along well with all my Catholic relatives as long as I did not talk too strongly about religion, something I found very difficult. I went to visit a Catholic charismatic prayer group that I used to attend in the seventies to see what kind of growth had taken place. The leader was not there that night, and nobody knew that I had been there years before. I was surprised they had no new revelation. The teaching was pretty much the same as it was in the seventies.

In the seventies I was studying at Duquesne University, the place where the spiritual renewal first started. I was one of the first Catholic charismatics in the modern era to receive the baptism of the Holy Spirit, with certain evidence of this baptism being the word of knowledge, tongues, and prophecy. There were just a few dozen Duquesne charismatics at the time, and the administration asked some to leave the school, including a priest. I went to a convention in Notre Dame Stadium in 1973, and there were thirty thousand charismatic Catholics in attendance.

I experienced this tremendous growth in the renewal in just a few short years. The Urantia movement should have experienced the Baptism of the Holy Spirit and the charismatics (Catholics and Protestants) should have come to *The URANTIA Book* and eventually to Continuing Fifth Epochal Revelation. But unfortunately they did not, and no new growth has taken place in the charismatic movement as far as acceptance of new revelation. To simplify, one is "mind," the other is "heart." Both mind and heart are needed for true wholeness and ascension.

I have many fond memories of my charismatic days in Pittsburgh and other cities, one of which is meeting a special soul. She was Agatha von Trapp, whom I met together with her mother Maria and another sister. This was the famous family about which the film *The Sound Of Music* was made. As a little girl in the forties, Agatha was one of the singing daughters of the Baron von Trapp family. I had lunch with Agatha on several occasions and with a Jewish evangelist friend who knew her. These were the days when people of different denominations all came together to worship the same God.

The movement should have evolved into the present Divine New Order and the Divine Planetary Administration. Many left and became involved in the New Age, but when they found that their Jesus was not there, they had nowhere else to go. Many went back to their former denominations. Agatha's love for Jesus was so beautiful. I even considered going to New Guinea with her as a missionary, where she had been serving her Lord for many years. Oh, to have that kind of heart and love for God, fused with the mindal knowledge of higher cosmic truth!

That is what my later work would do for the planet, and many souls would join our community with this kind of combination. Today the charismatic renewal is just another branch of the Catholic Church. The revelation stopped when most people in the Catholic Church did not join the renewal. As it was in the thirteenth century with Francis of Assisi, the modern renewal did not go far enough. It could have led the way to the first stage of light and life on Urantia.

One day, while still in Pittsburgh, I went to a Wendy's restaurant and there I ran into a close friend from the past. I had not seen her in twelve years. I was not planning on seeing her or her husband, although next to my human parents I had loved them more than any other people on the planet. I did not understand why I loved them so much, particularly the husband, who I felt at times took advantage of my love for him. In the past when I had become a born-again Christian they rejected me and my new philosophy. I do not blame them for that. Now here I was a Catholic again, but a New Age Catholic with some beliefs that they would not accept. However, God had other plans for us and having met again, they were my closest friends for the next year.

When I went to their home it brought back many memories, one of which is most important to this book. After the divorce from my first wife, at a time when my daughter Dina was three years old and still alive, I felt tremendous pain and grief. I was living upstairs in their home and praying to God for a reconciliation with my wife. Downstairs I heard voices of laughter. It sounded like my wife, my daughter Dina, my parents, and my in-laws.

In my mind I felt that this terrible separation from them was over. I heard footsteps coming up the stairs, and I thought I heard a little girl laughing and giggling who I thought to be Dina. I waited and I heard a knock on the door three times . . . rap, rap, rap. I quickly opened the door because I was standing so close to it. When I opened it, no one was there! I stood there in disbelief and was quite frightened. I listened to hear if there was still noise downstairs, and I heard none. I thought I was going out of my mind and felt tremendous pain in my heart.

At that moment I felt a presence near me, and it actually put its hand on my shoulder. This also frightened me, and I literally ran down the stairs. I felt this presence follow me. I pounded on the door downstairs and asked for my friends to come. When the husband came, I asked, "Where is everybody?" and he said, "Who?" It was then that I realized that something supernatural was going on. The familiar voices were not real, obviously, but who was the being with me?

It was years later, and because of Continuing Fifth Epochal Revelation, when I realized that because these close friends were part of my cosmic family and had been my human parents in a past life on this planet and because their home was located very near the energy reflective circuit of Mount Washington, that these combined energies had allowed the midwayers to come into closer contact with me.

I gave my life to God and Christ Michael that evening. In this lifetime that is where it began. I also learned that I would become their teacher-son, a role that has become very difficult for me as I am also teacher-son to my first-time Urantian parents Mary and Anthony. I could never understand why Mary and Anthony were a little jealous of these friends. What none of us understood then is that these dear friends were also once my human parents, but not my cosmic parents.

On another occasion when I went back to Pittsburgh, the first thing that the husband would say to me was, "I'm Catholic, born Catholic and will die Catholic." For the two weeks that Niánn and I stayed with them in 1988 there was very little spiritual conversation that we could have, as he closed the door immediately. The wife was more open, but at the time of this writing I have no contact with them. I have tried but they have not responded.

Another cosmic family member that I met in Pittsburgh was the brother of two old friends from my childhood. I had not seen him for fifteen years, and he was now nearing thirty. I was to be closest to him on a spiritual level during the whole year I was in Pittsburgh. There was an immediate kinship between us, and we understood spiritual things on a very high level. He was also deeply involved in Native American spirituality. He was making films and had just met Will Sampson, a Native American actor (now deceased) from *One Flew Over The*

Chapter 5

Cuckoo's Nest. He took me to a ceremony of a Central American Indian tribe called the Caney, and during the year, I visited the Caney circle many times and had open discussions with their shaman leader.

I would later find out from Paladin that my friend was my cosmic son and this shaman leader, a cosmic brother. In the shaman's group I met a Caney woman by the name of Tenache. When I first heard her name my heart leapt. I did not understand all that was happening at the time, only that I loved these people but we were all on different paths and we could not quite connect. A year or so later I was to learn from Paladin that Tenache was the name of one of my Apache Indian loves and wives and that this Tenache that I had met in Pennsylvania was my cosmic daughter.

One evening this cosmic son and I went to Mount Washington. While I was there in meditation, a vision came to me and once again I felt a close presence of an unseen personality. This was made possible by being with my cosmic son. (I would find out from Paladin, years later, that it was an energy reflective circuit, but until then I just knew it to be a beautiful view overlooking the three rivers of Pittsburgh.)

The name "Gabriel" came to me. At first I thought that the presence might be an angel called Gabriel. Then a vision of a circle came to me with dots in the middle of it. I shared with my cosmic son that I felt a presence nearby, but he was not "into it" so much, so I did not get deep into the experience with him at the time. I went home by myself and prayed about the vision. I felt that I was to change my name to Gabriel and that I was to return to my original Italian surname—my ancestors owned orchards and were farmers in Italy—of "Dell Erba," which means "of the grass or the earth." I sensed I was to name my future children Dell Erba—Amadon, my future son, would be named "Dell Erba," and he certainly was of the earth, the loyal one of Urantia.

As time passed, the dots that I saw came to be positioned in specific locations within the circle. I also saw a triangle within the circle and a solar cross connecting four points on the circle.

Outside the circle I saw a smaller triangle. This is the basis of the logo now used by Global Community Communications Alliance. I had no idea at the time what it meant. In my limited thinking back then, I thought it symbolized the seven locations around the planet where I would have offices for my spiritual musical ministry in which I was to become Gabriel, a messenger through music.

It was four years later, as I was reading a book by Billy Meier (a contact for the Pleiadians who was living in Switzerland) that I saw the seven dots within the circle was an ancient symbol of the seven sisters of the Pleiades. I would later be told by Paladin that these seven dots would actually be seven sacred/protected areas on Urantia that would be Divine New Order communities, the first of which would be in Sedona, Arizona (which twenty years later moved to Tumacácori, Arizona). Then I, as the leader, and the Eldership of Aquarian Concepts Community (which is now Global Community Communications Alliance) at the First Planetary Sacred Home would help establish the other six communities on Urantia.

One day I received a phone call from a friend who owned a metaphysical bookstore. He said a young artist, upon hearing the music I had recorded, wished to trade me *The URANTIA Book* for my album. When he said the word "Urantia," something leaped within me. I thought I had remembered it from when I was a Christian minister eleven years previously and had rejected it. Actually, it had been programmed into me by my grandmother that time in Guaymas, Mexico, when I was beamed up on a space vessel. So I immediately said yes, I would make the trade, and went down to the shop about a block away. The first thing the young artist said to me was, "You have to read about Gabriel." I told him my *Unicorn Love* album was only ten dollars and I believed the book cost much more. He said I should have the book without paying anything for it and that it was the clearest direction that he had ever received from God about anything and for me to please take it immediately. That is how I received *The URANTIA Book*.

Chapter 5

I decided to record my *Unicorn Love* album in Pittsburgh, and I used all the savings I had accumulated over the years to produce this spiritual/New Age Vocal album myself. It was, and is, meant to reach the mass consciousness and those who listen to rock, rhythm and blues, pop, folk, and jazz. All the musicians who played were spiritually-minded, and we prayed before each session. The experience over the months of making this album was one of the most exhilarating of my life.

I was glad the musicians did not recognize it as contemporary Christian music, but they certainly recognized it as something different and quite spiritual. I did not tell them of my other spiritual beliefs; as far as they knew, I was a Christian, expressing an art form different from the usual contemporary Christian music. I was the pioneer of New Age Vocal. The album was ahead of its time. It was the beginning of my current Global Change Music™ and sound of CosmoPop®. A short definition of CosmoPop® is "Music of the future for minds of the future."™

I had become quite settled in Pittsburgh with a nice apartment on the South Side. I had renewed friendships and made new acquaintances, including my cosmic son, who was very close to me and whom I loved very much. Yet I felt this tug and pull to go to Los Angeles. Right before I left, a producer from Hollywood was in Pittsburgh and offered me $30,000 cash and a five-year contract with his company that was open to recording commercial spiritual music. After praying about this I felt that it was not God's will to accept this offer, as it would have tied me down for the next five years. I also felt drawn to Los Angeles because I had met a female rock star and her manager at a songwriter's home in Beverly Hills in 1981; the manager and I seemed to click. My plans were to marry her.

Actually I did not understand the love I had for her until years later, when I found out she had been a wife in a previous life. God used my love for her to get me to Los Angeles (He does that). I did not know that third-dimensional success in music would escape me as would this woman. If I had remained in Pittsburgh I could never have met my destiny as the Audio Fusion Material Complement of the Bright and Morning Star, Paladin, and many other celestial friends, in order to bring Continuing Fifth Epochal Revelation to this planet. With much pain in my heart and tears in my eyes, I left for Los Angeles. I bid my farewell to all four of my Urantian parents, my dear sister and her children, to my cosmic son, and many others for whom I felt more than an earthly love.

CHAPTER 6

Los Angeles: The Diseased Heartbeat Of America And The Planet

I had been to L.A. before to learn about the music business and try to have my music heard by someone who could appreciate both art and talent. All three times before, I was defeated by the smog, traffic, and working minimum-wage jobs to survive. The abbot was right. I would have to become famous quickly, or I would end up in isolation somewhere as years before I had escaped to the monasteries. I tried not to think of failure. I was still naive enough to believe that if the right person heard my music and recognized its spiritual value in helping to change the planet, that commercial success was possible.

In January 1986 I decided to live by the ocean to get away from the pollution. I rented a small apartment from a ninety-two-year-old Jewish man in Santa Monica who still chased women. Saul Weck[1] said he knew a lot of famous people but outlived them all.

"You cannot trust people who have money or power; don't even trust me," was his first advice. "They will do anything to protect what they have, whatever the cost to you. When I first came here sixty years ago, the ocean was clean, and there was room to breathe on the beaches. What do you see now? Apartment buildings everywhere and places to feed the fat people who spend too much for the food they eat." He had a real way with words.

Saul continued, "I sold out too. I'm no better than the rest. I sold most of this land to developers so that I could wine and dine women. I'm still a dirty old man. Unfortunately the environment that used to be so beautiful is even dirtier, and I pray the Lord will forgive me. The weather is not the same here as it was sixty years ago. It is fifteen degrees cooler in the winter months, much hotter in the summer, and too humid on the beach. Only a fool would lie out in the sun. I lost track of the number of young people who contracted skin cancer. You do not hear the real statistics. Do you think the rich want the tourist-and-beach business ruined? They pay off big to keep it low-key."

It sounded as though he was very aware of the condition of the ozone layer without reading scientific reports. Saul was an interesting diversion while I pursued my music career.

Some artists who claimed to be doing New Age vocal sounded just like gospel. My music did not. Others just chanted and made unusual sounds with their voices, as if that was supposed to be "spiritual." I had real lyrics that brought the listener to a point of truth that some did not want to hear. I told people that it was not the planet that needed cleaning up, it was their own minds and hearts that needed a major overhaul. I sang about greed, envy, power, lust, false pride, and materialism—to name a few subjects.

I spent all my time either creating new forms of spiritual music on the Santa Monica beach or fighting the rat race of the Hollywood music machine. I wrote spiritual folk, pop, rock, and even country western. I told it like it was, but none of the music executives seemed to really care about making a change for the spiritual good of the planet. They liked things just the way they were. They were happy cheating on their wives and snorting cocaine.

A few in the business, who were removed from the Hollywood machine, were willing to give me a positive review: several DJs who liked the album but could not play it because they would get fired; a top producer who at the time led a famous TV orchestra but was out of the record business; an Academy Award-winning songwriter who gave my album a good review, but would not pick up the phone to make the right connections for me. Oh, he gave me names to call, but I could have gotten better contacts from Joe Blow on the streets of Hollywood.

Chapter 6

Envy And Greed, The Dark Soul's Needs

I was learning firsthand the real problem with our planet, and it had nothing to do with environmental issues, at least not directly. The songwriter hurt me the most because he was supposed to be a spiritual man, a teacher and leader. I found him to be no better than the rest of the glory hounds. What was he afraid of, that I might beat him for next year's best song award? I found out that the more talented one was, the harder it was to break in, unless they could own and operate you and mold you into one of their clones. People in L.A. would actually go out of their way to destroy you if they thought you were a threat to their career or inflated egos.

One female executive of a so-called spiritual record label actually saw to it that I would not receive a record contract from her parent company that wanted me at that time. She blocked a major contract for me by outright lying to her superiors about my personality. She did not know me from Adam, but I would not jump when she barked and she did not like my independence. When I had to work minimum-wage jobs to survive, one lousy job after another, I often wondered if I should have jumped just a little for that power-hungry soul, but I knew I would have failed the greater test I had yet to pass.

To keep my sanity I joined a black church and their gospel choir. I had done this before and loved it. I was even picked to sing lead a few weeks after joining. There were a hundred black people in the choir, and I was honored. Deserved recognition of one's talents is always a blessing on this planet, and when it comes your way, treasure it with humility and thankfulness. I felt outside of the Hollywood jungle with these real folks who just loved their Jesus.

Confusion And Delusion

I attended all the help-save-the-planet and New Age groups I could fit into my busy schedule. Most of them were pretty weird, even for me. One group believed in the coming earth changes and that California was going to disappear in a great tidal wave. They believed that the deva forces (whatever they were) were calling the souls who had died in Atlantis back to California to drown all over again. Karma, you know! Another group said that when the planet was about to explode, that they who had grown spiritually would concentrate and use their mind energy to walk out of their bodies into the glorious new world to come. These were the same people who would not even give you a ride home if you needed it or smile at you when you looked at them.

One Sunday a friend and I went to see a channel in a New Age church. Channeling was unusual then and just getting started. The voice that came out of this young man's mouth sounded like a drunken Irish man who told everybody that God was love and love was God. La-de-da. We laughed so hard we were almost asked to leave. If this guy was not an aspiring actor, he sure missed his true calling!

Many of the men who had the energy gift in their hands to heal—Reiki, they called it—wanted to touch all the pretty, sick, unbalanced females for nothing, no charge. The poor men and older or less attractive women would either have to pay or stay forever in an unbalanced body with their unaligned energies shooting all over the place. Psychics were a dime a dozen, and I did not want to be identified with them.

One day, just for kicks, I paid one five dollars to read my fortune. It was on the walk at Venice Beach. She used a Tarot deck, and while she was telling me that I would be rich and famous, would soon marry the woman of my dreams, and travel a lot in my life, I decided to "read" her. I concentrated and heard a voice that said she was from Indiana, that she was divorced and had two children, two boys. I spoke up and repeated what the voice said. "How in God's name did you know that?" she yelled. I answered, "You're the psychic; you tell me."

I began to practice learning how to listen and see how accurate I could be with people and events. I was amazed myself at the things I was able to determine by listening to that voice. But I had a long way to go before I really learned what was happening and exactly what this gift was.

I was guided to a spiritual group that studied the teachings of the ascended Tibetan Master Djwal Khul. This group was one of the few that made any sense to me. They talked about being a world server and about the shift that was about to come upon the planet. They taught that our body was really astral and that it had a central channel from the head to the pelvis that had seven spiritual centers they called chakras. I spent many hours reading all I could about these centers and how to clear this channel, which was called the antahkarana and was the link with the unseen beings who wished to communicate with all who spiritually advanced to this level.

This was available to all souls who were open and willing to learn and venture into the unknown—unknown in today's age, but once very common among the higher civilizations, which they identified as Atlantis and Lemuria. It was this disciplined practice that opened the way for the inner voices to come more often and for other voices to come, all more clearly than my initial contact. Eventually I was able to fuse with some of these entities, as an audio fusion material complement of these celestial beings.

It did not take long to discover that most of the New Age spiritual thought was actually ancient evolutionary religions with new names, nothing really new at all, a lot of it just rediscovered. That a New Age was coming I had no doubt, but bringing most of the old into "the new hip consciousness" I knew was a big mistake. Most of the old concepts that people were accepting as the new answers to their lives and to the world's problems had not worked for the past 200,000 years and could not work now. Even if the world would be fresh and clean from a future holocaust, I remembered what Christ said about new wine skins being needed for new wine. Our planet needed a complete overhaul.

I was about to be given some real answers via a book that the voices said was already in my possession, *The URANTIA*

Book. These voices said that this book contained part of a revelation that was given to a channel, actually an interplanetary receiver, over a period of years. I could not deny all channeling because of some corrupt ones. Something was definitely happening to me, and I looked forward to studying this revelation.

Hope Begins To Come

The URANTIA Book was fascinating and intellectually above any I had ever read before. Upon reading it, one had to come to the conclusion that no human could have written such concepts with such clarity and consistency. The language was new, at least for Urantia, which is the cosmic name for our planet. The beings who authored the book were of various orders, planes, and worlds. Some were angelic, some of higher spiritual orders than even angels, some semimaterial, and some nonmaterial.

I would later find out that it was the midwayers who were responsible for our planet having the Fifth Epochal Revelation (*The URANTIA Book*), of which this two thousand page book contained just a small part. Continuing Fifth Epochal Revelation would come through me. I could be used because of the language I had acquired by studying *The URANTIA Book* and by spiritually advancing to what is called the third psychic circle. That I would be chosen was an honor that was little appreciated by many of the people who I would try to reach with its message. It became a trial for my complement, Niánn, and me for many years, up until the final physical evacuation of our planet and the first appearance of our unseen friends to human eyes.

One day I made a phone call, trying to find a record producer. A man answered and told me his name, Duane Faw. I had dialed the wrong number, but the kind gentleman talked to me and said that he had a Urantia Book study group in his home in Malibu each Tuesday night. I told him I was reading the book but did not know that study groups existed. I also realized that some unseen hand had dialed that number. Out of 14 million people in Los Angeles, I believe the midwayers led that phone call to him. He was a remarkable man. He was a retired brigadier general of the Marine Corps, attorney, and a Bible teacher in his Lutheran church for more than thirty years. He was one of the world's leading authorities on *The URANTIA Book*. I was committed to learning this revelation, and I was blessed to be his student. Duane was just down Highway 1, as I was in Santa Monica. I began to attend every Tuesday.

Many times I have been led by God to reconsider decisions I had made previously. One of these decisions affected my music career because I had to devote more time to reading the book, and the black choir I was part of rehearsed on the same night as the Urantia Book study. And so, after a tearful good-bye I left the choir to join the study group. I left with a bang you might say. On Sunday the director had me sing a lead song, called *Waymaker*. It was a hand-clapping, foot-stomping gospel tune that had the whole church standing and shouting. I wondered why God asks us at times to make so difficult a sacrifice, in following what we believe to be God's will for us. Why couldn't I have both? Leaving that choir was one of the most difficult things I ever had to do. I prayed that the Waymaker I was following appreciated my loyalty.

The Big Test

One day I received a phone call from one of the major record labels to which I had sent my *Unicorn Love* album. A secretary said that they would like to make an appointment with me to talk to one of their big brass about my music. I was very excited for the next three days, until I went to the plush offices of the music kingdom at Universal City Plaza. I met with a man who introduced himself and told me he had been involved with many of the big names in music in the seventies as a personal manager and now with many as a record executive. The conversation went something like this:

He began, "We really like your music and style, and you have a great-selling voice." Then he completely changed the subject. "My wife and I belong to St. Mel's Catholic Church in Woodland Hills. I am a deacon there."

My hopes were up. Maybe he was going to tell me next how badly our nation needed music that could raise the consciousness of its citizens. I thought the best of him and my heart ticked faster than normal.

But then he dashed my hopes by saying, "We think the spiritual aspect of your music is not for the general public. We do not think they would buy it."

I shot back, "How do you know for sure unless you try it and give the music airplay?"

He did not answer but went ahead with his programmed speech. "Our company is prepared to give you $100,000 in advance and produce two albums a year for you for the next five years. All we ask of you is that you change a few of the words in your songs and take out all that spiritual jargon. What are a few words here or there, and who really cares about our planet?"

Before I responded, I thought for a few moments. I considered the lousy job I had as a message driver, wearing a funny red suit and fighting the L.A. traffic eight to ten hours a day, delivering messages to people who had "made it" in the system by compromising their values, never thinking they needed morality in their greedy world. I thought of how they treated me and others below them, as pieces of dung or objects to be used or bought. Some of them were musicians like me who did not have half my talent.

I thought of the people who looked at me as though I were a failure because I was not making the money they were or was not locked into the system they were or did not have the things they had. I thought of some of my closest friends and even my parents, who saw me as strange because I did not do it their way. They never saw the nobility of my motives or that I was trying to make a difference on the planet. I thought of all the years as a kid that I spent alone practicing. I thought of the many heartbreaks along the way to get me to this offer. And then I silently asked God to give me an answer. It came to me quickly—the riches of the world that Satan offered Christ and how He rejected them. I knew what I had to do.

So I said, "Sir, I truly appreciate your company's offer, but the world does not need another John Lennon or Elvis Presley. They did little to uplift our troubled planet or bring about any real spiritual change. The world needs a Gabriel, and with God's help and in His time that is what the world will get."

The big wheel shot back, "Kid, you are crazy! You may never get an opportunity like this again."

I knew he might be right. I had hoped to teach this older man that there was something to look forward to that had nothing to do with this corrupt and greedy world, and I very sincerely said, "Sir, a Divine New Order is coming upon this planet, a just order, you might say, where all dreams come true if they include the common good of your fellow brothers and sisters. One day you will hear my music being played around this planet on all of the radio stations and television networks, for they will be owned by the administration of a just system and operated by people with concern for our planet and the people on it. Good-bye."

It would take many, many years before the hope that I spoke of would happen. How many times when my family and I were near poverty did I wonder if I had made the right choice. I hated a world run on money, and I did not do well in it. I had so many doubtful moments wondering if God had forsaken me. But it was not God who had forsaken humankind, but people who had forsaken God and their brothers and sisters on this planet. Truly we are our "brother's keeper," and every decision that one makes for selfishness and greed affects every human being upon this fallen planet. I would come to understand the depth of that truth in the years to come.

Betrayal

I felt I had been forsaken by friends and my two wives, partly, of course, my fault, but never had I experienced an outright preconceived plan by someone to betray me from the beginning of a relationship. I had seen it done by cheap con artists in Hollywood, lustful men promising parts in movies to pretty, hopeful actresses for a night in bed, or a producer who never produced anything but a scam, promising record contracts with phony screen tests where the musician paid to have his song recorded. I thought I had seen it all until I met Miss X.

I was selling women's shoes in Beverly Hills, and she walked in one day. She was in her fifties but did not look it. She first came on to me sexually, and it worked. I was lonely and needy in all areas. When she found out I was spiritually more mature than the average man and that I was a hopeful singer/songwriter, she worked on both interests to feed me the bait that would lead me to be used by her until she was tired of me and found another sucker.

"I am a spiritual advisor and a dream-maker. I help make dreams come true for people like you," she said. She listened intently to my tales of woe about my Hollywood experience and said she knew people in the business who could help me. I had heard that before so I was not impressed, but she was good at giving people false hopes, and I was very vulnerable at the time. She acted as though she believed in me, so I talked on. I told her the desires of my heart and secrets I usually did not tell strangers. I told her about the name Tenache and how I was so attracted to the Caney Indian woman with that name. Miss X looked a little like an Indian that day and even had a headband on. So she picked up on this one quickly. "Oh I know that I've lived many Indian lives before," she said.

That was all I needed to hear. I gave her my heart—hook, line, and sinker. She would send me cards signed "Tenache." I spent most of my free time in bed with her and did not bother to pray and ask for guidance as to whether she was a past-life wife or not or whether this was a right relationship. She even took me to a psychic friend of hers who claimed to be able to tap into the Akashic records (the heavenly book of life). She said that I was her long lost twin flame and that we had shared many lives. Now, I was not that gullible, but the sex was good, and I had fallen into the lust of the flesh. My spiritual eyes and heart were blinded.

As it goes when one gets off the spiritual path for even a short while, I fell deeply into her web. I did not read *The URANTIA Book* or attend meetings, thinking that in time I would turn her on to the Fifth Epochal Revelation, and we would spend the rest of our lives together—I, a famous singer (thanks to her contacts) and an influential spiritual leader. Ha-ha! We were a great "spiritual couple"—under the sheets. We even prayed together on occasion, particularly about the oceanside apartment she wanted. I was the energy and catalyst she needed to get out of the city. She said we could live together and I could continue my music career and bring in some money by playing music around the area.

So for weeks we looked and finally found a place. I had given up my apartment, planning to move in with her. She asked me to give her what little money I had left and my last paycheck from the shoe store. (I was fired because of the stock market drop that year.) After I gave her everything I had and she put money down on the apartment, she told me I was no longer welcome to move in with her, but she wanted to stay friends, actually, to have an extra stud in her stable. I was heartsick. I had fallen in love with this woman and had never seen through her deception. She was the final blow to me in California, and I had no energy left to fight the Hollywood greed machine. My heart and mind turned to Arizona.

CHAPTER 7

The Superstition Mountains—
Recontact Is Made

I had roamed the foothills of some of the mountains in Arizona before with an old acquaintance who had a studio in Apache Junction. He was a famous artist, Ted DeGrazia. He died a few years later. He had lived with the Pima Indians and loved riding on horseback through the mountains. As I thought about my time with him, I remembered one thing he had told me. "These Superstition Mountains are magical and mysterious. Many who go in, never come back again." I felt these mountains drawing me in the winter of 1987.

I stopped over in Tempe, Arizona, to visit a group of *URANTIA Book* readers whom I had contacted when I was in California. A door was opened for me to stay a week or so. I needed time to figure out how I was going to exist in the mountains, as I was no mountain man. These new friends were far too intellectually oriented to believe my experiences with unseen celestial visitors. I wanted desperately to tell them, but I knew that I would only be ridiculed and considered a fool.

Several years later, when I did go public with part of the experience, I was not believed by those intelligent but closed-minded souls who read T*he URANTIA Book*. It was strange that they read a book that talked about the millions of inhabited planets in our local universe and the billions of celestial personalities, but they could not accept the fact that whatever is out there just might have wanted to communicate with little old us, you or me, or our next-door neighbor. Even my dear friend and teacher of *The URANTIA Book* in California, Duane Faw, did not believe in spacecraft from other worlds being seen on Earth/Urantia.

In the years to come, I felt all alone, with the exception of my friend and mate, Niánn, who believed with me during the faith years before many of the earth changes that Celestial Overcontrol predicted came to pass. People's very doubts blocked the door to the reality and to the possible contact with these marvelous superhuman personalities. These unseen mentors only wanted human souls who were brave enough to venture away from the established thought-forms, traditions, dogmas, and religions of misinformed and confused humanity.

The Ashtar Command of the Pleiades would call these contactees "eagles." The name was given by Paladin, the second in command of the space fleet, who had repersonalized on the earth plane and had lived several lives here—one as a Nez Percé Indian, in which his name was Sky Hawk. A hawk, like an eagle, can fly alone and does not need the flock. I had been told that we too must be able to fly alone with the new truth that our extraterrestrial friends were attempting to give us that would help bring about the changes our planet so desperately needed. I had so much to learn and so many changes to make myself. Soon Sky Hawk himself would tell me these very things.

I decided one day to go to the local food co-op in Tempe, and as I looked at the bulletin board, a flyer jumped out at me. It said that a community somewhere in the Arizona mountains wanted men and women to come and be part of a work/study program for at least three months. My heart danced. This was it. I contacted them and made arrangements to go there on Thanksgiving Day. Twenty of us met in a small country store to make connections with the community's leaders and some of the members, who drove us in their four-wheel-drive vehicles ten miles into the desert mountain region. I had left my car at a deserted ranch and did not see it again for about two and a half months. The nearest town was about thirty miles away via the main road.

Apart from wilderness survival skills and learning to live off what the land had to offer, the community also taught metaphysical principles. It was my first experience living in a tipi during the middle of winter with only a wood stove to give heat. Waking up in the early morning was always an experience.

After living in southern California, I had a hard time getting used to the cold. The afternoons warmed up, but the sun went down behind the mountain at about 3:30 P.M., and it got dark around 6:00 P.M. I had plenty of time to commune with nature and God, and I made the best of this time of solitude.

Those who lived in the community and those students who came to learn all prayed, ate, and sang together daily. It was a beautiful experience, with people actually trying an alternative lifestyle and really working on loving each other. Yes, we had our personality conflicts, but it did seem that these people tried a little harder to be allowing and loving. Forgiving each other when we were hurt could be so difficult for our proud hearts. Contrary to the popular belief that "love means never having to say you're sorry," we found that sincere apology and asking for forgiveness was a necessity for harmonious living. At the time, I thought that I wanted to stay there for the rest of my life. I truly loved many of the people, but soon my plans were to change again.

My job was supplying wood to the individual tipis and other simple living quarters and helping to construct a deer fence. One snowy day I was alone, as usual, splitting wood at the far corner of the land when I felt a presence come near me. I heard a voice outside of myself say, "Hello Gabriel." I turned around to greet whoever was there, thinking it must be someone from the group or a hiker. It was a strong masculine voice, but I did not see anyone. It was just too beautiful outside in the snow to be frightened, so I stopped and asked who was there. I first asked God to protect me and then waited, shutting my eyes and letting the snow fall upon my face. Once in a while I would look up for one more glimpse of the snowflakes that were coming down.

After a few moments of silent waiting, I heard a voice within me say, "*We would like to use your body to speak to you. Would you give us permission?*" I somehow felt that this was what God wanted me to do. So after asking how, they said to just move my mind back as far as possible and they would use my voice box. I did as I was instructed and felt the presence of more than one being around me. Soon I felt a strong essence in my mind and body, but I felt that I was also there, in control, so I had no fear, being on sacred Indian land of the Dineh—the People. I should have guessed at how they would introduce themselves, as I was interested in Indian spirituality at the time.

"My name is Sky Hawk, and I have had several Native American lives."

My voice was actually speaking! I was listening to my own voice, and I knew I was in some kind of trance, yet totally aware of what was happening.

"Is this called channeling?" I asked in my mind, and then heard this reply, *"That is a contemporary understanding of a very scientific interdimensional communication based upon ancient beliefs of spiritualism and mediumship. We are not only spirits, we have bodies. Some in our administration, however, are more spirit than flesh, but we will teach you these things in the proper sequence and time–space frame."*

I wondered what was meant by all that. I decided to tell no one there about the incident; besides, I thought I might be flipping out.

A few days went by, and I was working on the deer fence again when I felt someone near me. I quickly prayed and shut my eyes as before and mentally backed as far away from my body as I could. I then felt an urge to speak and out came another entity's communication. The entity (using my voice) said, *"I am a finaliter, sent by Michael of Nebadon to help the people of your fallen planet. You have much to learn. You must learn to become a clear vessel for our transmission to be one hundred percent accurate. You can interrupt us at any time or stop us. Some who will come will be much different than others. We are under orders not to allow you to see us until the proper time. I am the commander of a fleet of 3,000 spacecraft that will participate in the evacuation of your planet when the final change point comes.*

"You are needed to help us prepare for this evacuation. It will not be an easy task. You will be called a fraud and a deceiver, and you will find few to follow you until the earth changes or chaos of

some kind begins to touch the lives of your countrymen. You have the beginning data of the Fifth Epochal Revelation within your mind. We can use that and add to it to help change those who are willing to listen. We will make clear the concepts of the revelation and give you continuing revelation through experience. As you begin to walk into the fourth dimension, you can teach others to do the same. I leave you now."

This entity, who was Sky Hawk, began to come on a daily basis. He told me that I would soon be meeting a wife from a past Apache life in which my name had been Gentle Eagle. I was amazed.

Sky Hawk explained, *"Your spirit has remained the same for many incarnations now, as a result of spiritual advancement. This woman will be your highest complementary polarity, and together you will be teachers of the Continuing Fifth Epochal Revelation."*

"What is her name? What does she look like? How old is she?" I eagerly asked.

Sky Hawk calmly replied, *"All of these questions cannot be answered, for you must know her in a higher way."*

I had read what some authors wrote about soul mates and twin flames and was delighted that my time had come to meet mine. I did sense I had one. In the years to come, I would learn the cosmic reality of what would become known as complementary polarities. My female complement would become one of the world's leading authorities on the subject, which was part of the Fifth Epochal Revelatory truth that was to continually come to and through me from these higher beings of other worlds and dimensions.

I began checking out all of the available young women who came for the weekend retreats. I knew I would be meeting her soon. I also thought I knew how the dark forces worked against something good that was about to happen, but I had no idea how deceiving the evil unseen forces could be. And I too often forgot that we were all in such a battle.

The very next weekend, one of the most beautiful dark-haired women I had ever seen anywhere showed up for a weekend retreat. She was part Mexican and part Navajo. Needless to say, I thought she was the one Sky Hawk told me was coming. I was elated. I spent as much time with her as I could, for I knew she was only staying for a few days. One night we talked after dinner.

I quickly got to the point, "Do you believe in past lives?"

She answered, "Our group believes in Jesus Christ and the Bible. 'And it is appointed unto men [and women] once to die, but after this the judgment'."[1] I knew that verse well, as I used to spout it all of the time, just like she was doing.

She continued, "We are in the New Age movement because we do not believe in the rapture or institutional Christianity, but we do not accept all that is in the New Age."

"Good," I responded, "neither do I." She was so pretty. I did not want to argue with her about reincarnation; I did not yet completely believe in it either, though I had such a strong sense of myself having previous lives. And Sky Hawk had told me about meeting someone from a past life, but I did not share any of this with her.

Later I learned that there were millions of souls who had been incarnated back to this planet several times. The celestial guides gave me a "video tape" of a few of mine. I would later learn directly from them that the words they used to explain such phenomena were: "reconstruction," "repersonalization," and "rematerialization." Each method was much different from the other, and numerous variables of spiritual ascension of the soul would determine what method the universe administrators would order for a particular soul.

All I could think of at the time was making love to this beauty. So I changed the subject to the environment, and we talked about how messed up the planet was. Like most people, we never really got down to the bottom line, whatever that might be for the individual at the time, avoiding any issue that might raise the other person's hair a little, particularly spiritual hairs. I played the game well with Maria. She was quite good too. I guess she also learned how not to step on toes. I could not have been more blind at the time nor more in lust.

When I got back to my tipi, I was ashamed of myself for not being sincere with her, for leading her on, when all of the time I knew something was the matter with our communication on a very necessary spiritual level. But when I saw her again, I resorted to my beating-around-the-bush conversation. She looked so good! Even though she left without any physical contact between us, I knew that given the right circumstances and time, I could be making love to that beauty. I had made plans with her to visit her community in Phoenix at the first opportunity.

The very next weekend my true spiritual complement arrived with her three children. She was special and attractive, but not dark like I thought she should be. She seemed very Anglo, and I was looking for a Native American. Besides, she had three children from a previous marriage, and I wanted no part of that reality. That is, until her oldest daughter told me that her mother grew up on several Indian reservations and taught on the San Carlos Apache reservation—where according to Sky Hawk I had lived a past life—and where I had spent many weekends in this life when I lived in Tucson. I started a conversation and found her to be very spiritually mature. Her name was Nancy.

She told me, and made an open announcement to the group, that she had resigned from her teaching position at Globe High School because she felt God was calling her to do some other kind of spiritual work. She had no idea how, where, or with whom she was to do this work, but she planned on selling her home and moving from Globe, in search of God's will for her life. I had great respect for her already. Even though her family and financial security were there in Globe, she had the courage to venture into the unknown. I knew that kind of call. " . . . many are called, but few [choose and] are chosen."[2] After eighteen years of following that kind of call, I had to say that it was not getting any easier. I knew Nancy was in for growth and loneliness, for few of her family and friends would understand her or the decisions that God would ask her to make in order to follow that call.

I visited her in Globe as soon as I could. Her home reflected her Indian life on the reservations, with a variety of baskets, pottery, rugs, and paintings spread throughout. She was an intelligent and loving soul. If she had any faults at all, I thought that she was too trusting of people, too naive about the dark side of most of us. She could be easily used, and I found out soon that she had been. But she prayed for those who used her and tried to love them, even though they would still try to use and mistreat her. I thought that when God made her He must have thrown the mold away. Everyone loved her, except those few who hated her goodness. Those kind of people did the same to Jesus Christ when they crucified Him. I found myself wanting to protect and teach her about the evil in man's heart. I guess from the very beginning I loved her because she loved all she met and only saw the good in them. I even told her all the negative things about me I could think of, but that did not scare her off.

We communicated on a very high level, like we had known each other for years. Soon I forgot all about Maria, as I realized that I had been more in lust than in love. I felt a peace about continuing a relationship with Nancy, even though I knew intuitively that her children would not accept me. I just felt God somehow would work it out for the good of all. Their father had been talking to Nancy about taking the children because he wanted to be a full-time parent. This was difficult for her, letting her children go, but she also felt that this was God's will. As she was leaving her security for the unknown, the children would be better provided for financially with their father.

I knew that it would be a lifelong commitment with her and so did she. Both of us wanted God's will above our own desires. I knew that she was the one spoken of by Sky Hawk and the other guides, and she felt that I was the one spoken of in a psychic reading she had received a few months before I met her. So our new adventure together began.

CHAPTER 8
Meeting The Midwayers

I told Nancy all about what had happened to me concerning Sky Hawk and the other celestial visitors. Gradually, over the years they gave back memories, depending on how well I could be trusted with the information and reality of what had happened to me in previous existences. It was not until later that I remembered being on a spaceship or what had happened in Mexico. But I could not deny the experience in the Arizona mountains and felt that the beings, whoever they were, were real. Because of them, Nancy and I had met. That, for me, was beginning proof of their reality.

One evening in the Fall 1987 in our meditation time together, I decided to try and reach these unseen beings. I asked for God's protection as usual and left it up to Him as to whom He would send. Soon, both Nancy and I felt a different energy in the room. I listened for a voice in my head and soon heard one say hello and give me two names.

"We are Gabron and Niánn, primary midwayers assigned to your watchcare. Usually secondary midwayers attend to these administrations, but your task is special and your planet is in grave danger."

I wondered if what I had just heard "within" was real, as we did not hear audible voices at that moment. So I asked Nancy if she had heard within her mind the female midwayer's name.

"It sounded like 'neon,' like the light bulb," Nancy said.

I asked if that was all she had heard, and her answer was in the affirmative. Even though I had "heard" more, I was overjoyed that Nancy had picked up that much. I asked these particular entities to spell out their names.

One of them then answered audibly (using my voice), "G – a – b – r – o – n and N – i – á – n – n. And it is I, the male of the two (Gabron) who speaks to you. Nancy's cosmic name is also Niánn and from now on she should be called by that. It means 'cosmic woman of grace.' We were given birth by your ancestors who were the staff of the Caligastia One Hundred, who were here from other worlds many thousands of years ago."

"Do you live in a spacecraft?" I asked.

Gabron answered, "No, we have never left this planet. We await the first stages of light and life on Urantia. Our job is to help teach you the solution to the world's various problems. We are in contact—and have been for thousands of years—with beings that have far surpassed your planet in its spiritual and social evolution. But we have not been allowed, until now, to contact humans like you in this manner because they did not have the mindal capacity to understand the answers. Because of the vocabulary you possess of the beginning Fifth Epochal Revelation and some understanding of its concepts, we and others can use you as a vessel of communication for true change on your planet."

"But why me? There are others who know The URANTIA Book better than I, and they also have the vocabulary," I inquired.

Gabron continued, "There are many reasons why the Universe Directors chose you. The majority of readers have followed interpretations, from the founding organization, that are not completely correct. You are, and have been for many repersonalizations, a free spirit and open to hear from the Spirit of Truth that our Universe Father left here for all to understand cosmic reality. You are honest with yourself, with your neighbors, and with your God. You are not likely to accept even our truth without deep introspection and soul-searching with the Spirit of Truth. You have done this ever since you asked this Spirit to come into your present reality.

"You and Niánn are of the Cosmic Reserve Corps of Destiny. Your tasks will be to awaken others of the Corps, Urantian and Cosmic. Many of them will be called starseed by the New Age teachers and channels of lower-plane communication. In reality, in the universe of Nebadon, even some first-time Urantians have starseed genetics. If you have been here before, you are not from this planet. Do you know the ascension plan of Michael for the system of Satania in His universe?"

I answered, "I do understand the seven mansion worlds and the inward journey through space toward Havona and Paradise."

Gabron responded, "*This is good, but there are many on your planet who are not originally from Nebadon. Many have repersonalized here for special assignments. Because they are not from your local universe they are not required to adhere to the ascension plan for Nebadon, which includes Urantia (Earth) and most of its residents.*

"*This information is Continuing Fifth Epochal Revelation, and you must continue to study the Fifth Epochal Revelation* [The URANTIA Book] *that is now in print, so that we and others who will speak to and through you can use that data to widen your understanding. We want to bring to Urantia new concepts of Continuing Fifth Epochal Revelation at the highest level. Eventually when you are at the level of the first psychic circle, we can complete what is already written. Your worst enemies will be those in the 'spiritual' groups. You will not be accepted by most spiritual groups as a true Fifth Epochal Revelation channel for some time. You and Niánn will have many years of being accused of fraud and deception. It will be very difficult and lonely. There will probably come a period when you yourselves even deny our reality.*"

"But why would I do that?" I asked.

He said, "*Because your path will not be easy. Many of your cosmic children will be brought to you, along with sisters and brothers of cosmic origin. You will even meet a past-life mother and father that you love very much, but it is doubtful that they will accept your work until the trials come to your country. Some will stay and work with you for a while, but when the real tests come, they will deny you, us, and the work.*

"You will suffer much verbal abuse, and much of it will come from those to whom you have shown nothing but love. The majority of them will be cosmic family. You see, it is the will of the Universal Father of Paradise that members of the same family units live, work, and grow together. This is called the union of souls. When this happens on planets in the third dimension, such as Urantia, and particularly on the thirty-seven planets that fell during the Rebellion of Satania, then the planet is ready for the pre-stages of light and life."

"Do you mean the promised return of Jesus Christ?" I asked.

Gabron explained, *"First there will be the appointment of the new Planetary Prince of Urantia, whom we speculate will be Machiventa Melchizedek. The schools and administration of Melchizedek will be established using human personalities like yourselves. You two will have the Mandate of the Bright and Morning Star of Salvington, an overcontrol mandate. It is hoped that another couple you will be meeting in the future will be the first of others to have the Mandate of Machiventa Melchizedek as Vicegerent First Ambassadors to the Planetary Prince. Either Christ Michael will return as He promised, or Trinity Teacher Sons from Paradise will come. Michael will come, but we are not sure of the sequence."*

I asked, "When do you think this will happen?"

"Possibly, but not definitely, within ten years or around May of the year A.D. 2000 or 2001," answered Gabron.

"That is the date that was told to a prophet of this century by the name of Richard Kieninger. He started the Stelle Community in Illinois and another in Texas," I replied excitedly.

"That is correct," Gabron replied. *"The date is accurate according to cosmic alignment of the first seven planets of Satania to be settled in light and life, but much depends upon human choices. The earth will be totally cleansed of all negative diotribes within dark souls. The energies that will enter the physical earth as*

a result of this alignment will cause the plates to make their final shifts. There will be few survivors left on Urantia when this happens."

I drew a conclusion, "So, we must be taken away first?"

The midwayer's answer was, *"Correct, and as many as will harken to our words and the voices of many prophets of old in these last days of your present civilization."*

For many months afterward Niánn and I developed a relationship with the midwayers. In the meantime, we were being guided to Prescott, Arizona to live. We were told that we would probably be there for two years, no longer than three. I could have stayed a lifetime, as the area and the home we purchased were beautiful. But many factors would lead to our moving after two years, just as the guides had said.

It was not so much my willingness to be in God's perfect will as it was the unwillingness of others to be in God's perfect will. It is much easier to follow a godless reality, an energy or force, for in this manner there is no rule to follow but your own—you plan your own life. Then there were those who believed in a personal God but just did not seem to be able to hear from that God very well. They picked and chose their reality, just like those who claimed that God was just an energy. So many failed when the real tests came, mostly because Urantia consists of billions of individuals trapped in wrong thinking and hidden agendas. Lucifer, the fallen system ruler of Satania, believed in his Creator Father but did not believe in God's program for him—or for the other created beings of the grand universe.

A question that comes to many people's minds is "What does this all have to do with solving the problems of our planet? This is all so intangible and unseen. And who is 'the Devil'? The existence of Lucifer cannot be proven. Even God remains a mystery to most."

The midwayers had told us very clearly that one must come to the conclusion that there was evil in this world and thus wrong actions. In his Rebellion, Lucifer taught that there was no evil, all was relative, and there was no absolute truth, and so billions of beings of various orders fell into these lies.

About 200,000 years ago self-assertion and unbridled liberty had also been presented by Lucifer and been accepted by these fallen ones, and these Luciferic teachings would be accepted by many up until the final change point on Urantia. These falsehoods produced artists and heroes who told the public, "I'll do it my way." Mr. and Mrs. America followed their example, and so did the children, resulting in an explosive situation on the planet during the final change point.

I begged the midwayers to become visible, but they said that it was not time and that it would actually spoil my education and growth on this planet as an "agondonter" (one who follows God's will by faith). "A – G – O – N" were the first four letters to both agondonter and agony. I remember the word well because as the midwayers had taught us, agony is often the initial knowing of being in God's perfect will moment to moment as opposed to the memories of being out of His will. We discovered that soon after moving into His will the feeling of agony changed to emotions of joy and relief and a sense of deep peace. It made me think twice about decisions and slowed me down before I spoke like a fool.

Most souls who were aware they had guides, had midwayers, but often these people thought these beings were deceased relatives or spirits of past souls who had lived on this planet. Midwayers are not human, nor are they pure spirit. The primary midwayers are the offspring of the one hundred superhuman mortals from other worlds who came with the Planetary Prince. The secondary midwayers originated much later, from an offspring of Adam and Eve (the Material Son and Daughter) and a descendent of the one hundred supermortals who had come thousands of years before. These midwayers will remain on Earth until we humans get it together enough to bring our planet into the pre-stages of light and life.

According to the midwayers, up until November of 1988 our planet could have taken a quantum leap or made a spiritual shift in consciousness. The change then would have come in a much gentler way, without so much catastrophe to individuals and to the planet. But not enough people could move out of their old ways of thinking, their antiquated religious institutions, or their dogmatic views of reality that were based upon politics or social conditions. Thoughts create both pollution and healing. The root of the problems on Urantia was not the poisoned environment but the dirty and polluted minds of the inhabitants.

And the ignorant millions of people who were God-conscious but could not break away from tradition, what about them? They were just as much a cause of the problems, for they unknowingly were a part of the evil that keeps millions of souls in bondage to false beliefs perpetuated by leaders who enjoy their seats of power and prestige. Do all roads lead to the same God, as many have said? What many of these roads lead to is war, poverty, injustice of all sorts, environmental pollution, and spiritual confusion. Should all Catholics become Protestants or all Christians become Buddhists or vice versa? None of these systems of religious thought had really made a dent in the real problems of our planet. So, our question to the midwayers and other higher intelligences was, "Where do we go from here?"

"*The Fifth Epochal Revelation,*" was their answer, "*that which is already in print* (The URANTIA Book) *and that which will continue to come to Urantia for the next forty years. It contains all of the truths of the previous evolutionary religions and points out their non-truths. It gives the pure teachings of our Creator Son, Christ Michael, who is Jesus to you Urantians, and it speaks of the cosmology of His universe and His Father's grand universe. It reveals some of the worlds in the grand universe and some of the beings that exist on them. It explains the vast administration of the grand universe so that you humans on Urantia can feel secure in a friendly and ordered universe, even though the majority of the occupants on your planet are presently in rebellion.*

"*Getting the writings into your hands is hard enough; making the proper changes in your life according to the concepts of cosmic truth and reality is the real problem. Putting that spoken statement into practical service with the one you love is another thing altogether,"* said Gabron in one transmission. *"We have found that humans say one thing and show in their actions something else. All of you are your brother's and sister's keeper—when the majority of you can learn what this means on the highest level, your planet will change for the better, but not before.*

"Many who do practice love to the degree that it is real are stuck within a framework of religious dogmas that have other wrong realities that cause just as much damage to the one you are loving and giving to and usually negates the good you may have done for that person. It is like giving hungry people food without knowing that the food contains a bacteria that will slowly poison them."

Over the months and years to come, I would learn the problems in their specifics from the guides and from actual experiences with cosmic family members and others who would be sent to us by Providence. Learning to trust the guides was not easy, even for Niánn and me, for they very often pointed out flaws in our characters that we did not want to deal with, or they would have us do things that our lower natures interpreted as unpleasant.

I became a private channel for these beings to speak with the humans under their watchcare (actually, I am an audio fusion material complement). I did this reluctantly because people would say that they wanted to hear the truth, but when it was given to them, they had a million and one reasons for rejecting it. I too made my own excuses when these celestial counselors told me where I had to change things in my life.

I learned in my early days in metaphysical groups that the phony psychics or the ones with little spiritual understanding would either tell people what they wanted to hear (by picking up the vibrations of their desires and thoughts) or they would simply lie. But these particular psychics were very popular. Everyone wanted to come into some financial windfall and most, both single and married alike, were still looking for their soul mate or twin flame, their Prince Charming or Cinderella.

The guides who came through me told these people that their proper mates and complements were there for them in the future, but that tremendous changes had to be made in their individual lives in order for the Universe Supervisors to have them meet each other. Very few of those people were willing to make those changes. Also, many couples were already in relationships that they did not belong in, some with children. The problems were vast.

Much of the planet's confusion could have been healed in the proper relationship of the family unit, each member knowing his or her appropriate place. With complementary polarity unions between husband and wife and soul mate unions between friends and co-workers, all can be of like mind and purpose, working, playing, and growing together, but each still being individualistic. This was missing on our planet. With the help of our unseen but much felt friends, Niánn and I committed ourselves to educate individuals with these truths and realities in a world on the brink of destruction—truth and answers that very few wanted to hear.

CHAPTER 9

The Pleiadian Connection

The Ashtar Command

One evening several months after making contact with the midwayers in 1987, Gabron said that another entity wanted to speak to Niánn and me. I agreed, having complete trust in them by now. Soon a very powerful personality, much different from the midwayers, entered my body. I felt safe, however, before he ever spoke and told me that he was a Father-circuited being of the light.

He introduced himself, "My name is Ashtar, and I am originally from the Pleiades. I am a mortal who has become a finaliter from Paradise. I am in command of a vast space fleet of thousands of vessels called the Ashtar Command. I am under the authority of Michael of Salvington (capital of the universe of Nebadon) and His first administrator, Gabriel, the Bright and Morning Star. I take orders only from them or their direct superiors. My function is to help bring Continuing Fifth Epochal Revelation to Urantia and to help the angelic forces in the evacuation of humans during the earth changes to come."

The memory of my close encounter in Mexico had been erased from my mind at that time, and this was even harder for me to believe than the reality of the midwayers. I was familiar with the Billy Meier sightings and encounters in Switzerland from reading about them; they were also Pleiadian visitors. Spaceships! This I did not expect. I cut off Ashtar and prayed to God for guidance. For many hours Niánn and I talked about the experience.

Because my memory banks were devoid of the encounter in Mexico, I had never told Niánn about it. But I did remember the distant sighting of a vessel that had changed directions in the Arizona White Mountains. Niánn also told me about the sighting she had seen on Mingus Mountain, near Cottonwood, Arizona, one summer, and I recalled reading about many other people's encounters with UFOs. So I asked the midwayers to come and explain. They told me that they work directly with the Ashtar Command, which includes mortals on various levels of ascension status, as well as with other superhuman and angelic personalities. The leaders of this command—Ashtar, Zoltec, and Paladin—were finaliters, presently in seventh-stage morontia bodies so that they could exist in physical surroundings, like spacecrafts.

"The Ashtar Command is, you might say, in Christian terminology, like the hand of Christ ready to rapture the church at the time of the great tribulation," explained Gabron.

The midwayers said there were other methods that could be used to evacuate a planet's inhabitants, but, because of our fallen state and our evolution in body and spirit, we could not utilize these methods. Urantia was several hundred thousand years behind in development. When the higher or spiritual body is fully developed, the physical follows suit. Simply put, we were walking around in "degenerate mechanisms." (The midwayers have quite a sense of humor.)

After several days of soul searching, I decided to allow Ashtar to speak to me again. So I asked Michael to send Ashtar, if he was of God.

Ashtar came and spoke, *"I appreciate your sense of loyalty to your God and the forces of light. This is why we allow you to cut us off. We have no real control over you. If what we say is not truly agreed upon with the Fragment of the Father and Spirit of Truth within, then we are not of the light. But beings of the light can also be misunderstood by a channel or person who is not ready to die to self and get off the cosmic fence. This is why the highest and purest messages from the Universe Supervisors can come only to tried and tested vessels, and so you have much pain to go through."*

I did not like that message at all. I thought that I had experienced enough pain in my life, and so I shut him off again, for several weeks this time. I also turned off the midwayers who I felt would tell me the same thing. Why me? Why didn't they pick on someone else? How about some master in India or Tibet or somewhere "sacred"? We in America had become so comfortable and complacent.

So what if people were starving in other countries and dying off from diseases that we in Western civilization had long since cured? So what if twenty-five thousand people died in an earthquake in China? That night we could have a barbecue. In our fat country of American materialism the Haves controlled the Have-Nots. The Haves allowed the Have-Nots to work in unfulfilling jobs in order to buy the things they did not really need. But once the Have-Nots tried to get in on a piece of the pie, to get a position of influence, the Haves closed the doors. If the Haves thought they could own an individual, then that person might get in, but if they thought they could not control the person, that person became their enemy. So few dared to dream of great things or dared to think they could make a difference in the world.

After I had gone through these thoughts of realization, I decided to get back into the battle and stop feeling sorry for myself. I decided to accept the challenge of being an audio fusion material complement of the light and allow these beings to give the answers that few wanted to hear. So one evening Paladin came in and gave the following information.

Global Sovereignty Will Prevent Global Wars

"Good evening, my friend. My name is Paladin, and I am second in command to Ashtar.[1] *I come to speak to you this evening on law, liberty, and sovereignty. It is written:*

> *If one man craves freedom—liberty—he must remember that all other men long for the same freedom. Groups of such liberty-loving mortals cannot live together in peace without becoming subservient to such laws, rules, and regulations as will grant each person the same degree of freedom while at the same time safeguarding an equal degree of freedom for all of his fellow mortals. If one man is to be absolutely free, then another must*

become an absolute slave. And the relative nature of freedom is true socially, economically, and politically. Freedom is the gift of civilization made possible by the enforcement of LAW. [The URANTIA Book, p. 1490]

"When men who make the laws divorce themselves from their Creator and the will of the Universal Father, unjust laws are created. And these men gain office because they are voted in by the majority of people who have also disconnected themselves from universe sovereignty.

"Christ said concerning these times:

> There shall be wars and rumors of wars—nation will rise against nation—just as long as the world's political sovereignty is divided up and unjustly held by a group of nation-states....
> ... But global wars will go on until the government of mankind is created. Global sovereignty will prevent global wars—nothing else can....
> ... all notions of the supposed rights of self-determination [must be abandoned]. [The URANTIA Book, p. 1490]

I interrupted Paladin here and said, "But what about Nelson Mandela and his movement, is he not a great leader?" Paladin replied,

"Mandela should be trying to free the people of the planet, not just South Africa. It has to be a global movement, not just a national one. The context has to become planetary. All of you humans on Urantia are citizens of the planet and must begin to see yourselves as such. The supposed rights of self-determination must be abandoned by individual peoples. War is not man's great and terrible disease; war is a symptom, a result. The real disease is the virus of national sovereignty.

"World law must come into being and must be enforced by world government, the sovereignty of all the people on this planet.

Under global administration the national parties will be afforded a real opportunity to realize and enjoy the personal liberties of genuine democracy. The fallacy of self-determination will be ended. With global regulation of money and trade will come the new era of worldwide peace.

"Soon a global language may evolve and the hope of a global religion, or at least a religion with a global perspective. Collective security will never afford a lasting peace until all humankind is included. The political sovereignty of representative human government will bring rest to troubled Earth. The spiritual brother-/sisterhood of humankind will forever insure good will among all people. This is the way of the Universal Father of All; there is no other way."

The Cosmic Family Getting Over The Basic Problems

Over the months we found Paladin to be a very strong-speaking grandfather type with a great sense of humor. He said that his job was not to placate us humans with soft words and untrue hopes about our planet. He said that strong words were needed to awaken people, so that they could change by coming out of their complacency and false pride. This, he stated, included me.

Paladin explained, *"Most of the people of your planet believe in God, but in that belief they murder each other in God's name, lie, cheat, and steal, all feeling that they are right with their individual God. Those of you who have existed on other planets and are here now have forgotten that you are of one family. Those many billions here for the first time have never known what a family truly is and how wonderful it is to be surrounded by loved ones—grandfathers, grandmothers, uncles, aunts, cousins, brothers, sisters, and children—who care about you and would help you when needed."*

I knew what it was like to grow up around my family back in Pittsburgh, Pennsylvania. I had known both my great-grandparents, and also my grandparents on my mother's side. I realized they all loved me and all of their grandchildren, and they made us feel special. When I grew older and needed my car repaired, I called my cousin Vince; if we needed a plumber, we called a different relative. Families could live a lot cheaper when love and cooperation were working within the extended family community.

Paladin continued, *"Today in your planet's hour of need, the Universe Father is trying to bring cosmic family back together again to work and serve each other and humanity. If you seek the Father's perfect will, those of you now on Urantia who are originally from another universe—or from other superhuman origins—will be brought together to meet your first parents, brothers and sisters. You parents will meet your first sons and daughters, and those of you who have grown spiritually together in the past on Earth and on other planets will be reunited to live in communities and to teach the principles of the Divine New Order on Urantia.*

"Many of these teachings have to do with proper relationships between family members, which lead to right tribal government and global rule. Many of the great civilizations of the past functioned in this forgotten order. The Dalamatians[2] understood the cosmic family and the divine authority of the universe. A family needs a head and a body with arms and feet. When people come together today for environmental or other humanitarian concerns, most want to be the head. Those who do assume leadership are not the ones chosen by God to lead. Your Urantia governments attest to this truth, as do the majority of your religious and economic institutions. As the Native Americans say, 'the grandfathers will return to the tribes to rule them again.'

"And so thousands of souls are repersonalizing in this century to become first communities and then the cities of the future. But it will not be easy even for them, for they must find their God first, over and above all the false teaching in both the New Age and all religions. Then they must die to their selfishness. For many reasons

Chapter 9

such as self-will and misplaced loyalties, many will fail to find themselves or the perfect will of the Universal Father.

"Humans have a hard time discovering God's path in life, for they do not override their desires, usually based on lust (not necessarily sexual) of some sort. Even though a desire or motive is good, that may not mean it is of God. Many good works have been done in the name of God, when greater things could have been accomplished if God's plan had been followed. Many who achieve financial success are failures in the eyes of the Universe Directors, who have been trying to lead them into the simplicity of God's will.

"In Western civilization millions of souls seek careers for financial security and fail to learn the true security of being in God's perfect will. Many who try to walk the true path for a while, give up because of impatience. God's timetable is usually a lot longer than your own. In America, where one may be more able to seek one's true destiny because of more freedoms, the enemy becomes sin. Americans as a whole do not want to deal with or believe in the reality of error, sin, and iniquity.

"So millions of Catholics believe that they can go on being their dark 'normal' selves, as long as they confess their sins once in a while to a priest or receive last rites before they die. Protestants feel that because they have been saved, born again, or baptized, that this event has earned for them entrance into eternity or Heaven. Go to church on Sundays, and on Monday it is OK to act like the son of the devil. The world is full of conformists, people who play the game well within the framework of what is accepted. What your planet needs are eagles, those who fly alone without pleasing the crowd. Those few brave souls can bring about change on your planet of clones and robots."

There was that word again, "eagles." Why was it for the past year I had felt a fixation for the eagle? I did not remember at the time, but when I was taken by Celestial Overcontrol they told me that the coming evacuation of our planet was called "The

Evacuation of the Eagles." Paladin had lived several Native American Indian repersonalizations (he had introduced himself to me at first as "Sky Hawk") and had chosen the name eagles for those who would be called and be taken into the ships, then brought back after the cataclysms were over. These eagle souls would be the ones to build a new Earth, a new Urantia. What I did not know at the time was that it would be Niánn's and my job to help gather the eagles together from all over the planet. Others would be chosen to do similar things on different levels.

"Your level is the highest and most important work on the planet today," yelled Paladin one day when I was not believing the reality of what was happening to me.

I moaned, "I'm just a guy from Pittsburgh. My father was a steelworker. I have always felt just one step away from being homeless and on the streets, like so many thousands of other poor souls."

Paladin responded, *"The world tries to make you fit in, to conform, to get degrees from its universities of madness, to accept the Hollywood delusion, and to buy into the materialistic bondage of its false reality. If you do not, you are considered a failure or an oddball. Few are able to exist comfortably outside of this system, and if you succeed enough to make any kind of living in an alternative way, those still trapped in the system will tell you to get a real job. If you somehow become rich by becoming a 'star' Hollywood puppet, you will become their hero, oddball or not. Is this not the reality of your country, and the reality your country sells to the rest of the planet?"*

I had to agree one hundred percent with Paladin.

Paladin continued, *"Many in your country do not see the problems, not the real ones. They cannot even ask the right questions in order to begin to find the solutions. They see everybody else as the problem, but not themselves. If they, as individuals, would accept just a little responsibility for the mess this planet is in, change, true change would come.*

"The best way for people to see their faults is for a loved one to point them out. Even then the individual may not accept what is

observed about them by people who are closest and know them best. This is why community living is the highest ideal for the evolutionary worlds of time and space, like Urantia. If your pastor tells you what is wrong with you and you do not like it, you can go down the street and join another church without dealing with the problem.

"*In a family or community situation it is not always that easy to leave. But many families do split up and move away from each other and very little growth takes place. True leadership is missing in many families on the planet, and there is tremendous imbalance between the male role and female role in the home. Many parents do not want to accept the responsibility of raising their children in the highest way, and many are just ignorant about what they as parents should do. Admitting error is not easy.*"

I then asked, "You spoke of the imbalance between male and female in the home—what do you mean?"

Paladin answered me, saying, "*In America, many women want to be the boss, and they do not want to hear of submission to their husbands. They want authority both in the home and in the workplace. So they lose their femaleness and become like men. There is a good reason for this—there has been a terrible abuse of authority by males. But there is a very high truth in the concept of appropriate submission of a woman in the home to a spiritually balanced male. If this truth is not applied in the home, you have two men in daily combat, one in pants and the other in a dress. The children become very confused in this disharmony and misunderstanding of roles.*

"*You will see many women leading their men by the nose because the men have not grown into the spiritual leaders in the home and community that God has ordained for them. All suffer when this happens. For centuries women have taken the burden of spiritual leadership, as well as childcare and other tasks, and it has caused much imbalance and unhappiness within each family member. The home, the neighborhood, the city, the nation, and the planet all feel the effects of the unalignment of the male and female in their proper roles with each other and with their God."*

Throughout the many years to come, Niánn and I would discover the truth of those statements by Paladin as we tried to teach proper male and female roles in the home and community. It would take the collapse of our culture and economy, and war in our land, to really change the obstinate minds of men and women in America. Before the national tragedies, a high percentage of the couples who left our community did so because the women would not allow the men to take their proper roles in the home. They wanted to keep control and that was that.

All were attracted to the truths of the Fifth Epochal Revelation, and many were aware of the danger our planet was in environmentally, economically, and politically, but they could not see themselves as part of the real problem—the spiritual problem. After all, they all believed in a Higher Power. Some were teachers themselves of metaphysical principles that they believed to be truths. But most of them did not really understand the simple living reality of the teachings of our Creator Son, Jesus Christ, as applied to their daily lives.

The midwayers one evening quoted from *The URANTIA Book*:

> Some day a reformation in the Christian church may strike deep enough to get back to the unadulterated religious teachings of Jesus, the author and finisher of our faith. . . . The Apostle Paul later on transformed this new gospel into Christianity, a religion embodying his own theologic views and portraying his own *personal experience* with the Jesus of the Damascus road. The gospel of the kingdom is founded on the personal religious experience of the Jesus of Galilee; Christianity is founded almost exclusively on the personal religious experience of the Apostle Paul. . . . [*The URANTIA Book,* p. 2091]

> Jesus founded the religion of personal experience in doing the will of God and serving the human brotherhood; Paul founded a religion in which the glorified Jesus became the object of worship and the brotherhood consisted of fellow believers in the divine Christ. . . . [*The URANTIA Book*, p. 2092]

No matter how high an ideal or advanced an achievement society attains, it can never transcend Jesus' teachings. The ideal of all social attainment can only be realized in the appropriation of Jesus' kingdom of the brother-/sisterhood of humankind and the Fatherhood of God.

We humans do not have to be jealous or envious of one another if we realize that each of us has a special place in this world according to our Universal Father's master plan. But how many on this planet really ask our Father His will concerning even the simplest of things, let alone the most important? Many pray, "Thy will be done" and then do their own thing, just as society has taught them. Few understand the moment-to-moment walk with the Father that is necessary to bring peace to Urantia. There cannot be a religion by rote—it has to be a daily revelation with a living, real, and personal God. Only then will humankind understand brother-/sisterhood with one another.

"We are all in this together," a female musician friend once said to me. We certainly do not escape the law of cause and effect. What goes around comes around. If we had made the right decisions in the past, the right results would have returned to us. When decisions based on greed and selfishness are made, that is what is reaped. Give and it will come back to you; take and you will continue to lose.

Many souls are energy drainers and take from the very essence of other souls. They draw the energy from others and control them with their minds. These takers feed their egos with the trouble they cause others and the rest of the planet. They become so good at it that they appear as the good guys, doing others a favor. If a loud bell would have rung every time a wrong motive was the intent in someone's heart who seemed to be good, it would have been a very noisy planet indeed.

Our unseen friends, who know human nature better than most, gave us good lessons on the true heart of humankind. I thought I understood the human heart, but the midwayers said I had a lot to learn in that area. Soon they arranged for my education, as they did for many on the planet. God was trying to bring cosmic family together from all over the planet, and these people experienced interpersonal relationships as never before.

I had met people whom I liked or disliked immediately upon meeting them, but never with the intensity and in such numbers as began to come into our lives in Prescott, Arizona. In the past forty years there had been perhaps three really close friends in my life, but in just a few months there were a dozen or more people we had met who we actually wanted to move in with us, to become a part of our extended family. We met mother figures, father figures, sisters and brothers, sons and daughters. I loved Niánn with all my heart, but suddenly several women came into my life that I felt in love with and desired.

One woman I particularly loved with a deep, almost supernatural feeling. The guides called her Setta and told me that she and I were past third-dimensional complementary polarities and that we had spent several lives together as husband and wife. They said it was my job to bring these women into fourth-dimensional reality, but at the time it seemed impossible. The communication between Setta and me was poor, and we ended up in an argument in most conversations. I never once was unfaithful to Niánn, and she knew on a higher level what was happening.

Many of us starseed had come from planets in another universe where pluralistic marriages were the norm. Pluralistic marriages (triad units and trimonad units) of interuniversal cultures can only work when all involved are highly spiritual and emotionally mature. All would have to be aligned to the Divine Administration to learn the divine reality principles of triad marriages. These interuniversal realities can presently only be begun to be learned and lived at the First Planetary Sacred Home.[3]

These interuniversal cultures were very different from Western civilization on Urantia. These realities and memories were deep within the genes of our molecular being. Some of us would be the cosmic pioneers to bring interuniversal culture to Urantia, which would become the norm in many sector regions of the Divine New Order and part of the laws of the Machiventa Melchizedek Administration after the final change point.[4]

Niánn loved these people too, particularly Setta. They all would be very attracted to us, and then they would leave for one reason or another, many not even understanding their own feelings or our past-life relationships. Niánn and I had a slight advantage—as the guides would tell us our past connections with these people—but we could not tell them, as they were not yet ready. We prayed for them as though they were part of our family, even though many of them could not have cared less if we lived or died.

It was little consolation from the guides when they would remind us that this same reality would happen all over the planet to other people of the future Divine New Order communities. Cosmic parents would feel the joy of meeting their past children and other relatives and loved ones, then suffer the pain of losing them to the world system, their own selfishness, and the chains that Caligastia (the fallen Planetary Prince of Urantia) still had on them. Usually I would get all of the blame.

Those years were very difficult for me, as I had the gift and calling that very few wanted or even believed in at the time. I began to hate the word "channel," and calling me a contact personality or interplanetary receiver did not help things, nor did it put food on the table for my children. People were just so blind to the real problems and were so right in their own eyes. They could not see with the real love of Christ and with cosmic truth. True reality was far from them.

I felt so helpless in this world and so often wanted to give up myself. To join the rat race just to be accepted would have been so easy. You know the game. Get a nine-to-five job. Do not rock the boat (even if it is sinking). Do not talk about politics or religion. Maybe even become a musician for the environment, like many of the other do-gooders. Or maybe just preach the love message. It does not change the planet, but it rakes in the bucks. People liked to hear of a loving God who forgave them for being unloving and unforgiving with their neighbors, but they just hated hearing of a God of judgment and justice. They did not want to stand before that God one day. That is a truth that nobody wanted to hear.

CHAPTER 10
Complements And Pair Units Begin To Come

When Niánn and I were just about ready to give up the belief that cosmic family really existed or that, if they existed, they would never know their relationship to us, some came to join the community. Their legal names were not as important as were the names the guides gave to them. These new names would reflect the future person this soul was called by God to become. It was a cosmic name given before they ever entered this plane.

All over the planet, we were told, were thousands of souls like these being called to transformation, but few would really heed the call. Even in our small group in Prescott, these people would deny their own reality and fall back into the world system before they finally gave their hearts to us and our work. It would take the great tragedies that struck our nation for them to rejoin us, but they came back one by one. How Niánn and I suffered in the interim period! How we missed them, for in the brief six months they had been with us we had grown to love them as family.

In the beginning, before the tragedies, Mikal joined us. He did not live with us at first but remained loyal to us and the guides for many months, while others, who we knew were of the cosmic family, fell by the wayside. When he came to stay with us, he had a hard time living in close contact with others and in many ways was unbending. This was his downfall the guides said and would cause him much grief in the future. He was divorced and had grown children. He had a business degree but was working in a job far below his potential. According to the guides, he had the capacity to become a great administrator one day, and they urged him to quit his job and work with us full time. But he declined and eventually was the first of the original community to leave us, doubting the reality of the guides.

Paladin said one day, *"People on your planet, and particularly in Western civilization, think that by putting on different clothes, changing their hair style, or changing their foods, they have made a major transformation. Some even change their names, and jobs, and geographic location, but the root problem is always there. It is the spirit of the person that must change, all else will follow. The turtles must become the eagles. No outside transformation will grow wings on a timid soul."*

Jonathan and Evening Star were the first to live with us. They realized that they were supernaturally led to us but later would forget that and even deny it. Evening Star was from California, and Jonathan was from West Germany but was an American citizen. Evening Star was a clinical therapist, and Jonathan was a carpenter. We were told of the many lives that we had shared together in the past on this planet and others. All of us felt this to be true and grew to love each other. Niánn felt closest to Mikal and I to Jonathan. All three were our cosmic children. It was difficult at first to accept the role of father to Mikal, who was a few years older than I in this life, but I made the transition inwardly and loved him as a son.

[A Possible Future Scenario]

He never knew how deeply I felt about him, at least, not until I would share that with him one evening, when we were lifted by our space friends and we were about two solar systems away from Urantia. Mikal rejoined the community after the earth changes began to happen but remained a skeptic about the spaceships until one day he found himself in one. This was an unfortunate reality for Mikal; his doubts prevented many of his loved ones from joining our community and being spared physical death, as they too could have been taken in the ships.

Chapter 10

In this life, Jonathan's soul was first sent to be my brother through the womb of my mother, but the baby had died when he was three days old. Another similar couple had to be found as parents halfway around the world, and thirty-five years later Jonathan and I met for the first time. I loved him as both my brother and cosmic son. We really felt that with Jonathan we had a true friend and one who would be loyal to us and the work through the final change point and after. Evening Star had the tendency to be insincere with her words. We never knew when to believe her, but Jonathan invariably meant what he said.

He seemed to understand the teachings of the need for a union of souls better than the others, and with this one loyal soul we felt we had the foundation for a future Divine New Order community. The guides said that one loyal member of the cosmic family would draw another. That was a universal law—when souls of like mind came together for a common purpose, the power of heaven would be available to them on the highest levels possible. We would not only meet and become friends with these people, but their unseen guides would also become a part of our lives and reality. Angels, midwayers, and other superhuman beings assigned to the human watchcare could now speak to me and all of us about cosmic truth and the future Divine New Order.

We all ate together, prayed together, laughed, and cried together. But most of all, we had a common purpose: to inform the people of the planet about the future earth changes, the need for community life, and the necessary evacuation by spaceships or light body for those who would respond.

One evening an angel called Destin spoke: *"There will be sacred/protected areas all over the planet that will be supernaturally protected during the earth changes and possible final war. At a point in time even these areas will no longer be safe. It is hoped that thousands of people will be living in these protected and Divine New Order areas and that you will have the organization on an international scale to mobilize millions of others when the final evacuation will be necessary. Your group will be responsible for seven locations around the planet. It will seem like an impossible job in the beginning, and you will probably want to give up."*

Little did I realize just how hard it would be, and I almost gave up when Jonathan left. He was persuaded by a pretty ex-girlfriend who came to supposedly be part of our community. She wanted to travel and he had itchy feet (being a traveling man all of his life), so she played up to another young man, and Jonathan became jealous. She won Jonathan's lust for her and maybe his heart. The next thing we knew they left together, taking Evening Star with them. Before Jonathan left town with the confused triangle, he spread the rumor that I was a fraud and God knows what else. We were left with all of the bills and high mortgage payments.

Months earlier, we had been directed by the guides to sell the house (they knew what was coming) and move to Sedona, Arizona, which would become the key protected area and the First Planetary Sacred Home. Because these first community members left so suddenly, we had to take a twenty thousand dollar loss on the home. We also had to deal with the hatefulness of Niánn's ex-husband who had put an unjust judgment against the proceeds of the sale. By the time we were finished with lawyers' fees and closing fees, we did not have enough left to even dream of obtaining land for a community. We needed a miracle.

Evening Star was a very gentle female spirit, and our two babies, DeleVin and DeleVan had loved her. For several weeks after the group left, the children, who had grown accustomed to them as family, were very upset and cried a lot. It was as if they knew on a higher level that some of the family was missing. Evening Star just could not face up to her own lack of self-esteem and self-motivation. When we or her guides would try to share her precious potential with her and how to use her gifts, she would pretend enough to let us believe she understood, but inwardly she resented our instruction.

After these family members left, the guides shared with us that our community breakdown was a small example of the Lucifer Rebellion. Only God the Father, Michael the Son, and a few other Universe Supervisors knew what was in the heart of Lucifer and his potential to fall.

Niánn and I were in a state of shock for several weeks because we felt that despite any differences or hurts to one another, these first three community members would not leave us or the work we felt they were called to. We had much to learn about the human heart and its weaknesses. It was our continued learning that eased the pain over the years when many of the soul mate family members we had met would go their own way, and because of this we were being educated about the true problems of the entire planet.

We became wiser about the complexities of the human psyche when Terra and Sastar met in our home. I had first met Terra in California and immediately loved him. I did not know until years later, when the guides told me, that he was my cosmic son and had been in my human family as a brother in several past repersonalizations. He was a tall, dark, and handsome man, with a sensitive, kind soul. He had just received distribution on his New Age instrumental album from a major company in Hollywood, and he was at a high point in life. He left L.A. searching for another city in which to relocate.

We had been told in advance by the guides that God wanted Terra to join our community. Terra did not agree with that at all. Hollywood was still a bug within him, which he did not realize. He thought he just needed a bigger city than Prescott to reach the success level he desired. We prayed that he would at least not go back to L.A. He did for a while, but temporarily ended up in Tucson.

Sastar had been aware of the Ashtar Command when she lived in California and was directed by the Command through a lower-level channel to come to Prescott. She came to several private transmissions and was instructed by Celestial Overcontrol to become part of our community. The moment Niánn and I had seen her, we loved her. We spent the first Christmas in Prescott with Sastar and had many nights of high-level spiritual conversations. She was intelligent and well-read, divorced, with five grown children.

Celestial Overcontrol was very forceful in telling the people of Prescott about the upcoming earth changes, a message the conservative mindset did not want to hear, and so many of the New Age community there rejected our work. Sastar could not stand with us in this area, and eventually she denied the validity of our work and that I was a true Ashtar channel. We loved her very much, and she was Niánn's cosmic daughter. I was not her cosmic father, but in past lives on this planet I had been her older brother. She was told of my brother relationship with her by the guides, but they never revealed Niánn's true cosmic relationship with her.

Terra was staying with us, and we invited Sastar over for dinner one evening. Sastar was immediately attracted to Terra—as a matter of fact, she was beside herself with adoration for him. When they started talking, it turned out that they both were from the same Midwestern town and had attended the same high school. Although they both lived in L.A. at the same time, they had not met until in our home. It was a definite providential meeting. We were told much about their past lives together, but could only tell them bits and pieces because of their unalignment with our work and with Celestial Overcontrol.

~~~~~~~~~~~~~~~~~~~~~~~~~~~

[A Possible Future Scenario]

Years later, after the first big earthquake hit L.A. and San Francisco, killing thousands, they each, in their separate lives, found out where we were and joined us. By this time we were in Sedona and had several hundred in our community. Terra was instrumental in helping to produce several motion pictures of high consciousness, saving thousands of lives and reaching millions with higher truths, as the people of the planet were then ready to hear the answers few had wanted to hear before.

Chapter 10

Within the body of the community we were able to accomplish great things in many areas, because we had so many minds working together for a common purpose. It was too bad it took the deaths of many of their loved ones before others could accept the answers themselves. So many of us, including myself, would have had the desires of our hearts answered if the alignment of cosmic family could have come years before the cataclysms and economic upheavals. The joy and fulfillment we did experience was mixed with great sadness because of the death and destruction all over the planet and in our own backyard of America.

CHAPTER 11
Commitment To Global Change And Service To Humankind

More of the cosmic family began to come to us in ways that we realized at the time were divinely directed. One day in the winter of 1988 a gentleman came to look at our antique furniture and spent several hours talking about spiritual things. He immediately liked both of us. We even talked about community living and purchasing land, and he said that this was also an idea of his. His name in past repersonalizations was Woman's Eye because he was easily led astray by women; his wife's name in a past repersonalization was Kala, meaning cautious one. In that past life Woman's Eye also had married Kala, who had led him many times to do other than what God's will was for him, for she was fearful and cautious. Because of this, Woman's Eye never became a leader among his tribe, as he was always busy trying to please Kala.

In this present life we saw the same circumstances being the reality. Woman's Eye loved learning and growing spiritually, and although he said his wife did also, she was actually more interested in other things that pulled her away from spiritual growth, and she would not commit herself to any study that would take time away from her other involvements. Woman's Eye was not enough of a leader to lead the way, thus both of them never aligned themselves with our work.

We saw this same scenario take place with so many other couples who came to us. A question was posed by the midwayers, "Does God ask us to come to a cliff in life and just jump over, leaving all behind with no guarantee of landing safely except the faith that one is in the perfect will of the Creator?"

The answer to this is an unquestionable yes. But we found few who were willing to take the dive. Usually the men were the first willing to jump, but misplaced loyalties to their women and their own lack of courage kept them from their destinies and held them in their own smallness. We saw the reality of what could have transpired if they had stayed with us.

Urell and Anignea came to us. He (Urell) was an intellectual, and she was an intuitive, sensitive controller. She was willing to allow him freedom as long as the freedom that he pursued aligned with her own wishes. Whenever it did not, she would assume authority over him. This same spirit was in the souls of many women in Western civilization and was one of the greatest imbalances in the family prior to the final change point and Divine New Order. The love shown between us was felt not only by Urell and Anignea but also by Urell's two star children who were cosmic children to Niánn and me. These children even said that they really wanted to live with us. They sensed a higher reality and past association with us. But all of the love they experienced was denied by Urell and Anignea when she began to lose control of him.

Apo and Apoleaha came to us knowing that God was calling them to a new way of life, particularly the husband, Apo, who knew that he was being called into a life of spiritual destiny. The first plans were for them to move into our new cottage, in which they would have had to invest a few thousand dollars. Apo was more willing to do this. They were also told that an opening would come up for them that would be a metaphysical bookstore and spiritual outreach for the community and would be a sufficient source of income for them. Apo was willing to dive in, and at first made the necessary steps, but Apoleaha was reluctant to go the distance and persuaded Apo not to join our work and our hearts.

One week after they left, the next door neighbor told us that they were moving and would be renting their home and asked if we knew of anyone who would be interested in renting. Also there appeared in the local newspaper an ad for a metaphysical bookstore. We saw that the destiny of this family had been missed. We also felt we had lost something, as we loved them very much.

As each person we met left us, we felt much pain and grief because we could see a little of the future and believed in the actualization and fulfillment that would come with our union, but this new future was being held back because of their obstinacy and misplaced loyalties. I particularly had a love-hate relationship in my heart for those whom I knew had erred in their judgment, not only hurting themselves but those who loved them. In their unalignment to the perfect will of God, fulfillment of destiny could not be realized. When one soul is out of divine will, out of the eternal purpose, it affects the whole planet starting at the level of the family unit.

Zordon and Zella came to us with much pain and brokenness of past repersonalizations, and both in need of counseling. We immediately loved Zordon and felt in this gentle but manly human being a courageous loyalty that needed direction. When Zella saw his affection toward us, she became overly protective and eventually caused the breakup of our relationship with them, using a number of accusations, as people will do who do not want to look at the real problem. Both had tremendous potential to become counselors for the afflicted and addicted. Had they remained with us, within five years they could have been authors and leaders in this field.

In all of these cases, the men were not spiritually strong enough to follow the will of God and allow the women to follow the men's examples. All of these men were kept on a leash by their women. As the tragedies of the earth changes increase and the deaths of many of their loved ones possibly occur, it is hoped that some of these men will become courageous enough to leave these women, after realizing that these domineering women not only hold them back but hold back the consciousness of the planet and their own children's future growth.

CHAPTER 12

Inappropriate Relationships

Judas and Magna came to us and entered our classes. We had a great love for Magna from the very beginning. We were told by the guides that her relationship with Judas was a mismatch and that she had a Native American complement who would be led to her as she aligned herself more perfectly with her God. We could not tell her this until the proper time, and when we did, she was angry with us, as she was still with Judas. We believed at the time that his name, given to us by Celestial Overcontrol, was an indication of the type of person he was.[1]

Although we showed him love and respect, he denied us the same, gossiped about us, and saw problems in my character, where perhaps there were none—all this because he subconsciously knew that we were aware that they did not belong together. Physically, Magna was a tremendously beautiful woman with a sensitive heart and giving nature. Judas was a selfish individual and an opportunist.

From time eternal, there was in the mind of God a plan for a union of souls—males and females—on all evolutionary worlds where the birth of the children and the spiritual growth of the planet was the primal order. This perfect plan, a masterpiece, was upset by the Lucifer Rebellion, the subsequent fall of the Planetary Prince (Caligastia), and the later default of the Material Son and Daughter (Adam and Eve). Because of the spiritual decadence and genetic imbalance, Urantia became a planet where marriages and mating between the opposite sexes were not marriages of cosmic origin and spiritual attunement but marriages of animalistic origin and materialistic expediency. That was true of twentieth-century civilization, especially America, and on into the twenty-first century.

The teachings of complementary polarities and soul mates go far beyond the scope of my sharing in this orientation. I will briefly state that it became quite evident that there were few males and females who were united in true fourth-dimensional complementary polarity unions. Even those who wrote books on the subject of twin flames and soul mates and who were initiators in the field were not united with their true complementary polarities and in fact had divorced the wives with whom they co-authored their first books.

Most individuals, having married the prince or princess of their dreams, soon discovered that they did not get all that they had hoped or bargained for in their mate. The reasons for this were numerous. The spiritual growth of the individual, or lack of it, is the foremost reason for either obtaining a high-stage soul mate/complement or a low-stage mate (a partner who is not a complementary soul mate). Since the various cultures of the planet and the existing realities within them were far from fourth-dimensional cosmic reality on an international level, souls had to be educated with new concepts and new ways of looking at reality, particularly interpersonal relationships.

It was the belief of certain individuals that those who looked good, were in good health, and were financially successful would be able to find their perfect mate. A good look into that Hollywood delusion should have shown Western civilization that this was not a true reality. The universe is consistent in that it gives the motive of the heart the answer it deserves. Most of us found that life did not go exactly as we had planned.

Many of those who succeeded in certain career choices were spiritual failures. Character faults were present in their personalities to the extent that those individuals were only a shell of what they could have been. Better to be a happy plumber in the perfect will of the Creator than a miserable surgeon out of the Father's will. Many females who had become imbalanced in their energy dominated their men and chose men who had become feminine in their character. Many men chose the successful businesswoman with a similar career, thinking that this would be a common denominator in their relationship and discovered that they had only obtained a combatant and competitor.

Many couples who came to us simply did not belong together, and those who had personal transmissions were told this. These people had become trapped in their own circumstances, and truth was something they said they wanted to hear but in reality were not willing to accept when it was given to them. Until these people as individual ascending sons and daughters had chosen to take the first steps of dying to their own wills and seeking the Father's will for their ascension to Paradise, they would never be ready to accept the truth. This search for the Father's will begins on the evolutionary worlds in the lowest stages, such as Urantia.

Inappropriate relationships and friendships of any kind between male and female begin at an early age and continue in the peer group, education, business, and recreational activities. Some close friends are selected simply because of their ability to do something that the other cannot do or because of their accomplishment in a particular field. An example of this would be the teenage boy who hangs around with those who play sports well and becomes a close friend with the best athlete because he is the most highly respected, in hopes that some of that respect will rub off on the nonathletic boy.

It does not matter that the athlete is an angry person with a character disorder. As long as he is accepted by the peer group, it does not matter that he might be a thief. If the nonathletic boy could see the future, he might see himself accosted in the store along with the athletic thief and accused of shoplifting because of his association with his hero. If his parents had directed him to choose his friends based on other values—firstly spiritual—then the universe would have drawn these friends to him, because his thoughts and desires would have created the energy that the unseen guides of these other souls could have used to bring them his way.

But great truths still have to be learned by the people of Urantia, who will not be ready for them until the near collapse of what we know as civilization. Sometimes the very longings within the heart can draw the object of that longing into our sphere. The degree of alignment with God is the degree that the object of your desire will come to you.

Many people who are sitting on the cosmic fence—the choice between total surrender and partial surrender to God—will draw energy to themselves in varying degrees. For instance, a woman who is in 75% alignment with her God might draw a mate from another corner of the world into the very city where she lives, but never meet that man until the other 25% of her will is aligned with God (and of course the man would have to be properly aligned).

One summer evening Niánn and I were drawn to a Native American Indian powwow. While we were there watching the dancing and enjoying the drums, I felt in the very essence of my being the reality of my past complementary polarity relationship with Setta. She was in many ways at that moment the very essence of the music I was hearing and the heartbeat of the drums. Niánn pointed out to me that Setta was sitting in the corner of the bleachers. A strange coincidence, as at this time she was living in another city.

It was Niánn who first felt the urge to go to the powwow, for Setta was not only longing for her complementary polarity but also for a sister relationship, and Niánn was her highest sister. The motives of her heart may have been good, but in third-dimensional reality her thoughts were quite confused by what people thought and said she needed, and what society said she should do. The universe will always do what is most correct, perfect, and loving for the motive of the soul that sends out these longings to God, but few there are who—when those longings are answered by God to some degree—recognize the answer within the cosmic family souls that God sends.

Personal Audience/Office Transmissions: Giving Souls Their Point Of Origin (A Major Part Of My Mandate)

It would be our job to teach the people of Urantia. Both the souls born here and those from planets of other universes needed to know their reality of existence, and all needed to be brought together in a planetary consciousness based upon individual origin and divine destiny. Paladin and the midwayers told me to request a full-face picture from those wanting to know their point of origin, whether you were from this universe or another.

Gradually I began to know the difference in soul age. Paladin came through and gave specifics. My opinion was, and still is, never final. Celestial Overcontrol wanted me to learn the discernment on my own by looking at a picture if the person was not present. Later I would do many transmissions by mail. It became impossible to see each person who wanted a personal transmission and have a private audience and bring Paladin through. Celestial Overcontrol wanted to eventually speak to only the most humble and those who really wanted to follow the will of God.

For several years, however, Paladin would confront many proud souls (who considered themselves spiritual teachers and leaders) about their own darkness. Not only did they receive information about their points of origin, they were also shown their areas of evil, sin, or iniquity that they did not want to see. No one else loved them enough or was brave enough to tell them, or perhaps no one saw. They were told about their immediate destiny and what they needed to do to reach their highest destiny. The majority of them were in inappropriate relationships. I would be blamed by parents, grown children, and grandparents for breaking up families. However their relationships were spiritually and emotionally broken long before they came to Global Community Communications Alliance. The community just made it physically and emotionally possible for them to make the necessary separation.

However, many dear souls knew Paladin was right and did what was needed to join the Divine Administration in which many of them had important roles to play. But for those very many who did not want to hear or accept the answers that would bring them more personal fulfillment and sense of spiritual destiny, they did not want anyone else to consider them either.

On February 25, 1999, Niánn and I wrote a letter, and below is an updated version of that letter.

> To Parents, Grandparents, and Other Family Members and Friends of Those in the Religious Order/Community of Divine Administration,
>
> We have prayerfully come to the conclusion that our Lord is asking us to write all of you with the intention of creating a bond of understanding between the Eldership of Divine Administration and you, as well as between your family members and friends of Divine Administration and you.
>
> Jesus said, "Blessed are the peacemakers, for they shall be called the children of God."[2] It is in this spirit of peace that we write all of you. We know that there are attempts by some of you to hurt this religious order and its leaders, especially Gabriel of Urantia/TaliasVan of Tora. Misrepresentation of any kind continues to cause us both emotional grief and financial loss to all in the community—adults and children alike—for we live under one common "purse."
>
> We understand that some of you have been in communication with each other, possibly contributing to each other's fears and misunderstandings of Divine Administration and Eldership.
>
> I, Gabriel of Urantia/TaliasVan of Tora, would first like to state that I had to leave my very close Italian Catholic

family when I was twenty-four years old to follow where my heart and personal relationship with God led me. My parents wanted me to be a priest; I attempted that twice in monasteries. Have any of you read my autobiography? If you have read it and thought it was one of the strangest books you ever read, I can understand that, for my experiences and understanding of life are probably very different from most of yours. Also, our claims are difficult to believe concerning who we are. But this does not make me a dangerous cult leader. For example, contrary to some of your fears, I do not tell anyone what to think. If you visit and meet all of us, you will observe that the community members are quite diverse and expansive thinkers.

Some single parents bring worries, stresses, and financial problems they had developed before they came to us, now wanting our help. The mother or father as well as the children benefit from our extended-family effort to help raise the children. Some couples separate soon after arriving because they could not financially do so before they came here, or they could not take the disapproval from their parents or siblings or other relatives who would not agree with their separation back home.

Our first and foremost wish is that couples or parents can work out their difficulties so that they and their children can stay together in a nuclear family unit. However, for many reasons this is not always the case, but they do remain in an extended-family unit, relating to each other in a harmonious and loving manner as friends rather than being separated and in conflictive situations that affect them and their children in a harmful way.

The first loyalty of your adult family member or friend in Divine Administration is to Jesus Christ Michael. That is why they are here, and that is why they stay here. Many of you who choose to be united to each other in your misunderstandings and fears about Divine Administration would be very divided among yourselves in your religious beliefs, and some might even think some of you others are not even "saved." We do not make such judgments. On the contrary, our work is to ultimately unite people in the nature and understanding of our Universal Father of All.

I, Gabriel of Urantia/TaliasVan of Tora, know what it is to lose children; I lost a seven-year-old daughter to open-heart surgery. My father died without he and I having been reconciled, for he never forgave me for leaving home at twenty-four years old. Neither has the rest of my family forgiven me for leaving home to pursue my ministry.

We did not separate your children from you; this planet has philosophies, theologies, and career choices that do that. We have some of our own biological children here in Divine Administration and are trying to create a society here where they will not have to make choices to leave their family. When children grow up they choose for themselves.

The movie October Sky is a prime example of a son going against his father's wishes in his choice of career. In the movie, the father finally comes around and creates a relationship with his son that is stronger and within the higher will of God. Another movie, called **Rudy** (which is also a true story), shows the courage of a young man from a very poor environment who follows his heart rather than the expectations of others close to him. Rudy's example inspired five of his younger brothers to follow their hearts and earn college degrees, something they probably would never have done if Rudy had not set the example.

Chapter 12

I, Gabriel of Urantia/TaliasVan of Tora, will close with this. It's hard for me to understand that if any of you have heard my music, that you would deny my relationship with God or think for one moment that I can bring any harm to your children or grandchildren in any way. My whole adult life has been just the opposite. This information is on our Web site for the world to see. I am proud of my life's service to humankind, and my ministry still continues.

I, Niánn Emerson Chase, am a parent also. I have birthed six children, all of them young adults now. Like many of you, I daily experience the love and concerns that a parent has for her children, even when they are of adult age.

Three of my oldest children have made choices that I do not approve of, that I feel keep them from being truly happy, healthy, and fulfilled within God's divine pattern. But they made those choices, and I do not attempt to interfere in their lives or prevent them from pursuing their dreams. I just love them and want to enjoy them wherever they are, but in their choices, they have chosen to separate themselves completely from me; thus we have no communication with each other. Of course I experience sadness in not being part of their lives, but I would not go against their freewill choices to live their lives the way they choose or force myself on them when they are not interested.

So, I do understand the pain of the separation you may be experiencing, but that separation does not necessarily need to exist. Separation is created within the minds of those involved and need not exist if we all overcame our own unfounded fears and misunderstandings. In separation there are sides, and it takes all sides wanting to break down those walls in order for a beginning understanding and unity to be formed.

Families can come together in love and enjoyment without completely understanding each other or even approving of some of the family members' choices, but honoring and respecting each others' individuality and right to choose how they will live, regardless of whether those choices fit your plans and beliefs or not.

Our wish for all of you is that you would be united with your children, grandchildren, parents, and siblings of Divine Administration as family, overcoming your own unfounded fears and misunderstandings, and allow your loved ones in this religious order to pursue their chosen lifestyles and careers, while enjoying their unique beauty and light that they shed upon your lives. We want all members of the community to be able to feel united with their biological families, accepted and loved by you in their choices to be with Divine Administration, and likewise, they being loving and accepting of you.

In the spirit of peace and understanding,

Gabriel of Urantia/TaliasVan of Tora
and Niánn Emerson Chase

CHAPTER 13
Universal Origin

Our unseen mentors began to share with us the vastness of the grand universe, its administration, and its inhabitants. One day Paladin came through and said, in his normal and humorous way, *"All humans are mortals in the universe of Nebadon, but not all mortals are human. You humans with penises and vaginas will find this reality quite different in the Orion system. What may be quite common in lovemaking on Urantia may be quite uncommon on planets of another universe where the physical reality may be quite different.*

"Along with the Urantian Adam and Eve progeny on this planet is the life plasm in the progeny of the Adams and Eves from planets in other universes. Material Sons and Daughters from other universes are quite different from Material Sons and Daughters from Nebadon. Where the ideal of monogamy may be the highest ideal of Nebadon, it may not be the ideal of Avalon. Not all humans present on Urantia are from Urantia; some have been here for centuries but are not originally from Urantia. They have been mixed with humans of Urantian origin or humans from any of the other planets in Nebadon and then expected to function normally, accepting not only the social and planetary norms, but the local universe norms.

"In all of these areas you have an alien trying to function by the standards of what is to him an alien world. On planets that have not fallen, there can be an amalgamation of not only interplanetary but interuniversal relationships, marriages, and administrative functions because the natures of these individuals are understood and allowed. On these worlds of unfallen reality where no major rebellion has occurred, circuits have not been cut off between them and other planets in their universe and outside of it. But on the thirty-seven

fallen planets of the system of Satania in Nebadon, cosmic chaos exists in all manner of socialization, integration, and actualization of its planetary citizenry."

At that moment in time Paladin asked me to remember when I had visited some Mexican prisons, all of the prisoners, no matter what their crime, were thrown together in one social structure. In the same cell may have been a murderer and a shoplifter, a rapist with a tax evader, a gentle sensitive soul with a violent one. In this kind of environment it was like the animalistic societies of primitive man. The strongest ones were in control. The most sensitive and gentle ones found themselves either dying or changing into a character harder than who they really were and having to accept the norms of that particular deranged, cruel, and uncivilized prison.

Having to accept and live by the norms of the majority, over the years I began to feel like a prisoner on Urantia, and I saw others who also felt like prisoners to those norms. The difference was that I had realized it to the degree that I wanted to no longer be in prison. I was not happy there and tried to awaken those, at whatever level I could, to their own imprisonment. It was an impossible task. When they began to realize that what I was saying just might be true, their family, friends, and societal structure would all draw them back into the Luciferic thought pattern and the Caligastia timetable.

Once back into that so-called "reality," individuals denied their cosmic identity, earning their living in unfulfilling jobs, looking for sex partners (because the appetites needed feeding), eating the wrong foods, drinking impure water, and associating with souls far below their highest potential that they themselves had not realized to the fullest. Those souls, like the majority in the world, either needed a major tragedy to awaken them or for the universe to arrange a slow series of constant disappointments and trials, with the hope that they would be enlightened to true fourth-dimensional reality.

One day Paladin again gave a powerful teaching.

"Since Caligastia's staff of one hundred came to Urantia, and after the fall 200,000 years ago, their progeny have had instincts, talents, abilities, and genetic inheritance far different from humans of Urantian origin. It was hoped by the Universe Supervisors, even up to the twentieth century, that these descendants would be able to flow into, not only the norms of the planet, but the norms of the other planets of the universe of Nebadon, the universal code and law in which their ancestors had learned to function while they actively served and administered. They were also those who were only on an assignment and would have to go back to their own universe and superuniverse for completion and total actualization of reality.

"It was determined after approximately the mid-sixties of the twentieth century that these descendants could not function under the Nebadon code. They could come to the highest spiritual attainment, far surpassing their Urantian brothers in many areas, but could not be totally fulfilled or complete within the norms and morality of Urantia and its social structure. So it was determined by the Universe Supervisors and mandated by Michael of Salvington that those who could be used as contact personalities would be given Continuing Fifth Epochal Revelation at various levels that would complement that which was already given in the 1934–35 papers [The URANTIA Book].

"We all live in an evolving universe, and in an evolving universe no one book can contain the total truth of the cosmic reality of any one planet, let alone a system, universe, superuniverse, or master universe. This is what the schools of ascension are for, to supplement the answers to questions that could only be partially understood in the previous plane, to synthesize the omnipresent reality of the Absolute and the Ultimate God of Paradise who has reached out of His reality to teach His creation, in a continuing process, the secrets of eternity. No one lesson, no one text, no one life upon a planet or plane can encompass that lesson, that total truth, for it is a gift and a process of growth.

"In the larger cities of America there is ethnocentrism in one's neighborhood, and some can tell what neighborhood a person is from simply by conversation. Others may not be able to do this outside of the city, but those within the city who know the various neighborhoods are adept in this discernment. We of Celestial Overcontrol—with an objective view not only of a system of planets, but a constellation of planets, a universe of planets, a minor and major sector of planets, a superuniverse of planets, and a grand universe of planets—can tell what universe and neighborhood you are from and can totally, with one hundred percent accuracy, recognize your talents, abilities, how you think and react to reality, and your quest or non-quest for God."

CHAPTER 14

Leaving The Old Behind, Changing Your Name, And The Cost Of Becoming A Change Agent

I remember that back in Pittsburgh in 1985, the transition in changing my name to Gabriel was not easy. I found out very quickly that few of my old friends would call me Gabriel and definitely not my parents or close relatives. The reasons varied. I did not even realize at the time that I was beginning to shift in consciousness from the third to the fourth dimension. At least one of the apostles of Jesus was given a new name to make his transition, Simon became Peter. And later, Saul became Paul, a powerful leader among Jesus' followers. I realized that as long as I stayed in Pittsburgh I would be Tony.

Actually, the name given at confirmation in the Catholic Church is a name symbolic of a spiritual rebirth. At twelve years old, when most Catholics of my generation supposedly made their commitment to God, the only things on their minds were looking pretty or handsome in their white outfits and what gifts they might get. It had become just rote for the adults also.

There is a cosmic reality that remains the same. A cosmic name is our inheritance from the Universe Father, not only for the mortals of the evolutionary worlds like Urantia, but for all the ascending sons and daughters of God and all orders of beings in the grand universe, in which we of Urantia are like a grain of sand on a seashore.

One of the reasons why people would not call me Gabriel was plain old sin. To be more specific, they had envy, jealousy, greed, and false pride. I began to find this out while in Pittsburgh. I met a record producer of New Age music from San Francisco; let's call him Mr. Lost. He had all of the previously mentioned faults. He would not admit that my album was good and picked on the bad timing of the drummer in some of the parts of a couple of songs. When I asked him to pinpoint exactly where, it turned out to be a drum machine part and not the drummer. I did use both, but drum machines do not lose time. He called me Gabriel until he found out my birth name was Tony. Strange, I thought.

I realized that in Hollywood jealous hearts would not recognize another's struggle to become a success. If they could not make the metamorphosis themselves, they did not want you to either. But if you became rich or famous, they wanted to be your best friend. "I knew you would make it" or "I believed in you all of the time" were their comments when you succeeded.

I met many Mr. and Mrs. Losts all over the country, and they could be very painful for any soul trying to evolve spiritually. Yes, I wanted to have my music heard by the masses; yes, I wanted to be influential in music and films so that I could help our planet and other struggling artists, but I could not have cared less about being famous. As a matter of fact, the Hollywood persona that colored the world with materialistic and sexual lust nauseated me. I think it would have sickened any spiritually healthy person.

Other people would have liked to have made a change in themselves, but because of misplaced loyalties to a spouse, job, religion, or career, they subconsciously would not accept the eagle's courage. I began wearing an earring in my left ear, a long hanging one, to show my desire to be different. The earring was an outward sign of an already inner decision. A lot of men I met who had jobs where this would not be accepted and macho men who claimed it was not manly snickered at me. The reality was they did not have the courage to quit the jobs they were unhappy in or leave friends who kept them on a lower level.

Christ said that old wine skins were no good for new wine. New thinking brings about many changes in life, and one must look forward to each challenge of newness. In Pittsburgh, for about a year, new friends were calling me Gabriel and old friends stuck to calling me Tony. I had to leave my hometown for good to complete the metamorphosis, and it took several years before I actually knew I was the Gabriel that God wanted me to be.

Chapter 14

The Cloak Of Respectability

Try to buck the system in any way and see what happens. When terrible things happen to the innocent, people would say, "What a pity, what a shame." Like the respectable lawyer who overcharged his clients or his secretary who knew she was working for a legal thief but did not see herself as part of the problem. What about the television and radio commentators who sell out to corporate interests rather than presenting the truth? How about the people who worked for title companies that took a good part of people's hard-earned dollars, all in the name of service? Did they quit their jobs in protest of their company's policies? How about those who worked for war weapon corporations or liquor industries? Why did they stay? "For the money," they said. "I have a wife and children to support; I have to survive," said Mr. and Mrs. America.

Would God have wanted you to survive by placing a gun to someone's head and taking their food if you had none? The moral complacency of Americans helped to destroy the modern world. When greed was allowed to rule in the hearts of neighbors, peers, and business associates without confrontation by ethics, civilizations were destroyed. How many died in the latter half of the twentieth century because they could not afford proper medical care? The answer is tens of thousands in America. Even those assistants who worked for so-called men of healing could not afford their employers' services themselves.

All of these formerly-complacent ones were called "voices crying in the wilderness," bums, radicals, and cultists when they left their jobs or careers in the establishment in order to try to make a change. The true artist who helps bring souls to God-consciousness is a dying breed, and in the name of art, so-called artists with materialistic values have helped to choke the life force out of billions of souls around the planet.

When you become a material girl or boy, man or woman, you do not become the true you—the astral or spiritual you—

and you do not become a candidate for a higher plane of existence as an ascending son or daughter. But you do have to spend another lifetime on a planet much like Urantia or worse. If you are lucky, you may get to choose your next hell.

CHAPTER 15

The Protected Areas

We had been told by Celestial Overcontrol and by various celestial intelligences that all throughout the planet there would be interlocking grid systems and ley lines of supernatural origin that would create a web that only a few of our modern scientists were beginning to recognize. Protected mountains and valleys on the planet were interconnected to others in different geographic locations on various continents. These interdimensional portals, these sonic tunnels, these tunnels of cosmic energy, unknown to man, served as passageways for extraterrestrial and interdimensional travel on Urantia.

At the very center of each transport area was a surrounding circular area that put out energy. This depended upon the kinds of beings that entered the vortex or energy reflective circuit. We on our planet had named these places of incomprehensible energy vortexes, but the finaliter, Paladin, gave us the new term of energy reflective circuits, and this is the term I will use to describe an area under the divine supervision of intergalactic and interdimensional authority and protection. It may be as small as an acre or as large as a thousand acres, with tributaries shooting out in all directions connecting with complementary energy reflective circuits in other geographic areas, perhaps on the same continent or on another.

We were told that the consciousness of the people in that area, the mass consciousness in relation to their link with their Creator God, would determine what representatives of the cosmic family would be sent to that area and what supernatural forces would be working there. Just because an energy reflective circuit had been so in the past did not mean that it would remain one. It could function in the present only if the humans in that area recognized the Cosmic Father of All, His authority, and the authority of those whom He had mandated in human form. These leaders were yet to be recognized, but we were told that in the days of crisis that lay ahead they would become manifest and known.

We were moving from Prescott, an area that had lost its chance of becoming divinely protected, and for the next several months it seemed that all the forces of evil were bent on keeping us from entering the protected area in Sedona where we were guided to go. Let us call it Secret Valley. For two and a half months Niánn and I, with our twenty-three-month-old twins and two-month-old son, lived in a tent while forces of good and evil battled through the red tape of obtaining a loan approval. The home that was selected in an affordable price range was near a protected mountain in Sedona, linked to Salvington, the capital of our universe.

The energies manifested in this area were of a balanced female circuit, even more so than the nearby male circuit that was also of cosmic balance. Hundreds of interdimensional beings who had mastered the female aspect of God had entered through this area. The very soil itself was being artificially injected by the Life Carriers to produce food under subnormal conditions. The area would also receive rain when other areas in Arizona would experience drought. Great gusts of wind would come from time to time to clear away the pollution in the air, and this was all taking place before we ever lived in the area.

Finally we acquired the home and moved in. The forces of evil were still fighting very hard to keep us in financial despair and fear, for they did not want our work to succeed. We had no idea as to how other members of the cosmic family and our human family would come to live in a safe area with us, as we hardly had enough income to sustain our basic needs, let alone purchase more land. Yet we were told that this would happen, and we began to see the reality of it in the months and years ahead.

Chapter 15

[A Possible Future Scenario]

Certain communities that were led by extraterrestrial guidance were asked to go to specific geographic areas. Some of those areas had already experienced earthquakes, volcanic eruptions, and tidal waves. When they arrived, the people living there were in chaos and fear. Many had no hope of survival and did not care because their loved ones had already been killed. The true spiritual ones of the planet were guided by the extraterrestrials to explain what was really happening to our planet and to prepare those who would listen for evacuation by spacecraft, so they could be brought back to a new world, a new earth. Some were able to transcend by light body transference rather than by spacecraft evacuation. Those who would listen would indeed survive and give hope to all who had to be awakened.

~~~~~~~~~~~~~~~~~~~~

Tragedies—natural and otherwise—do not happen due to God's wrath but through the cause-and-effect pattern of negative thought-forms with which man had disfigured this planet for 200,000 years, since the fall of its Planetary Prince. Man's inhumanity to his brother, his greed and pride and lust for false power, his lack of understanding of cosmic truth are now making Mother Earth explode within and without.

Celestial Overcontrol told us that it is hoped that certain special areas will serve as a shield of divine protection for all who are committed to come out of the old ways and into the Divine New Order and administration of the Planetary Prince. Where Niánn and I live is the first of these areas. We found that when those interested in living in the community began to commit themselves to higher truths and higher teachers, they were able to put aside their false pride and intellectual nuances and accommodate within themselves the humility to become students with questions to ask rather than with answers to give.

Unfortunately, until many individuals find that they have no food for their stomachs or no roof over their heads, they will hang onto their illusions of the Great American Dream that is influencing the whole planet. Materialism and mechanistic technology have totally replaced the extended family, and the values of humankind have deteriorated as those in control of governments desire even more power and material gain. Cancer of the soul is much worse than cancer of the body, for it causes the possible everlasting separation from its Creator, while death of the body can actually bring the soul closer to its Creator.

Both in Prescott and in Sedona we observed some of our neighbors moving away soon after we moved in, especially those with fundamentalist ideas that could not be easily changed. Still, we were very discouraged when we would meet members of the cosmic family who yet did not understand the necessity of commitment and adherence to our counsel, which was always the counsel of the higher intelligences who spoke through me. As they proceeded in their own way, we saw much turmoil take place in their lives, all of which could have been avoided.

While living in the tent in Sedona, we met people from all over the world and found them to be pretty much the same—materialistically oriented, with misplaced loyalties to human family members and to careers that promised security and misplaced loyalties to spouses and to dreams that were based upon the same Babylonian principles that had destroyed civilization after civilization. Many heard the truth when they had private transmission sessions with Paladin. But since he told people what they needed to hear, not always what they wanted to hear, many of these souls did not accept the higher teachings, though some would when tragedy struck them personally. Unfortunately, many will begin to accept the higher teachings when they realize that Earth is falling apart.

It was amazing to see the condition of a lost soul. To the higher intelligences a lost soul is defined as any soul who is not totally experiencing the divine fulfillment and total actualization of all of his or her dreams, talents, and abilities and who is not in a right relationship with the Creator. It would be safe to say that most souls on the planet are lost souls.

[A Possible Future Scenario]

During the beginning days of the purification, dozens of families and single people were beginning to be moved from the area by unseen forces. Many homes in the area of Planetary Headquarters were repossessed by banks and left empty; the occupants of many others just moved. The energies of truth and love within the Third Radius, and in particular the First Radius of the Planetary Prince, were so powerful that those less loving, nonbelievers in absolutes could not resonate there. Slowly these vacant homes were occupied by cosmic family members who were awakened and were still allowed by the Universe Supervisors to come into the area of safety.

It was common during the later years, before the final change point, to see smaller spacecraft land, bringing representatives of Christ Michael in human form who walked about the land with me, discussing the organization and administration needed in governing the community and in the future evacuation that would take place. With some of the unseen friends becoming visible, the role of leader became much easier.

In the following years, as more souls loyal to Christ Michael arrived (those who truly loved Him more than anyone or anything else), the ministry began to prosper financially, enabling us to acquire more land and facilities. It was not always the most loyal who arrived first, but souls that tested Niánn's and my faith time and time again. Some were mandated for their potential loyalty to God and their mindal ability to comprehend Continuing Fifth Epochal Revelation. In many cases their virtue did not match their mindal ability.

The first two older cosmic family souls to arrive in Sedona came six months after they contacted us by letter in November of 1990. They had been with us in past lives. One was my cosmic half-brother. He would provide Niánn and me with much education as to discerning the individual and our responsibility to love unconditionally. The Bright and Morning Star said that my cosmic half-brother had great capacity for both good and evil. We unfortunately have had to deal with the unstabilized spirituality of this soul and others. We have found that in dealing with cosmic relatives, there has been a certain agony and ecstasy of experiences in interactions with more experienced and powerful souls. I began to truly learn the mercy of God.

CHAPTER 16

The Adjudication Moving Into Full Swing

Against all odds, Niánn and I and the children had finally moved into our new home in November of 1990. The house was situated facing dead center of the energy reflective circuit and mountainous rock structure called Cathedral Rock. This area is considered one of the most beautiful and sacred sites on the planet, and people from all over the world come to experience it.

It was so good to be in a home again after living in a tent with the three children for almost three months. After having used all of our savings to make the down payment on the home, we had only $25 to our name to provide for all our necessities, but I had faith that since the guides said we should be there, it would all work out. We started meeting neighbors, some of whom were cosmic family, but they were not at first responding to our work.

By the next month (December) I had become very depressed. Now that we were here in this protected area in our home I felt so lost. Where were the higher souls that were promised? Where were our cosmic family members? There seemed to be no one in the area who gave a hoot about us or what we had to offer them. We felt so isolated and alone.

We had to continue to sell many of our sentimental items in order to exist. Finally, Niánn obtained a position as a teacher in a Montessori school. I believe that the midwayers helped us by hiding our mortgage transaction from the loan company for three months until we were able to make the payments. The lending institution did not even know we existed. If those initial cosmic family members had aligned themselves, there would have been no need for some of the actions taken behind the scenes by the midwayers.

During this time we received our first letter from the two older souls mentioned before. We hardly believed what we read;

they were actually *URANTIA Book* readers and teachers and were interested in Continuing Fifth Epochal Revelation and wanted to talk to us further! We began the correspondence, and I felt that sooner or later we would disagree on something major, but to my surprise our relationship only got better. We began having long telephone conversations, which we always looked forward to, and it soon became quite obvious that somehow we would all have to be together.

Paladin made it clear that these two men would indeed come to Sedona and began to tell me of our cosmic connection. It did not take long to realize that this was the pair that (three years before) the midwayers had mentioned we would be meeting in the future. In May of 1991 they joined us in Sedona, Arizona and were living within walking distance from us in a central location of the energy reflective circuit, compliments of the Midwayer Commission (a location not so easy to obtain by human methods).

We all saw the hand of God begin to work with us. They recognized that I had the Mandate of the Bright and Morning Star, and I recognized that they had the Mandate as the first of the Vicegerent First Ambassadors to Machiventa Melchizedek. None of us at the time really understood exactly what that meant, but we learned much more about these mandates as the years progressed. With our joining in the union of souls, the four of us created our own energy reflective circuit that enabled other representatives of the Machiventa Melchizedek Administration, including Machiventa Melchizedek, to speak to us.

Soon, other cosmic family members from around the world began corresponding and had a desire to join us and become part of The Starseed and Urantian Schools of Melchizedek [a.k.a. Global Community Communications Schools of Ascension Science & The Physics of Rebellion]. Soon to be with us from Australia was the former editor of *Six-O-Six*, Delpheus, who was Niánn's and my cosmic daughter. We awaited with great expectation her arrival and the arrival of others at her level of spiritual ascension.

Chapter 16

In September of 1991, a married couple came from Santa Fe. In Sedona, several others aligned after the coming together of the first four Elders. When Delpheus arrived, the energy reflective circuit created by the union of souls became stronger and drew others from various parts of the planet who resonated with that vibration.

                                              ✧⋄✧⋄✧⋄✧⋄✧

At this time (October 9, 1991) I am being asked to interrupt this narrative to present a transmission by the Bright and Morning Star, Gabriel of Salvington.[1]

My adjudication began in the Earth time approximately 1911. This occurrence had been prophesied through other prophets. It began with the early transmissions of the Fifth Epochal Revelation and slowly, throughout the years, with representatives of my administration—under the mandate of Christ Michael, our Universe Sovereign—rematerializing on Urantia. In 1934 and 1935 a higher vibratory frequency was established. In 1955 an even higher vibratory frequency was established.

In 1967, quite unknown to the Urantia movement, another vibratory frequency was established. By this time the Urantia movement had fallen from the clear reception of their Thought Adjusters and the Spirit of Truth within them. Had they been open to the voice of God, many of them, and so many other millions, would have received the baptism of the Holy Spirit of my Divine Mother, the Universe Mother Spirit, and would have manifested the gifts of Her Spirit.

It would have enabled them to receive and understand Continuing Fifth Epochal Revelation now being given through the mandated personality, Gabriel of Urantia/TaliasVan of Tora. Many Protestants and Catholics alike received these gifts. If the obstinate URANTIA Book *readers had asked for it, they too would* have received the manifestations of the Mother circuits and could have been an aid to those Protestants and Catholics to help them in the understanding of the Fifth Epochal Revelation.

I call upon all URANTIA Book readers to receive the baptism of the Universe Mother Spirit and humble themselves and seek learning from God and Continuing Fifth Epochal Revelation, which the Spirit of God is pouring out upon this planet for all who have ears to hear.

It is Her last gift before Her rebirth. It is a complement to the Thought Adjuster and the Spirit of Truth within. It is the dance of the renaissance. It is the fruit of the Tree of Life. It is the cleansing water of the soul. It is the mirror of complacency and pride. It is the fire for the slothful. It is milk from the breast of the Mother for the obstinate, and the final covering of the divine hand from our Paradise Father. It is the awakening light in the eyes of all souls who receive Her—the essence of true respect and submission to the Father and all personalities that are elders within the Father circuits of time and space, particularly to those who are mandated within the Administration of Machiventa Melchizedek, the present Planetary Prince of Urantia.

It is not within the text of this transmission to define the Mandate of the Bright and Morning Star, given to Gabriel of Urantia/TaliasVan of Tora, or the mandate of Machiventa Melchizedek, given to other future ambassadors. However, what I do give is for you who are chosen to read this paper to activate that which is within you as Reservists and awaken you to your proper destinies and soul urges.

It is the Mandate of the Bright and Morning Star, given to Gabriel/TaliasVan, to manifest to all of the vast cosmic family quite real physical blessings, to change circumstances and to come against any of the evil forces on behalf of any of those cosmic family members who wish to align themselves with the First Cosmic

Family and the establishment of the Machiventa Melchizedek Administration upon this planet.

It is a mandate that brings the highest love mates together, their highest spiritual complements. It is a mandate of fulfillment to individual personalities and souls. It is a mandate of perfection that comes from the overcontrol of thousands of unseen celestials on this planet. It is a mandate of universe administration unified on a third-dimensional plane upon entering the fourth dimension. It is a mandate of interdimensional and interplanetary communication. It is the reopening of the circuits of Nebadon and Orvonton with your world, Urantia.

There is only one personality on any one planet who can have my mandate, co-shared by his highest spiritual complement. It is a mandate of healing of the soul, astral body, and all other bodies that you will come to learn about including the physical Urantian one. It is a time-and-space-warp mandate that knows no boundaries within its universe of existence, that being Nebadon. The past, present, and future are coexistent within this mandate.

You will come to learn of these things since you have this personality with you, and I am with you (Gabriel of Urantia/TaliasVan of Tora being the Audio Fusion Material Complement for me). Until your planet has entered the first stages of light and life, a process that is being greatly accelerated by this adjudication and within the administration of Machiventa Melchizedek, I, the Bright and Morning Star, take personal representation and overcontrol.

All those within the First Cosmic Family who align themselves perfectly with their God—first-time Urantians and those from other universes and particularly those of Avalon—to some degree can manifest the power, harmony, and love of this mandate. I bid you all come, from the four corners of this planet, who are to be part of this great work and manifest destiny. *The harvest is ripe, but the harvesters are few.*

A second transmission then came through from Machiventa Melchizedek.[2]

It was decided by Christ Michael, the Bright and Morning Star, the Acting Governor General of Urantia, and the Chief of Seraphim that it was time that I announce to human personalities the reestablishment of the seat of the Planetary Prince on Urantia. It happened on December 9, 1989, in Santa Fe, New Mexico, USA, an area very close to several energy reflective circuits near the Four Corners area in which hundreds of celestial visitations had been made by physical spacecraft and seraphic transport alike—an area that had slowly deteriorated in mass consciousness from the spiritual position it had been designated to obtain.

We had previously found our audio receiver in 1987, and he was given the complete Mandate of the Bright and Morning Star and all that went with it. Now it was time to appoint the first two of the potential hologram receivers, who would act as representatives of myself after A.D. 2040–2050. Other celestial personalities would form images of themselves through the light body of all future Vicegerent First Ambassadors.[3] They were appointed to be the first two to serve Gabriel of Urantia/TaliasVan of Tora and Niánn Emerson Chase, with the Mandate of the Bright and Morning Star. These two potential Vicegerent Ambassadors were apostles of Jesus in the first century. Far from saints, they still had much spiritual growth to obtain.

It was decided that my announcement would first be made to these two as they had the higher mindal ability to comprehend and follow up with an announcement of my appointment to the rest of the world. Now the virtue of their hearts would have to match their minds. They would be given the opportunity to complement the virtue of Gabriel of Urantia/TaliasVan of Tora and Niánn Emerson Chase and the Mandate of the Bright and Morning Star. Several others had been contacted but failed to step completely out of the Caligastia system and make my announcement public.[4]

Caligastia was told many things that I cannot give in this transmission, but what I can say is that he was not allowed to try to take their lives or cause any physical accidents to the first two potential Vicegerent First Ambassadors or any others in the future. Also upon their leaving New Mexico, neither he nor any of his representatives would be allowed within a five-mile radius of their physical bodies. A half dozen angelic beings were assigned to protect this radius until these two would eventually come to the protected area at the First Planetary Sacred Home [at that time] in Sedona, Arizona.

The reason I give this information is because those who read this transmission and know you are also supposed to be in Tubac/Tumacácori, Arizona might wonder if Caligastia could try to do the same thing to you. Fear not, for if your alignment is in the will of the Father, you will have that same protection until you reach your destination within Global Community Communications Alliance at the First Planetary Sacred Home in Tubac/Tumacácori, Arizona, USA.

What these two did not know then is that my administration would be established in Sedona [and then move later to Tubac/Tumacácori], and I physically would live there, although unseen at this time but ever present within the same Third Radius of Gabriel of Urantia/TaliasVan of Tora and Niánn Emerson Chase and other family members. This first community will be the prototype for the first cities of the Divine New Order. It is not just an administration of human beings but an administration with divine overcontrol and design, using mortals to exemplify the administration of divine projections within a lower world framework.

The signature of any mandated Elder to the Mandate of the Bright and Morning Star carries with it a warning to those who assume to be spiritual teachers but whose motives are far from divine. It is a warning to those who call themselves messengers of the Brotherhood of Light, channelers of archangels or even of Michael or whomever they claim to be contacting, that they must humble themselves and become students at The Extension Schools of Melchizedek [a.k.a. Global Community Communications Schools of Ascension Science & The Physics of Rebellion]. They first must find their true God and the Creator Son of that God, the ruler of their universe of Nebadon, Christ Michael, and then submit to His appointed and mandated human personalities.

The first of these is Gabriel of Urantia/TaliasVan of Tora, the second is Niánn Emerson Chase, then the Liaison Ministers followed by all other Elders—men and women alike—who have first aligned themselves with their complementary polarities and cosmic ancestors at the First Planetary Sacred Home. If they refuse to heed the request of these mandated Elders then they have refused me, for their signature carries the complete authority of the Office of the Planetary Prince of Urantia just as Gabriel of Urantia's/TaliasVan of Tora's name carries the complete authority of the Office of the Bright and Morning Star of Salvington.

Each of them will come to learn of the complexities of their own mandates in the years ahead, and so will all of Urantia. We suggest to those who are interested in the healing of their physical bodies that you study Paper 205 of The Cosmic Family, Volume I, *for Gabriel of Urantia/TaliasVan of Tora works within the astral; tron therapists and stabilized third-circle Vicegerent First Ambassadors with the etheric.*[5]

"Sananda" was the <u>title</u> of Christ Michael on another planet when He took the office of Planetary Prince in one of His bestowals. It is not the <u>name</u> of Christ Michael and never has been, not on this planet or any other.

If you receive a personal letter of request from either Gabriel of Urantia/TaliasVan of Tora or other personalities of the Divine Administration, I pray that you treat it with the utmost respect, for any reason they would have to contact you is in accordance with the true spiritual government of this universe and the lines of communication therein, starting with Christ Michael and proceeding from the Bright and Morning Star to myself, Machiventa Melchizedek, on Urantia.

We have at our fingertips thousands of supermortal and celestial personalities to see to it that you begin to respect their requests, for this indeed is the adjudication of Urantia. Truly, let the love of God brighten your horizons. Let the discipline of God guide your thoughts, and let godlike humility direct your decisions.

CHAPTER 17

The Chaos Begins
A Possible Future Scenario Chapter

When thousands of American troops were being sent into Saudi Arabia, it was hard to believe that the majority of Americans were still waving flags and wanting war. Little did they know that thousands of lives would be lost (mostly Iraqis, but that was OK because they were the new bad people) and all because a few families in control of the world's third-dimensional structure wished to keep that control. The rest of the voices that cried out for God and country were as puppets on the strings of those in power, and these voices willingly sent their sons and daughters off to die so that the rich could stay rich, while they themselves wondered where the next meal was coming from and could not even afford proper medical care.

The majority of those sent to war could not afford a proper education, and that is why the military had been an option. They had few other choices. This was the way that "Big Brother" decided things for those who had voted them into power and kept them there. The powerful ones' sons and daughters went to the exclusive colleges and were able to choose a career of their hearts' desire. They lived in the grandest of mansions and wore the finest clothes. It was unpatriotic to talk against one's country, and some said it was even ungodly, for surely God was with America.

What America did not know was that their sons and daughters were being drawn into an immense trap by those who hated them and all that they supposedly stood for. The game was being played. In their palms were the sons and daughters of the patriotic puppets, not only in America but in all of the countries in the world where nationalistic tendencies led people to believe that their nation was God's country. The whole concept of being a *planetary citizen was lost except to just a few so-called idealists, who sang songs of planetary brotherhood and the Fatherhood of God, but the music of these songs was only silence to the deaf ears of the proud, arrogant, and spiritually blind.*

The stage was set for the almost final destruction of humankind. It did not matter who fired the first shot, the shooting began. More and more troops were required to go to the Middle East and, since nuclear weapons were banned by the United Nations, in the beginning it was conventional war. Although the war ended in a few months, over the following years the Arab countries one by one began to turn against the United States, and wars escalated. It was an unbelievable mess. The nation of Israel, that so many fundamentalists said would not be destroyed, was overtaken by the united Arab powers and genocide took place in the millions. It was a long war, lasting far into the twenty-first century. American men in their forties were being drafted and so were many women. Children were being left parentless as a result of this long war.

By then our community was growing all of our own food and supplying all our own energy by solar power and another technique, which I will not mention here. This technique was given to us by Celestial Overcontrol. Hundreds of cosmic family members were now living in the First Radius. Many who came got in by the skin of their teeth, and many of them did not last long as there was much discipline and sacrifice required. The only ticket into the fourth dimension, which our planet was about to enter, was the study of Fifth Epochal Revelation and Continuing Fifth Epochal Revelation.

The dying of the self that God demands of each individual was a prerequisite to the continual stay in Secret Valley. We do not quite know how our unseen protectors kept away the lawless and criminal element from our valley. All I can say is that throughout the years the only problems we had were with those we allowed in to become a part of us and who were not sincere and had to be removed.

When the Chinese saw that the United States was finally weakened to the point of almost helplessness on the home front, they attacked our country.[1] First they allied with the united Arab nations and marched into the Arab lands and attacked the Americans there. It was the Chinese who also led the attack against the nation of Israel, but by this time "the new Israel" was safe in the protected areas around the planet under the human leadership who were, in turn, in submission to their supermortal leaders.

It took a certain amount of faith for the cosmic family members to remain in the protected areas when the food supply was low and when at times it seemed that there was some stability in our country—at least that was what the news media reported. Those who were not in one hundred percent compliance with the will of God would fall back into wanting the desires of Babylon and of the flesh. It was these who had to be discovered before the final evacuation.

Little did we know that our planet was a great testing ground and that our communities were the final laboratories for those entering the fourth dimension. Many came to me during these times and said that they could better serve the community back in the world by making money and therefore being able to buy the things that we needed. Others said that they would be able to become influential in getting the things we needed. Some even said that they could go out there and outright steal the things. Many were impatient in waiting for their proper complementary polarity to come, and some were envious of those who had their complements or even two complements, and they had none.

It took a while for me to see that life within the community would not yet be heaven, that I could not trust the human heart. I gave the benefit of the doubt to

Chapter 17

all who claimed they wanted to walk into the fourth dimension but sooner or later would show their true selves. As I did not want to become callous in my heart or cold in the handling of those I loved, I allowed myself to be vulnerable, choosing to be hurt by those who would betray me, rather than be a brother and leader who could not love or trust.

I knew that one day I would be able to have total trust in those with us who had been tried and tested by God. I longed for that day when not one Judas would be left among our company. As I have mentioned, faith was necessary for those of the community. It became increasingly obvious that it would be advantageous to identify those souls who lacked the faith needed to grow into a fourth-dimensional person.

When the Chinese attacked our country, most of the communication lines were down and we received very few (and later, no) channels on the television. So we really had no idea of what was happening. We would see overhead hundreds of aircrafts and had no idea whose they were, but we took our guesses in the beginning. Later we knew—for they were pointed out by our celestial friends who were not allowed at that time to interfere in any physical manner. In the end they would intervene to stop complete nuclear destruction, but only then would they take part. By that time, however, one-third of humankind had already annihilated themselves.

Nevertheless, on some occasions, the unseen forces did protect us from intruders in a very visible way. On one occasion several thousand Chinese troops were about to come over the mountains into our valley. We climbed the mountain and watched them as they came closer and closer to our protected area, and we prayed for intervention. I had contacted the midwayers upon hearing of the Chinese arrival but did not receive an answer. We had very few weapons and were not prepared for physical battle and certainly not with an army of trained soldiers.

It was early morning and the Chinese began to awaken from their slumber and to break camp when we spotted on the horizon three vessels that crisscrossed the skyline and became visible to our eyes and to the Chinese. These ships were approximately as long as a football field, and as they came closer to the earth we could hear the hum that their mighty energies caused. The elements of the earth, the trees, and rocks shook with the winds of the force—similar to the effect of a landing helicopter, but with much greater power—and these ships were about a mile above us.

They lined themselves up between the invaders and us, and shots were first fired by the Chinese. We even saw what looked like nuclear rockets being fired at these vessels, but nothing seemed to penetrate the energy field around them. The next thing we saw was a light coming out from these ships and extending to the earth. The light grew brighter and brighter until it became almost like red energy and seemed very hot. We did not know what it felt like to the Chinese, but I can tell you that in a matter of a few minutes of being in this red energy the Chinese abandoned their weapons, turned, and fled. Thousands of them ran, taking off their clothes, which soon burst into flames.

The next day we went down into the field where the Chinese had been. All we found was abandoned equipment, weapons and clothing, but no bodies. It seemed that no one had lost their lives. They knew as we did, that a superhuman intelligence did not want them to go any farther into our valley. They also saw the three magnificent ships take off and disappear into the sky in a matter of seconds. Whatever this force was, the Chinese did not want to mess with it again.

On another occasion it was winter and very cold. Our wood supply had dwindled down to nothing, but we did

Chapter 17

not feel that it was safe to go out of our protected area, for by this time everyone in the community felt it was insane to venture into the world. After we had come to this conclusion, for the next several summers we stocked up on our wood supply and thought it would last until the turn of the century. But we underestimated, and there had been much abuse by those who were used to living in gas and electrically heated environments. Many were beginning to doubt the sacredness of this area, and I prayed for an answer.

About nine one evening, it was quite dark with a quarter moon, we saw lights coming across the sky. A huge ship appeared and then a smaller one came out of her and landed where we were. Out came Paladin. After receiving some instructions I was given two metallic items that looked like briefcases. Inside of them were pellets that Paladin called Velecian pellets, from a planet called Velecia in a distant solar system. These pellets burned for weeks at a time without being recharged. They could be lit by a match and recharged by putting them into sunlight. There were enough in the cases to last for the next five years and wood to burn for heat would no longer be necessary.

On another occasion we had heard from a distant source that there was a band of looters and rapists coming our way. These gangs were led by those criminals who had escaped from the prisons and formed armies of thieves bent upon attacking anyone who had any semblance of goodness and morality. Police were rarely available, being more concerned with the imposing Chinese forces and the protection of the inner cities and wealthier areas within them.

Many militia groups were formed by the so-called honest citizens, and many little battles occurred between such groups. We had heard various rumors about this band of cutthroats taking young women and killing everyone else. The men of this band prided themselves on their physical prowess and often gave captured men a chance to live if, in physical combat with one of them, the captured man won.

As this renegade band drew nearer to our valley, we wondered if God had abandoned us, the Machiventa Melchizedek Administration included. We prayed to the Father of All for divine intervention. When the band got to the pass that led into our valley and began coming down, the men in our community decided to fight them with whatever we had, so we were positioned behind rocks and trees.

As our community did not believe in storing firearms for protection, we had very few weapons, particularly the kind of heavy artillery that the mob coming against us had. We had only a few rifles and shotguns that we would use for hunting if, for whatever reasons, the necessity arose. Up to that point necessity for hunting had never arisen, as we grew our own organic fruit, vegetables, and meat. Unfortunately, the word got out, and they were coming to take it.

We fired a few shots in the air hoping that up in the canyon top they would hear it and be scared away. Our scouts came back and told us that they were still coming, that they were not intimidated by what they heard. They knew they had us outgunned. After a long session of prayer, trying to determine the will of God, the men in the community gathered up what few firearms and weaponry we possessed, and moved forward up the hill to meet them. The women hid in protective cover on our land before we left.

Going up the hill, I had many thoughts. I remembered a situation, long before we had the land, when a community member, whose property we had used for gardening, got angry with me because I and Celestial Overcontrol told him that neither he nor his wife were to help themselves to the vegetables or fruits. Even if it was their own land, it was a community garden, and the *community member who had been appointed at the time to be head of garden produce distribution was the one to make that decision. We found out that when there was no food in the markets, even members within our own community, who were not closely aligned to the principles of the Divine Administration and my mandate, would sneak into the garden and steal food.*

Many of the decisions that I had to make several years before the hard times came were not understood by those at lower levels of understanding. I knew that if we did not implement those necessary rules from the beginning, that when the terrible times came there would not be enough aligned individuals to stop the unaligned ones from stealing and eating all the community garden food or either giving it to their unaligned loved ones locally or taking it and storing it for their families in other states.

We were on our way up the hill, not knowing what we were going to face. We saw them coming from a distance once we got to a certain point. We were greatly out-numbered and out-weaponed. I knew that our only chance for victory was to surprise and ambush them. I asked the men to climb to higher elevations, which they did. We got above them and waited. The plan was first to start a rockslide, and to run down the hill at full strength in a surprise attack. As we waited, we all prayed for a miracle, as the hungry, angry band of men came right beneath us.

I was about ready to give the order to start the rock slide when I noticed they had stopped in their tracks and were looking straight ahead. I looked through my binoculars and noticed their eyes and faces showed fright. I could not imagine what they saw. Many dropped their weapons and ran back up the hill. Others scrambled in various directions. A few came toward us, but realized it was a hard climb and began running down the hill and up another. They were completely frightened by what they saw. It took all of ten minutes for them to disappear behind the hill.

All of us quickly ran down to the point where they had stood. We stopped, and began to move more slowly, as we tried to see what they had seen. We looked straight ahead and saw absolutely nothing but the beautiful forest mountainside and our wonderful secret valley. I was shocked. I went down on my knees at that point and prayed. I asked Paladin to come in, which he did. He told me that thousands of midwayers had materialized, enough for these oncoming robbers to see them. I was ecstatic! We all were.

Once the word got around, we were like a bunch of silly little boys, jumping up and down, shouting and yelling, making jokes. We knew from that point on, that we were as safe as a baby in its mother's arms, but we had to be tested. The tests God puts us through! In the end He always supports us if we do the right thing. "The act is ours, the consequences God's," The URANTIA Book says [p. 556]. We are to take action, as protectors and leaders of our women and children. And when we do, God takes the next step.

Many of us old warriors, at least the majority, were relieved as we knew for sure, that we would never again have to pick up the sword, and that our days fighting with weapons were over. We knew God's invisible army would protect us from then on.

I remembered the war of 1967, when Israel defeated the Egyptian army in six days. It was reported that hundreds of Egyptians got out of their tanks in the same kind of fear. They too thought they had seen a larger army of tall, mighty men. The truth was they outnumbered the Israelis, had more guns, and from their position could not even have seen the Israeli army.

We heard reports that many of those who did not align with our community were dying of starvation. Many of them robbed and murdered attempting to get food. Some were too proud to come and ask us for help. Many *were too weak to even attempt the trip. The only sanity left in the world seemed to be at Planetary Headquarters and the other safety areas where we had set up the other six communities.*

What had happened that day was the talk of the community for many months to come. We all needed that physical event, for despair was great among us. The lawlessness of the land and the death around us was unimaginable. Many of our relatives, friends, and acquaintances were not allowed in the protected areas and had to face all of that by themselves. There were few survivors. Had they only listened years ago! Had they gotten their priorities right in the previous years, they too would be experiencing the fourth-dimensional reality of God's other children from distant planets and dimensions. They too would have been fed, like the Israelites of old, with manna from the sky and would have been led by a pillar of fire by night.

CHAPTER 18

A New Garden Of Eden

It increasingly became very evident to me—during the 1970s, '80s, and '90s—that the vegetables and fruits of the planet were losing their taste and nutritional values. Only in certain locations where communities had learned to get in touch with the Mother essence of the earth and Her helpers (the elementals and Life Carriers) were fruit and vegetables produced that could give the nutritional value and medicinal usage they were designed for by the Universe Supervisors and the Creator Son, Michael, so many hundreds of thousands of years before.

When the Material Son and Daughter, Adam and Eve, came here, they and their children lived in an environment conducive not only to physical growth and health but also to spiritual development. After the fall of Adam and Eve, a second garden was started, but it never had the Tree of Life nor the aid of the Celestial Overseers. Because of the Caligastia Rebellion the circuits were cut off from this Material Son and Daughter, as they were to the rest of the planet.

Perhaps the Fountain of Youth that so many tales have been written about could have been realized if the superhuman complementary polarities, Adam and Eve, had not defaulted. Eating food that was vibrant and full of unique potentialities would bring life and healing to those who partook of its nourishment and our planet would not have developed all of the various diseases that have caused so many untold deaths and suffering.

As the Father of All cut Urantia's circuits—which made available cosmic knowledge, wisdom, and interplanetary communication to the inhabitants—so had the Universe Mother cut off the essence of the healing properties within her garden. As the evil, sin, and iniquity increased in the twentieth century, that which people ate became worse, and that which people drank, polluted. We had been told that only in the protected areas would food be grown and water drunk that was not poisoned with the greed of man's impurities, which manifested into the very soil of the earth itself.

~~~~~~~~~~~~~~~~~~~~~~

[A Possible Future Scenario]

We did not know much about gardening when we first began to plant our first little garden (this was before we had acquired many acres surrounding us and also before we were talking to interplanetary botanists), but what we found was that whatever we planted seemed to grow twice as big and yield twice as much. We usually had enough left over to serve many other mouths besides our own. Little did we then know how important this garden would be to so many.

When food shortages became common in America and gasoline so expensive that it was difficult to travel to buy food, the garden became a very sacred and protected place. We found out that many who came by to investigate actually needed food and secretly hoped that we would offer them some. We began to see that if any real trouble broke out, many would come by and not ask but just take. So we became more secretive about who we told.

Those who came by were given food, and some purchased it by donation. We asked these individuals to keep our gardens a secret as we did not have enough for the outside world. We also asked them if they were interested in joining our community with its spiritual emphasis. Those who were not interested in spiritual things did not come back. Those who were interested in spirituality joined, because they saw, by the growth of our plants, that God was blessing our work.

One day, as Niánn and I were busy working in our garden, we noticed a wet area that was unusually damp for a hot sunny day. We asked each other who had turned on the water, but all denied doing it. We thought someone had secretly done it or perhaps one of the children had and did not tell. Several hours later we went back to the same spot and it was still very wet, so we took a shovel and began digging. We could not have dug more than a foot or two when water began shooting up. We had discovered a high water level coming from one of the tributaries of the nearby creek, an underground spring.

We later found out from our unseen mentors that this spring was a gift from them to us. We used it for irrigation and our area became an oasis within a matter of months, with running water at all times and all of it drinkable. We were told that if the people all over the planet had been in alignment with their Creator, as individuals and nations are supposed to be, this would be their reality: every thorn a flower and every thistle a blade of grass, as the earth would be in harmony with herself. She would not want to spit up volcanic rock and so would be soft to walk upon and gentle to the bare foot.

We began cleansing the area of all little stones, pebbles, rocks, and thorns. At first just an acre was cleared and one could walk without shoes and not be harmed. Even the weeds seemed to obey the Divine New Order and were replaced by new plant life that developed at the rate the earth wanted it to. We had no names for these new plants, so the Universe Supervisors told me to name them. It became a hobby of mine to understand all of the plants, fruits, and vegetables, and I became extremely interested in botany.

I came to enjoy all aspects of agriculture and farming, particularly getting out and working with the soil and watching it respond in the harvests of the divine hand. Some of the foods that were new had a consistency and a taste very much like steak or other meat. It was most amazing. One could swear that we were eating meat. The only plant that came close to this before was eggplant.

Chapter 18

We began to discover that certain fruits would do things to certain people, for the foods that one eats can also aid in the spiritual development. Medical science began discovering this in nutrition and diet studies many years before, but never to the degree that we discovered it from eating pure foods. In the organic growing of foods people were being cured of various diseases caused by eating foods that were produced from soil far below the standards of the Creator's original design.

When our foods began to come near that original design, a whole new world opened up for us, and it was a unique and wonderful experience. Some people who ate the red foods, such as beets and watermelons, became full of energy and physically stronger. We began to see near superhuman feats take place. People slept less and arose early with vigor. Hard labor became no problem, even for people who were physically lazy; once their bodies became pure and they ate of these garden-original fruits and vegetables, they manifested the properties thereof. So the universe guides told us to feed red foods to certain of the slow moving people who had been reluctant to pick up a shovel and dig. When they ate these foods they became like a machine, working physically all day long, whereas before, they just wanted to use their brain power.

When we fed the green fruits and vegetables to the hyper and physical people, they became more mentally oriented and wanted to do more creative, artistic work and administrative functions. It took quite some time to learn which diet should be given to what people. We learned a lot about natural ability as opposed to learned skill. The one thing we did not have to worry about any longer was motivation, for all one had to do was eat a magic piece of food and presto we had a volunteer for whatever the project was.

We tried with older people, and sure enough, even those in their sixties and seventies and eighties wanted to do a young man's labor. If they had not grown old in a dying body on this dying planet, they would have been able to do what their light body was telling them to do. So we had to be careful with these foods and have supervision over what and how much was eaten. If mistakes were made in the food distribution, more careful supervision was needed in assigning work duties by the leaders and supervisors, and I had the greatest responsibility. I did not want a seventy-year-old having a heart attack trying to do a twenty-year-old man's physical task. Nor did I want a skilled laborer trying to paint a masterpiece on canvas when something had to be built in a hurry. It was quite a lesson for all of us to learn what these foods brought out in the latent potentiality of both mind ability and physical prowess.

~~~~~~~~~~~~~~~~~~~~~~~~

We were informed by our celestial friends that the pure foods of a "Garden of Eden" would definitely cause reactions in the spiritual and psychological realities of humankind. Thus food took on a new meaning for us as we realized its potential for sacredness, and we began to eat accordingly. Our chemical-free food and livestock has continued to grow in quantity and quality over the years. Flesh eating will continue to be the reality for many whose genetics are from flesh-eating worlds of other universes, like Avalon, Fanoving, and Wolvering.

In the Divine New Order that will be set up on the planet, those in the agricultural sectors who distribute these foods to the world will be overseen by the oldest and most trusted souls of constellation status and above. In those early days I, as an audio fusion material complement, relied heavily upon my connection and communication with Universe Supervisors.

CHAPTER 19

The Closing Of The Door Of The Ark—
The Physics Of Rebellion Leads To Total Chaos
A Possible Future Scenario Chapter

Up until the times of the final wars and continued deterioration of the food supply and other basic needs in our country, many of those to whom we spoke about our work responded negatively. Some even stated that they were not at all interested in our work. When hard times came, many became our "best friends," and those we had not heard from for years began communicating with us by letter and phone, until telephone communication was no longer available. Hundreds from all over the world came without notifying us and ended up on our doorstep. I found that those community members who had questioned my leadership and wanted to be leaders in situations and circumstances before this time, now did not want to take the responsibility of helping make a decision as what to do with these people and their children.

Many of those who came were the biological and/or cosmic sons, daughters, brothers, sisters, and friends of those already here, and so with each person who came uninvited, I had to connect with celestial intelligences to aid me in knowing what to do, for each circumstance was different and each person unique. Some of them I automatically knew I should turn away without giving them the opportunity to stay even one night.

For these decisions I always was judged by those in the community with misplaced compassion and unclear discernment. Many community members came to me, expecting me to feel a sense of obligation because of their relationship to me or their relationship to God and wanted me to allow some of their relatives to stay. I wondered why the democratic process of voting and *going with majority rule could not be implemented in these situations. The guides told me to try it with one situation, and so I did.*

At that time there were 150 adults over the age of twenty-one in the community. First of all, trying to get 150 adults together to have a vote was not as easy as it sounds, even when we were within walking distance of one another. The person in question had to come in to stay for at least a night and day, and so I automatically lost the option of not allowing the person, in the first place. Accepting that, the community was open to whatever negativity that person might bring.

Even though it was top priority for the adults to come together, it took three days to get the majority of the people together, but only fifty-five turned up. Some of the women had to care for their small children. We then realized that babysitting by the older children had to be implemented so that more women could in the future attend important meetings, and this brought up more problems. But for that first time, we voted with the fifty-five.

It was decided by the majority of mostly men that this person, who just happened to be a male himself, would be asked to leave after being fed and counseled. I also had made that decision, but I never would have allowed the person entrance in the first place, yet had agreed to it for the sake of the experiment. The person showered, was given a healthy meal, and was counseled by one of our Elders. Even so, he was noticeably bitter, and when he left, he set fire to a corner of our land. Luckily, it was noticed in time and almost no damage was done, but the intent was there.

We also discovered that the decision of his staying or going was a much talked-about topic of many of the members for days afterwards, taking them away from their other duties and tasks, especially since he was the biological son of one of the men in the community. Years ago he had been notified by us to join our community, and this was done time and time again. So this one intrusion seemed to create a disturbance among us for at least a week after the incident. I asked the Midwayer Commission if I should continue with the democratic process. They said why not leave the decision up to the community members, and so a regular meeting was held, for which a week's notice was always given.

In the meantime, would you believe that there were other uninvited guests who came to the community, and I had to go through the democratic process again? An emergency meeting was called with proper childcare and other community functions covered. All 150 adults showed up within a two-hour time period. Things were looking up. This time it was about a young couple who obviously did not belong together. No one in the community knew them, but they had heard of us.

After talking with this couple for just a short while, my immediate response was that if they agreed to have no further sexual relationship together and abide by the community rules, they could be given a trial period to stay. I then contacted my unseen mentors, and they told me something that the young couple did not tell me, that she was pregnant by her true complementary polarity of a third-dimensional seventh stage alignment and needed to return to him or for him to come to our community. So I was correct in my analysis. I did not mention this to the group.

Both of them were quite charming. All of the women liked the couple, and everyone invited them to stay. She confessed openly that she was pregnant, and the couple was congratulated by all in the community. Of course the facilities for married couples were offered by some of the members to these two people, for it was taken for granted that they belonged to one another and that he was the father of her unborn child. At this time I wished that everyone in the community had that "relationship with their God moment to moment" like they said they did so that their inner guidance could tell them what was actually happening.

I quietly prayed for an answer, hoping that I could come to some quick decision of what to do, knowing all the facts. I tested the waters of the community members' open channel to their Thought Adjuster and guides. I asked that we all be in prayer for a few moments to make sure that this majority decision was a correct one. I personally thought that surely now some of them would be told by their guidance that this woman was pregnant by another man, her higher complement. After five minutes of silence, no one spoke up. So I said, "Has anyone anything else to say about this couple staying in the married quarters?" No one responded. Some of them began to clap, welcoming the couple, and soon all were applauding in agreement.

I became silent for a few moments and connected with the midwayers. They told me to ask the young woman if she had anything to say to the community. She just thanked everyone and said that she and her husband would be assets to our community. The midwayers then told me to ask her which husband she was talking about, this one or the true father of her child? She looked at me in shock, and so I openly asked her who the father of her child was. She then broke down and admitted to all of us that her "true" husband was a URANTIA Book *reader and that was how she had heard about us in the first place. He also read our Continuing Fifth Epochal Revelation literature and wanted to come join our community, but she had not truly been interested in studying the Fifth Epochal Revelation.*

Of course I realized then that she had come to us only for food and shelter and not for spiritual reasons. She was personally ready to come into a fourth-dimensional relationship with her absent higher mate, but could not do it without her mindal willingness to become a student of the Fifth Epochal Revelation.

It was then easy for all of us to see that the whole process of screening these applicants would take time, and only those who were highly clairvoyant, mandated, connected material complements would be able to save the community much time and needless heartache. That was the last time that a democratic process took place. I made the motion to vote on whether this should take place again. I spoke out strongly against it and pointed out that the extent of my authority needed to be fully understood at the gates of our community when our lost friends, family, and acquaintances were knocking at the door of our compassion. The vote was a unanimous 150 against the democratic process.

During the months and years ahead many were allowed to enter the gates of our community and stay with us. When I was in doubt, I always accepted the guidance of my unseen superiors, and many times I questioned the mercy of their decisions, for it was quite clear that it was these who caused the community the most problems and were themselves damaged physically and spiritually by the obstinacy of their thinking. Some of them physically transcended while with us, for they could not be healed, as the diseases progressed rapidly in their bodies and could not be corrected or reversed in time to save them. We also saw many miraculous healings. When some who had physical illnesses changed their inappropriate thinking and false views of reality, their bodies began to respond and their diseases to be cured.

I thanked God that finally all aligned in Divine Administration understood my mandate.[1] Soon our first community would grow into the hundreds, then have satellite communities worldwide. By the turn of the century, millions were aware of our work and our communities. The understanding of the authority of the mandate by Christ Michael, at whatever level, was absolutely essential. Initially, before mail services were no longer available, our mailing list had been in the thousands, and it had become impossible for me to read all of the literature sent from people wanting to enter our community. We simply did not have the time to respond to them personally.

At first we tried responding with advice as to where they and their families could go for some supernatural protection. But after a while, I was told not to send information to people, as that particular door was closed, because those communities that were set up around the planet were beginning to be overburdened with the entrance of newcomers. The exodus from the cities of newly awakened souls was now in the thousands, and in the near future it would be in the millions. But by then, new communities would be out of the question as chaos and confusion would rule.

One of the communities that we helped set up in England decided that they wanted out from under my and Celestial Overcontrol's supervision. They had decided that in their community, in all decisions the democratic process would be the rule over and above the authority of the designated leader I had sent there. You might say that this was a repeat of history: parliament and Oliver Cromwell (who was called Lord Protector) versus the king. That England was the country where this kind of rebellion was to take place in one of our communities should have been anticipated, because the people still had an earthly queen and well-developed parliament.

The reality is that if certain monarchs are not in contact with their God, parliament should indeed rule. That is why Divine New Order communities are set up with a board of Elders and/or Ministers as parliament, in cooperation with the Soul Watcher[2] or Director of the community. In areas where the leader feels he (or she) needs counsel, he (or she) does not have to go to the angelic realms and above, he (or she) can simply go to the parliament. But if the parliament all feels one way and the leader feels another, that leader who is chosen of

God to be in that position should be able to have full authority to act upon his or her inner and outer guidance.

A leader who is an active and functioning administrator simply cannot come before a parliament of six, sixty, six hundred, six thousand, or six million every time certain decisions need to be made. It is understood by the six and the six million that the decisions made by the leader are made in the best interests of all concerned. The leaders of God will be put into those positions by the hand of God. It is up to God to decide the ways and means and for all to recognize the mandate God has given that individual. The leaders humans put into authority, humans can oust. Their authority lasts as long as the humans who put them there want them there. The governments of humans get away from leaders because they become too large, bureaucratic, and impersonal.

Eventually a strong leader can indeed become very powerful. Unfortunately, if these individuals are not moment to moment in contact with their heavenly Father and the heavenly Father's Universe Supervisors, these leaders create dictatorships and impersonal rule over underprivileged, undereducated, and underemployed people. Divine Administration must be set up, and those humans appointed to be leaders in this Divine Administration must have a relationship with their Creator and be appointed vessels of the Creator for that administrative position. The appointment by humans alone will not and cannot guarantee good leadership. People who have been appointed by God, at whatever level they know their God, and appointed by humans, have the cohesion to some extent to bring harmony, justice, and peace to the peoples of their country.

Imagine governmental leaders who understand the vast cosmology of the grand universe with all its various beings created to aid in administrating a local planet and are able to call upon these celestial beings for aid and advice. I was told that this would be the case soon. These leaders would be working with Machiventa Melchizedek, the Planetary Prince of Urantia, and be overcontrolled by the Bright and Morning Star himself. All of those who had gotten into the ark before the door was closed were able to help Urantia set up this administration.

Years later, as we were returning to Urantia and looking through the portholes of the spaceship, we realized many millions had died and gone to the mansion worlds, which we had an opportunity to visit before we returned to the earth. It was an unusual experience, of course, since they had died to get there and we had been transported there in a ship and/or in light body. They had received new bodies, but we had our old ones still functioning on a higher frequency—pre-morontia or light body—with the anticipation of receiving new ones when we returned home to Urantia.

The amazing thing was that we would not have to die to get one. We were told that we would walk into a very highly advanced technological device in the resurrection hall and somehow drop our old bodies and receive a new one. The complete technological process is only known by certain seraphim who were entrusted with this Divine Administration. I looked forward to receiving my new body and put in my order, so to speak, for one of at least six feet, for I was tired of being 5'6" and having a metabolism that seemed to gain weight just by smelling food. What seemed to be in only the minds of science fiction writers was happening before my very eyes.

Humans being humans, there were many jokes among the women about what size and shape of breasts they would obtain, and men, of course, joked about their future penises. But we all, with great expectation, desired these bodies that would need less sleep and less food and would be lighter. These bodies would complement our new ascension to the fourth dimension and the first psychic circle, with the addition of two extra higher circuits (chakras), so that we would be able to communicate with some of the higher intelligences who would administer the government of our planet.

CHAPTER 20

The Heavenly Court
A Possible Future Scenario Chapter

It was an awesome sight when billions of souls were brought before the Ancients of Days on Uversa, our superuniverse capital. You might say everybody was there. Mortals and beings from millions of inhabited worlds came, some by seraphic transport, some rematerialized, and some by spacecraft. I cannot describe in human vocabulary the majesty of grandeur our eyes beheld. The court consisted of the three Ancients of Days and millions of their assistants—from angels, to Mighty Messengers, to finaliters of all stages and planets. Midwayers were also there, all visible to the mortal eye.

Indeed every knee did bow before the representatives of the Universal Father, the Ancients of Days. They were the most beautiful beings I had ever seen. When they entered the arena, the natural colors emitted from the already beautiful surroundings and beings became totally white. It seemed as bright as the Earth's sun, and everyone had to adjust their vision to look again. But it was not sunlight, it was the Sons' light—the Sons of God lit up not only the outward but the inward. I saw every sin that I ever committed in the next hour of total quiet before these judges of superuniverse justice.

Since this was a judgment concerning the rebellious planets in the universe of Nebadon (including Urantia) the next divine personality to arrive was Michael of Nebadon, the Creator Son—who Earth knew as Jesus Christ—along with Immanuel, the Union of Days from Paradise, as well as Gabriel, the Bright and Morning Star and head administrator of the universe. We could not determine the mode of transportation, but it seemed as though one moment they were not there and the next minute they were. Once they were seen and their divine presence felt, billions of beings of all orders fell to their knees.

From this position I gazed and saw three distinct colors: white (yet different from the Ancients of Days), a violet, and what is considered an ultraviolet. When the colors of these beings began to combine with the already brilliant colors of the supermortal beings, it was like looking into a kaleidoscope. No words were spoken by these beings, nothing needed to be said, for all present knew that for all practical purposes they had met their God and that every secret within their hearts was known to them.

As I began to clear my vision, I saw hundreds of thousands of mortals getting up at once and moving to the center of the arena. I felt internally that these were some of the millions of fallen starseed, who partook in the Lucifer Rebellion and now they had been called in their hearts to answer for particular sins in their lives. For what seemed about half an hour of Urantia time, all stood in front of these beings, bowed and then I heard very distinctly an archangel make a proclamation and read the ruling of the Ancients of Days that all of these souls be sent to planet 609 of Satania, a planet in the primitive stage of development, and that these souls would enter as primitive mortals with the hope of learning particular things they did not learn as more civilized beings on Urantia. I was so glad that I was not among them.

The next thing I saw was some sort of gigantic craft hover above them. I could not tell, when I looked closely, if it was mechanical or not. It made a musical sound and was beautiful. Within twenty to thirty seconds several hundreds of thousands of mortals who were kneeling before Michael disappeared. I said a silent prayer to God, "Dear Father, forgive me again for anything I have ever done." Before I continued, I felt the voice of God within me say, "Be still and know that I am God, faithful one, for you know that you are to return to Urantia." So I quieted myself and felt greatly relieved.

Again I saw several hundred thousand from this vast array of billions come to the center. The same scenario took place. I heard another proclamation from the archangel who said, "You will be sent to planet 617 of Satania, the planet of warlike tribes, hatred, and cannibalism. It is hoped that during your lifetime there you will realize the things you did not realize on Urantia and change your own cannibalistic attitudes that not only killed the flesh of your brothers and sisters but their souls as well."

Then I saw a red flame coming from the archangel, engulfing every one of the several hundred thousand in the center of the arena. Again I saw a great ship gather all these souls and in a matter of seconds they were gone. Similar scenarios followed. Several million were sent to fallen planets. The sons and daughters remaining were those who would ascend to a higher plane.

When all of the rebellious souls who should have been ascending were gone, the magnificence of the moment became even greater. I cannot put it into words. There was present a feeling of eternity. All my fear was gone. I knew that every wicked soul from that vast array of billions was gone.

Next, I saw millions of angels of all orders coming into the center and dancing, you might say, in the spirit. I wondered what they were dancing to, and as soon as I had the thought, I began to hear music—music like I had never heard before. I and others started dancing, and like a domino effect, when each began to wonder about it, they heard the music too, and began dancing. I saw Christ Michael, Immanuel, and Gabriel dancing, holding each other's arms going round and round. They seemed to be above anything material, as were many of the other superhuman beings. But all mortals were confined to the material ground and matter. This went on for what seemed like more than an hour of Earth time, all laughing with joy unspeakable.

Then the music stopped, and there was quiet. Hundreds of thousands were again called to the center of the arena, but there was a different feeling as those in the center began dancing again, for they had no fear of the proclamation from the Sons of God, whose angel then proclaimed that these souls would advance to the first mansion world. At that moment I looked with superhuman vision and saw many I knew, those who did not make it into the ship with us. I wanted to go to them, but I knew that I could not at that moment, yet I somehow knew that I would soon visit them on the first mansion world. I could not explain my knowing, I just knew.

Then the great mother ship came above, sang its song, and in an instant all these souls were gone into the arms of Morontia Companions. For several hours, billions of souls were sent to the seven mansion worlds. All temporarily visited mansonia number one. According to their spiritual attainment they were then assigned to a specific world.

After those who were assigned to the mansion worlds had departed, I felt it was my turn to go to the center with several hundred thousand, not only from my ship but from others. We got up and walked toward the center with no fear, knowing we had been forgiven. This was not a judgment of descension but of ascension. We heard the proclamation, "Go back to Urantia, fulfill your dreams and the dreams of your children, and make manifest the kingdom of God. Power will be given to you. You will be put into positions of authority, rightly earned. Because you have been scorned as latter-day prophets for my name's sake, you shall be justified. Well done my good and faithful servants.

"Your planet is no longer the planet of the fallen, but of the righteous. You will be instructed by your superiors, and you will be the superiors of others. The chain of command will be a chain of cooperation, love, and

understanding based on wanting the best for each of your comrades and respecting each individual soul for his or her unique abilities and talents. What one cannot do, another can. See your brothers and sisters as extensions of yourselves, for there is only one mind, that of the Universal Father, the Absolute and Ultimate of All. Join in that mind and teach others about the mind of harmony and joint effort in goodness, kindness, humility, and unselfishness. Let this be the new portrait of Urantia. Allow yourselves to be the brush of God, your words to one another to be the paint. Return to your planet and create the masterpiece."

It felt as if I moved in slow motion away from the divine Sons to the ship, the Star of Bethlehem. Awaiting us were beings who had received their judgments before in other universes and other superuniverses. I somehow would know them better. Whereas they could not speak to us before on certain matters, I felt there would now be more of a sharing, for truly the veil was lifted. The present reality I was experiencing was worth every ounce of pain, suffering, and tribulation I had ever gone through. I would have gladly gone through it again to arrive at this place.

CHAPTER 21

Coming Back—The Landing And The Divine Administration
A Possible Future Scenario Chapter

    As our craft drew nearer to Urantia, I felt certain feelings, memories, and pains of all kinds lifting. We had been briefed by the Universe Supervisors that this would happen as our third-dimensional bodies began to lose the lower circuits and we moved into the first psychic circle, as Urantia was now on a fourth-dimensional plane. Lucifer had always tried to make the body more than what it really was—that was why we had tried to dress it so well in all shades of color. If man had been more concerned about feeding his soul the spiritual food necessary for its ascension survival, the terrible tragedies that took place on our planet (particularly in its climax during the tribulation period) would not have had to occur. Was it not Solomon who said, "Vanity of vanities, all is vanity"?[1]

    I could hardly wait to set foot on Urantia again, which had been realigned with the basic cosmic concepts of absolute truths that would be the foundation for all of the human race living upon it. As I pondered on these things, many hundreds of thousands of mortals were being prepared to land.

    All of the humans who had been evacuated from Urantia several years before were being prepared to descend in smaller vessels from the mother ships. The beings of higher morontia and spirit bodies would be beamed down, and still others would go by seraphic transport and other methods of light-body transference. As I watched from the portholes of my vessel, I saw descend in a mighty armada, thousands of crafts of different shapes, each representing the planet from which it came. We were told that Gabriel, the Bright and

Morning Star, and Christ Michael would be coming in their own way of transport and to prepare ourselves for a most magnificent spectacle.

But there was no way that I could ever have imagined just how magnificent this sight would be. An array of colors—hundreds of which I had never seen before—began coming from a distant point in our system, traveling many times the speed of light. As it came into our local system of Satania, it began to slow down, and when it approached our proximity, we could see that it was so large that it looked like a planet or a satellite world. It seemed to dance in the sky, and it was evident that the gods rode in this vessel. Indeed they did, for accompanying the Creator Son, Christ Michael, were Immanuel, the Union of Days, the Constellation Fathers, the Bright and Morning Star, hundreds of finaliters, thousands of angels of all orders, and many others too numerous to name.

This tremendous craft took the lead and began to descend over the old United States of America, which now would be the United States of Urantia, with one planetary government. When the craft landed it became a permanent structure, a city within itself that would not ascend again. I estimated that it was the size of New Mexico, Arizona, Colorado, and Utah put together. We were all told right then and there, if we had any doubts, that its name was New Jerusalem. All of the thousands of vessels landed in close proximity.

After celebrating, thousands were organized and sent to different parts of the planet. I was glad that I would be one to help administer the new government, along with those of higher intelligence who would head the leadership in a higher ascension. I was so happy to have been chosen because of my choice to be in the perfect will of God.[2] Also, for several years I had studied the Fifth Epochal Revelation and Continuing Fifth Epochal Revelation and learned about these beings. Soon the *official inauguration of previously mandated human personalities would begin, along with mortals from other planets and former Urantians who chose to come back from the sixth and seventh mansion worlds as part of their ascension to help upstep the process.*

This new administration would be ruled by the precepts of cosmic absolutes and law, which I had come to understand many years ago on Urantia. Now some basic cosmic rules would govern our planet:

- *the Fatherhood of God and the brother-/sisterhood of humankind*
- *the continued knowledge of the existence of an ascension plan for ascending sons and daughters of various systems and universes*
- *the training and sacrifices needed from these souls*
- *the recognition of Christ Michael as the Universe Sovereign and God of Nebadon*
- *the understanding of submission to higher authority and elder wisdom, and knowledge and reverence for such (not only for the higher intelligences who have such attributes but also for those mortals who had attained such spiritual virtues)*
- *an awareness that immortality was not inherent in the master universe and that all beings had to earn that immortality by their love for God and their neighbor, whether that neighbor be of this planet or another*

We could no longer think of ourselves as nationalistic citizens or even as planetary citizens, but as universal citizens, all living together on the decimal and experimental planet called Urantia with one goal: to reach the Paradise center—the home of all those who choose with their free will to ascend to this divine womb,

Chapter 21

where we were once in the mind of God and then became a living, thinking reality.

As I began to see the hundreds of orders and thousands of beings from other worlds that I had never seen walk around Urantia before, even though I had talked with some of them as an audio fusion material complement, I knew that this was indeed a new beginning, an Orvonton celebration. I knew that the master plan of the Divine Father for this little planet called Urantia was beginning to take shape and that some kind of marriage was taking place. As soon as I had that thought, I saw falling from the heavens what seemed like rice, but in reality it was the tears of the Universe Mother Spirit drenching Her new planet with Her cries of complete and total joy, for She now had given birth to the new seed for Her Divine New Order.

Color prints of original art available for sale.
Call CosmoArt Studio (520) 490-2554 or email info@cosmoart.org

Part II
The Continuing Story

The next six chapters—22 through 27—were written after this book was first published in 1992. These six chapters deal with subsequent events that happened since then, though there is much reference to events previous to 1992.

CHAPTER 22

What Will My Friends Say This Time? When The Saints Come Marching In

I do not know if I could have written this chapter before July 21, 1993. I still feel it will be very difficult for me, yet I feel it is what God wants me to do. Our humility can be an enemy to us, as well as a friend. It was easier for me to accept that I was an unbalanced chief called Samba (pronounced "Soom-bay"), in Arizona, six thousand years ago, because I see all the imperfections in my character. I work on them daily. I have come a long way, but know I still have a way to go. I have asked God often why I was given the human Mandate of the Bright and Morning Star and why God invested me with such great responsibilities. I had a very difficult time when the celestial guides told me that I was someone who had been labeled a saint in the past.

At first I was not able to share this with anyone. So many people in the New Age go about claiming to be saints, kings, queens, pharaohs, and Indian chiefs that I did not and do not want to be associated with this company. The negative side of humility, if we are an ovan soul, is that we can never really tune into the now-opening memory circuits as long as we see ourselves as just a farm boy or girl from Iowa, or just a steel worker's son from Pittsburgh. We cannot come into our cosmic mind if we are rooted in insecurity. I still am not ready to share with the world all of my past existences, but I know that God wants me to share some of them at this time as well as some of the past lives of other Elders in our community of the First Cosmic Family.

The Catholic Church and other facets of Christendom have made saints out of very ordinary men and women who had many faults in their character, but through legends they have become bigger than life and more perfect in character than they actually were. Many miracles ascribed to them have been made up or exaggerated.

Chapter 22

I must start with the first personality Paladin said I had been, one that I had a hard time believing to be true. I must say at this point that this chapter is a lot easier because of another book that came into my possession through a cosmic brother, in February 1993, called *Secret Places of the Lion*. The book spoke of a "Goodly Company" who have come into Earth existences time and time again to assist humankind for thousands of years, and the author correctly linked several of my lives that Paladin had told me I had lived. I just love it when I find confirmation of information about anything with another source that resonates with every atom of my body.

The author, George Hunt Williamson, correctly linked Ikhnaton (Akhenaten), Pharaoh of Egypt—who tried to bring the One God, Aten, to his people—with Peter the apostle. He also linked Joseph of Jacob, King David, the prophet Daniel, and Joseph Smith as the same soul. Over a period of time Celestial Overcontrol has revealed that I had lived all these lives. The author also linked Nefertiti and Peter's wife correctly as the same soul. Niánn, Paladin said, was Nefertiti, Ikhnaton's (Akhenaten's) wife and Hanna (or Perpetua as *The URANTIA Book* calls her), Peter's perpetual wife who had shared many lives with Van as this book will point out. Anyone who has seen the bust of the beautiful queen Nefertiti should certainly recognize the same bone structure in Niánn's face.

In the beginning of our experience in Prescott, Paladin and other celestial entities had dangled the carrot often as to who Niánn, I, and others (then with us) were. Now I realize that the reason they do that is that they want us, if possible, to come to conclusions by self-discovery. It should have been quite clear to me who I was, but Peter was too awesome a character for me to walk in his footsteps. I actually looked forward to meeting him one day, and I was quite willing to believe that he was someone else on the planet.

When I lived in Tucson I played one of the apostles in a play called *Simon Peter*. At the time I felt I should have played Peter and that I could have portrayed him better than the actor who did. Now I know why I felt like that. However, the actor who played Peter was a classical singer and he gave an outstanding performance.

Since I wasn't much of a fisherman in this life, this fact also bothered me, but Paladin told us that many of the talents and gifts many Destiny Reservists once had are kept from them, or else they would be doing something other than what God wanted them to do. Of course Peter went out in a boat and threw out a net. That I can see myself doing—laying back, feet up, reading a good book, waiting for the fish to bite. Yup, that's me all right.

I certainly identify with Peter's impulsiveness. I have asked our Lord for forgiveness so often in this area. I can see a tremendous improvement in my forties as compared to my twenties and thirties. Since Jesus forgave Peter for denying Him three times, I have always found it easy to forgive others. I am disappointed when they think I have not forgiven them, mostly because I realize they have not forgiven themselves.

One former apostle was told by Paladin that he had been Menes, the first dynasty Pharaoh of Egypt, and Ramses I, the founder of the Nineteenth Dynasty. I had no problem believing this. On Easter, April 1992, the Bright and Morning Star, who fused with me, gave this apostle's identity as John the Revelator of the first century. Shortly after that an Elder and teacher in our community was told he was the Apostle James of the first century. In that life they were brothers. In this life these two individuals had been friends for more than thirty years and together taught about spiritual truths for twenty-three of them. (See Preface)

Peter, James, and John were aides to Jesus. We, who were the inner circle with Jesus in the first century, were reunited again in this current life. Our lives had touched bases in many repersonalizations. We had much to work out from our astral (past-lives) past. *The URANTIA Book* makes it quite clear that the apostles were imperfect men. I think the details of their imperfections were written in the Fifth Epochal Revelation so that we today can understand the interrelationships between one another in a higher spiritualized mind.

Character growth can be quite slow, sometimes taking up to the seventh mansion world of Satania. I found that, as a songwriter/lyricist/singer, it is easier to write and sing the words than to live up to them. It could take lifetimes. I sometimes began to doubt the whole reality, because I saw imperfections in myself and the other apostles and disciples, but I could not deny so many wonderful serendipities that have happened with the Bright and Morning Star, Paladin, and others.

I began to forgive myself and prayed to be able to love others unconditionally, despite their faults. One of our community prayers was and still is that: *community members become more conscious of past-life interactions with each other, so that present interactions with each other can be more highly understood.*

Now to top it off, Paladin one day confirmed, after dangling the carrot for four years, that I was also Francis of Assisi. Here we go again. I saw Franco Zeffirelli's film *Brother Sun, Sister Moon*, and the famous director had Francis far too "female" for me. Peter the Apostle, Francis the Wimp?

Niánn was told she was Sister Clare. That I could see for sure. Community members, particularly the females, still come to Mother Clare and confess their most hidden secrets and perhaps what they consider sins. Niánn, of course, has never solicited this.

When I read that Francis was a warrior before his conversion and was in prison for a year, I began to realize that most accounts of him left out his male strength. Trying to find the balance between the male and female circuits can take many lifetimes, both in other universes and on the higher mansion worlds of Satania. For some ovan souls it has taken ten lifetimes or more to reach a balance or stabilization.

Francis had to incarnate as an African warrior, who was taken to North Carolina to become a slave. Earlier in this book I spoke of being picked to sing lead in a one-hundred-voice black gospel choir in Los Angeles and how hard it was to leave and become a serious student of *The URANTIA Book*. The soul of my astral, past black life was very much a part of me in this life.

Francis also incarnated as Gentle Eagle, an Apache warrior. I identified with Gentle Eagle easily. I feel at home in Arizona, the home of the Apaches, and still feel very much the warrior. Peter was ready to draw the sword at any moment. In several lifetimes after Ikhnaton (Akhenaten) and before Peter (which I am not ready to reveal to the world as yet), I settled disputes by the sword. Jesus' words to Peter, I believe, began a real change in him: "Peter, put up your sword. They who take the sword shall perish by the sword." [*The URANTIA Book*, p. 1974]

In this life I have tried to learn the way of the peaceful warrior. Perhaps Peter, repersonalized as Francis, should have connected more with the Father circuits to bring about the renaissance that God wanted, in a much larger way. As it happened, the soul of Peter, in trying to become more Mother-circuited in that life, became too effeminate.

Francis later realized that he did not have to go to the Pope for permission to do God's will. He realized that his movement did not have to be endorsed by the Catholic Church, that he should have left the Catholic Church with its many false doctrines. He was already sick from his travels in Africa when he tried to share these thoughts with his closest friends. They believed that he was delirious and some thought he was losing his mind. "Leave the Catholic Church? Why that is heresy!" they told him.

He realized that God had tried to reach him when he first started his ministry, but he shut that part of God off. Just like in this life, when a young man tried to share *The URANTIA Book* with the then "Reverend Tony," I defended the Bible with the same misplaced loyalty. As mentioned earlier in this book, I considered becoming a Catholic priest and lived for a short period of time in two Benedictine monasteries, one in Arizona and one in New Mexico, and a Third Order Franciscan community in Montrose, Colorado. In this life the Catholic Church still had quite a hold on me.

In Prescott in 1989, an entity came through me as a walk-in and introduced himself as Francis of Assisi. I did not know at that time that this was a part of my astral self. He indeed was a past part of me that was much more at peace with himself than I was at that time. Francis never had to live in contemporary America. Francis of Assisi's movement spread rapidly in the thirteenth century; the time was ripe, and there was not much competition. Today in the religious arena there are thousands of self-proclaimed prophets, healers, etc. The equation "marketing + fame = avatarness" seems to be the unfortunate rule. After twenty years of ministry I had only a handful of students and did not feel successful by my standards.

One day Niánn witnessed a wonderful thing. Our parakeet escaped from the cage and was wildly flying into windows and walls. He had never come to anyone before when this occasionally happened. The essence of Francis in me called the bird and the little bird flew immediately to my finger, just like you see on so many pictures of Francis. What an experience that was for me, somewhere in between dimensions observing this. It was not until several days later that I was told that I was Francis. I am so blessed when others say they see that kind of gentleness in me.

Many men with various levels of gentleness think they have to suppress it because our society has distorted views of what a man is. I still feel that I went too far into an imbalance of the Father circuits in later repersonalizations and am now trying hard to balance myself out. Our planet needs balanced men, balanced fathers and husbands. Our community is trying to understand from a cosmic perspective the uniqueness of what it is to be a male or a female, an ascending son or daughter.

I began to see that my success as the balanced human being with godly virtue I was becoming—even if it is not recognized by others—is more valuable than gold. I would prefer to have a few students with the highest understanding of God, who are actively trying to deal with their lower natures, than ten thousand who really do not want to deal with their own baggage.

In November 1993 I became aware of another repersonalization. What Francis was not able to do in the thirteenth century, this same soul was able to do in the sixteenth century. This time as a Catholic priest, he started the reformation in the church, which led to the Protestant movement. Martin Luther, like Francis, was a musician and wrote many songs of worship that are still sung today. In this life he had a greater balance between the Father/Mother circuits and was able to take the courageous step away from the Catholic Church and lead others to do the same.

He regained his Father circuits without too much of an imbalance and recaptured the essence of the meaning of his name; Martin means "ancient warrior." I had many lives as a warrior swinging the sword, and when the apostle Peter literally drew his sword, Jesus told him to put down the sword. Jesus was talking about Peter's past lives, and of course He was also talking to all of the future generations of warrior souls on this planet. I am not ready at this time to share publicly the identity of the two most well-known warrior souls.[1]

I can say that both tried to unify the then-known world. One almost accomplished it but died young. Many in the community know who I was as these warriors. I still am trying to unify the world and conquer it, now with the sword of truth: the Fatherhood of God and the brother-/sisterhood of humankind.

Luther was asked by Christ Michael to translate the Bible of the Catholic Church. This took tremendous courage and reflected Luther's confidence in his relationship with God. Today I am asked to bring through Continuing Fifth Epochal Revelation of which *The URANTIA Book* is the first one-tenth! Many believe *The URANTIA Book* to be all there is—complete—even though the book itself, on page 1109, refutes that claim. I have felt this calling to make the world a better place since I was a little boy.

I do not feel it is important to share a past life unless something constructive can be communicated to benefit you. If you are a starseed, it may help you to tune into a possibly noble past aspect of yourself. It does not matter if you were a saint or a great person in the past; it is today that is important. However, it is time for starseed to find their past noble selves.

I am sure many of you have similar feelings of something you need to accomplish to aid our planet. We must also recognize other, negative traits that perhaps we had in the past, so we can understand ourselves better in the present. Luther was prone to bouts of depression, like I was in my former lives as Ikhnaton (Akhenaten) and Francis. Like them, he was often sick.

Trying to change oneself is not easy, but it is a must before you can begin to help others change themselves or try to help change the world. Ikhnaton (Akhenaten), Peter, Francis of Assisi, Martin Luther, and the two warrior souls all were leaders of men and women because they first dealt with themselves. Each soul was like a Bright and Morning Star in their time. With each life the same soul became brighter and brighter in the reflective image of God. Remember, it is not ego to "know thyself." It is ego to think too highly of one's self. I know I still have a long, long way to go.

There have been a few interesting coincidences in my present life. I was named Anthony Joseph at baptism. Anthony of Padua was Francis' closest friend. I am also the Joseph of Jacob. In the book *Secret Places of the Lion* the author has Francis and a half-brother of Joseph linked. My real name in Italian is Dell Erba, which means "of the earth or grass." My son Amadon was given my original Italian name, Dell Erba. This is the Amadon of *The URANTIA Book*, and he is certainly of the earth. "What of Amadon of Urantia, does he still stand unmoved?" [*The URANTIA Book*, p. 762]

The Catholic Church that I was baptized in as a child was St. Peter's. It was on Fernando Street, which is a derivative of Francesco (Francis). The church was Franciscan. My confirmation name is Thomas. In Prescott a son of the Apostle Thomas, Mikal, was with us. Mikal is my cosmic son. Celestial Overcontrol led me to believe that Mikal was Thomas the Apostle, I feel, because Peter and Thomas were very close friends.

In this life I almost died of grief when I lost my beloved second wife, Jerri. Now I know she was a cosmic complement, a past-life wife to me and a cosmic wife to me. She was a cosmic sister to TiyiEndea (my present wife), and I always hoped that Jerri would join us in Divine Administration, but as of this writing it has not happened. Ikhnaton (Akhenaten) and Francis both died in a state of grief. Ikhnaton (Akhenaten) felt rejection from his loved ones and the people of Egypt because they would not accept his God—the one God—Aten.[2] I still have a tendency to be depressed with life in general.

It always seems that I should be somewhere else, no doubt on a distant planet. People can be so cruel to one another. This saddens me deeply. It is much easier to love than to hate, to give than to take, to be an instrument of peace rather than an instrument of war.

CHAPTER 23
The Return Of The Cosmic Family

One of the greatest proofs of the reality of what is happening here at the First Planetary Sacred Home is the high quality of people in Global Community Communications Alliance. This indeed is a blessing for me and all of us. Niánn Emerson Chase, who shares the Mandate of the Bright and Morning Star with me, is one of the most generous persons I know and brings clarity to most interpersonal conflicts. She was a professional tour guide for Dorian Tours, the original vortex touring company of Sedona, Arizona, now owned by Global Community Communications Alliance and called Spirit Steps Tours.

Niánn was able to incorporate our spiritual teachings in her tours. She was quite suited for this, as on her biological father's side she is a descendent of Meriwether Lewis of the Lewis and Clark Expedition. She was Sacagawea, the Native American guide in the Lewis and Clark Expedition. Literally and figuratively, we have both climbed many mountains together. On the biological maternal side of her family she has the genetics of Ralph Waldo Emerson. In the last century Niánn was Ellen Tucker Emerson, the eldest daughter of Ralph Waldo Emerson.

She is the educational director of The Starseed and Urantian Schools of Melchizedek [a.k.a. Global Community Communications Schools of Ascension Science & The Physics of Rebellion] for adults, teens, and children. Years ago I watched her spend four to six hours each Sunday writing up curriculum for each child. Now we have other instructors who design curriculum and teach for our children's schools. Niánn continues to spend many hours writing quality curriculum for the various adult classes offered. That is dedication!

For current profiles of the Eldership of Divine Administration, please visit: http://gccalliance.org/eldership/

Many of the members of Global Community Communications Alliance here at this time have had past lives together. Many of the old unsettled disputes still surface. All of these souls are here because they have connected with God's will enough to find us at the First Planetary Sacred Home. Here the real struggles between good and evil begin—the struggles of the lower self with the higher self. Most believed they had lived past lives before they came here. Many of us recognized each other on some level when we first met.

I felt God wanted me to write this chapter for many reasons. One of them is that you who read this may open memory circuits to your own past if you are an ovan soul. Perhaps you have an inkling of some past-life experience. It is within my mandate to help you open those circuits. The beings who speak through me, mainly Paladin, want to tell you about your destiny, now. Perhaps you are a Destiny Reservist or a Cosmic Reservist.

In the very early days, a profound experience happened to all of us when Isis, a woman in her seventies from California, visited us. Although not a *URANTIA Book* reader, she had for a long time thought she was Joanna of the first century. Her presence among us brought out old patterns of behavior between us apostles of the first century, which shocked all of us. It seems she was a buffer in the first century between the apostles, and she again played that role very briefly, for that one day she visited us! Paladin confirmed she was the Joanna of the first century.

If you stay around people who think you are nuts for even slightly suggesting you may be picking up on feelings of a past life, you will not find your destiny purpose in this lifetime. You need to be around others who are discussing their past lives as well as working hard to fulfill God's will in this one. What is really important is who you are now. We do not realize our past and who we were or what we did just to brag about it. Much of the past can be used to help us understand ourselves in the present. If what we learn about the past helps us to become more Christlike and function in a more spiritual mind, then that is what knowing past lives is about. The light or darkness of a person's past should add to the light of a person's present.

I used to think that when you died and woke up, you were like the highest angel—perfect. Now I know that ascension is just that, ascension. You wake up just like you were and start from there. We starseed (and second-time Urantians) are not consciously aware that we have been here before. We have no memories of our former life; we are not yet eternalized. With the opening of our memory circuits, we are just beginning to find out about our past-life experiences. The circuits are just beginning to open since the upstepping of the adjudication. It is a very slow process.

Even slower is growth in virtue. The mind can actually develop intellectually and you can still be a very ungodlike person. For centuries you may hang onto various forms of pride and other evil ways. In *The Cosmic Family* volumes this is explained by the finaliter, Paladin, very scientifically. I speak now and all through this book from my heart, bringing what wisdom I can in layman's terms.

I also used to think that when the apostles returned, they would perform many great miracles and bring many people to God. Now I know that they were, and still are, very human, and that the greatest miracle they could perform would be to change themselves. The apostles are back on Urantia—some by choice, some because they had to. Believe me, none are as perfect as the Master they once followed. Some have fulfilled part of their destiny being in the Urantia movement but have not yet accepted the Continuing Fifth Epochal Revelation. Some may not make it to Planetary Headquarters and others will. Many come, stay for a while, then leave and default. It is so painful for us to see this happen. When we confront certain individuals who have been seared in their consciousness about their iniquity, they behave like the criminal in prison: sorry they got caught, but not sorry they did the crime.

Soul Diagnosis And Soul Surgery
— My Hard-Earned Ability

True clairvoyance comes from being like God. Greater virtue, fused with mindal ability, seasoned with experience over hundreds and thousands of years, gives an ascending soul clairvoyance. An aspect of this "seeing" is soul discernment. The New Testament calls it "discerning of spirits." In the Christian interpretation many see this as the ability to discern an evil spirit of some kind, when you could not before. They teach that this gift came at Pentecost with the reception of the Spirit of Truth. Others teach that it comes with the additional baptism of the Holy Spirit. I feel both interpretations are correct. But it is an evolving ability, not a complete gift upon reception. It continues, I am sure, to finality of personality development.

The understanding of the soul is a cosmic science, and few have the ability to truly recognize good from evil and error from iniquity at the level necessary to become a good counselor of the soul. Many of us can sense a very iniquitous or a very good person to some degree, as there are indeed many levels of good and evil. Many beautiful people die of various diseases because of incorrect thinking. Others are very iniquitous. Many are quite obvious in their evil, while others have become skilled at deception—so skilled they even deceive themselves in their wrongdoing. They are hard to detect. Many appear to be angels of light. They know the right words of the metaphysical/spiritual/religious circles. They can deceive the very elect of God. They are in the circles of the good seed and consider themselves teachers and leaders of those more humble and not sophisticated in mind and manipulation.

These are the millions of starseed and some of the second-time Urantians. The older the starseed, the better they are able to deceive others. When the problem is self-deception and they feel they are in the right, they will go to their graves with their own self-righteousness and various forms of pride. Some souls who have been called saints by the Catholic Church fit this description. Some souls, who reached a higher spiritual ascension in virtue at some point in their past on this planet, have fallen backward, and never really stabilized.

The first apostles of Christ are not exempt from having to stabilize on the psychic circles mentioned in *The URANTIA Book*. Many have the tendency to see only the good in others, and perhaps that is all they want to see. I too have been fooled by cosmic brothers and sons. I did not want to see the other parts of them that the Spirit of Truth was trying to show me. I did not even want to hear it directly from the beings I was in contact with. That is what most of us do; we cut off what is unpleasant to look at. I had to learn to listen. Usually we love them too much to see the wrong in them. Unfortunately, if they are not as evolved as we are spiritually, they end up hurting us by turning against our higher truths and virtues.

The souls who have the greatest ability for good, but have not stabilized, can also cause the most problems and have the highest potential to go either way, toward evil or toward good. Sometimes the more virtuous venture into error for a few days, weeks, months, years, or decades, sometimes even for lifetimes. A second-time Urantian with the highest genetics can ascend to levels of mind superior to that of a two-hundred-thousand-year-old starseed who has continually fallen backwards. This was the hope of Celestial Overcontrol for second-time Urantians who were allowed to return to their native planet during the adjudication.

Urantia is a planet of either rapid spiritual growth or deterioration. When I see into the soul of a certain individual and know that he or she is possibly months away from changing in some areas and years in others, I have to practice unconditional love when that individual says that he or she has changed but does the same inappropriate thing a few days later.

Some of the most iniquitous will spend many more lifetimes on fallen worlds, perhaps worlds worse than this one. The same judgment can happen to those who are so right in their own eyes and are not intentionally harmful. Pride results in blindness to many forms of error. Pride is worse than any drug addiction. Many heroin and cocaine addicts or alcoholics will go to the higher mansion worlds, long before a prideful soul. The prideful and arrogant will be quite lucky if they make the first mansion world.

So many claim to be spiritual. They may claim to be healers, and shamans, and priests. I get nauseated when I read most New Age literature. There is so much plagiarism. There are catchwords that everyone "in the (metaphysical) know" uses. They expound on a bunch of garbage they do not even believe or understand. They distort new revelation and real truth that they read or hear from a higher teacher.

I have already seen my work plagiarized and books published that became major sellers with lower-level and distorted information from the concepts of Continuing Fifth Epochal Revelation (*The Cosmic Family* volumes) that we had published in *The Salvington Circuit* and other public mailings, before we even published the First Edition of *The Cosmic Family, Volume I*. There is no credibility. The majority have no fear of God because they do not truly know Him. They teach instant healing and sell themselves as those who walk and talk with the angels. I could understand why many would think that I am just another kook, without having properly investigated my work and our community. There are very few real spiritual teachers and healers on the planet.

At this time I feel it would be very appropriate to insert part of a transmission on spirituality from *The Cosmic Family, Volume I*.[1]

What Is Spirituality?

First of all, we will tell you what it is not. It is not a dress code. No form of dress makes a person holy, or wise, or indeed spiritual—not robes, not collars, not turbans. It is not the way a person walks. It is not their height or their weight. It is not in their ability to speak nor their intellectual acquirements.

No degree given to man or woman can make them spiritual. No university on this planet can proclaim in their schools of theology that a person is now spiritual. No fasting over a period of time or sacrifice can make a person spiritual. Neither can the diet of certain foods or vegetarianism as opposed to meat eating make a person spiritual. No substance found in the earth and ingested can make a person spiritual. No modern chemical injected can produce a spiritual personality.

No amount of wealth, fame, or prestige can bring spirituality to a person. No appointment of position by man to man in any capacity can make a person spiritual. No self-sacrifice alone, no matter how great, can make a person spiritual—not the giving of a son or daughter or their rightful husband or wife to God, nor the giving of one's income, nor the continued public announcement to others that you are God's chosen. No amount of adulation of man for man can make another spiritual.

True spirituality or virtue is a process that begins based upon certain universe laws and procedures. True spirituality cannot be defined so simply. For example, even those who appear to present the fruits of the spirit may not be so spiritual at all. The virtues said to bring about the fruits of the spirit can be disguised at various levels of deception in the third dimension. It is not so simple, and many factors have to be taken into consideration.

Virtue for an ascending son or daughter is an acquired thing. It is learned over a period of time and that time may be hundreds, thousands, and, indeed, millions of years. It does not come upon you as the Baptists and Pentecostals say, in a moment of time upon the reception of the Spirit of Truth, making you perfect. It is an eternal process.

When you reach finality you can begin to say that you are spiritual. Throughout the grand universe the degree to which you are truly spiritual is the degree of your own individual blessedness. Blessedness is the beginning of individual happiness, but blessedness is higher than happiness, for one can be happy in sin.

For too long on Urantia Lucifer has tried to replace spirituality with other things, thereby decreasing happiness for so many millions at whatever level they could acquire happiness. Whatever level your spirituality is, it creates the reality in which you find yourself and what you have and what you have not. It separates that which you desire from that which you will get. As your spirituality increases, your desires that are based upon the desires of God will become manifest.

The Spirit of Truth is the beginning of higher spirituality on Urantia, and the hearing of it—moment to moment above all else—is the activation of that spirituality, which leads to your individual happiness and fulfillment. Spirituality is a golden box and within it can be found treasures—treasures that cannot be bought by ascending sons and daughters, for this golden box is owned by the Supreme Deity, and its gifts are bestowed based upon each individual's willingness to seek his or her God in whatever way one can, based upon that search and knocking on the door of the heart of God, and then the golden box begins to be filled.

As you become honest, the gift of honesty is given. As you become patient, the gift of patience is given. As you become giving, the gift of things are given to you. As you seek wisdom over pride, wisdom is given, and the golden box begins to shine with the light of God, and we shall call this box the heart circuit.

Wisdom, which increases one's spirituality, cannot be purchased. Even when written, words of wisdom may not be understood, for wisdom is given in and through the Holy Spirit to those who put others first above their own selves, for it is written that love should not seek its own welfare but the welfare of others.

Motives in harmony with divine ordinance increase spirituality and bring the body into higher morontia realities and above. Individuals, who are trapped in third-dimensional patterns in regard to religious thinking and even livelihood, cannot even begin to reach the higher motives, for the higher motives deal with others outside of one's own nuclear family, where most of the people of Urantia are presently obligated. Even worse than that, millions do not even have concern for their own families but only concern for themselves as individuals. The more people whom you can place into the sphere of your responsibility, the higher your spirituality.

This is a divine thing, and it is divinely understood at different levels, and at whatever level you can now begin to grasp it, it is given to your planet. Certain spiritual leaders of the past have understood this, but it is available for all to understand, and when the mass consciousness of a planet can realize that we are each others' keeper, the suffering of that planet will end. Words can be written and taught but little understood.

For thousands of years, philosophers have philosophized upon very high spiritual statements written by prophets and wise men of God, but few manifest the power of those words within their own realities for the benefit of the planet as a whole. At certain periods on Urantia at the time of certain renaissances, many ovan souls who had once come to the realization of selfless service to humankind were again brought to this planet and repersonalized as contemporaries, sometimes together and sometimes in different countries. It has been necessary on Urantia for these ovan souls to come back, for they have been the only voices to cry out against the established way of Caligastia.

What is spirituality? Many may think it is rebellion; and indeed it is. It is rebellion against Caligastia; it is rebellion against Luciferic reality; it is rebellion against evil, sin, and iniquity. Jesus was a rebel who came against the established norm. Today on Urantia the Spirit of Truth is even more so a rebel. Today the societies of the planet are much worse than they were even in Jesus' time. Then, the people suffered in slavery and poverty. Today the people are also blinded because of materialism and foolish self-pursuit.

Spirituality is faith—the faith to be humble, the faith to give of one's talents and abilities to the true spiritual teachers and elders on this planet when they can be found and recognized.

Spirituality is gentle when it has to be and forceful when it has to be. It is Father/Mother. It is not just Mother nor can it be just Father, and when the son or daughter is in balance with both, spirituality can be perfected, for the fusion of childish youth then is incorporated with maturated age, and a liveliness of spirit presents itself instead of rigidity and inflexibility.

Spirituality enjoys a good laugh, and some of the most highly spiritual personalities of time and space are great comedians. But the comedy is pure and is based upon cosmic fact of the relationships of the evolutionary process that is most humorous on the higher levels.

Spirituality is discipline. Discipline and perfection are wonderful as long as within this perfection one does not become so stagnant that one cannot change when necessary.

Spirituality to those who recognize it commands authority, and we bow to those of higher spirituality because of that spirituality in relation to the God of all. Spirituality and authority cannot be escaped, neither can spirituality and responsibility. Many refuse to become spiritual because they realize, even at a lower level, that they cannot escape responsibility for themselves or for others.

Spirituality begins in knowing one's place with God at any particular moment in an individual's existence. The saints of the past may have been spiritual, but as they ascended to the higher mansion worlds and above, their spirituality increased, as it does with ovan souls who return to this planet and others, and who do not default in their reasons for being on Urantia or on their missions if they are Cosmic Reservists. Spirituality is strong character, and strong character is the fusion of the Universal Father, the Eternal Son, and the Infinite Spirit in mortal likeness.

On some planets there are beings whom you would consider quite obese, but in comparison to any spiritual Urantian mortals at this time they would be like one with a Ph.D. compared to a kindergarten child in terms of their spirituality. It is because spirituality is a nontangible thing. You cannot touch spirituality, nor can you always judge it by appearance, and when you do you have erred greatly.

On some planets, those who are highly spiritual may be in a body form that would be so different from yours that they would actually frighten you. But those of us who have ascended high enough to sense the essence of God within them, once again, bow to their spirituality at whatever level they have attained it.

Chapter 23

Spirituality cannot be technically acquired or scientifically produced. It can be scientifically analyzed in accordance with higher understanding and ascension science analysis, but it cannot be programmed, for only God can create a perfect being and the Creator Sons are the only ones given this power.

There is a difference between courage and foolishness. True courage demands some form of spiritual attainment. The more courageous one becomes in true spiritual alignment, the more one will accomplish for the benefit of all on a particular planet.

Spirituality is colorful and creates in the astral realms the purest perceptions of divine colors that can resonate around any one particular individual personality. These colors in turn manifest healing to that individual and to those who are blessed to be near them. On Urantia, the highest spiritual personalities most often become drained of energy, for so many others unknowingly draw from their life force.

True spirituality is fragrant with odors that higher celestial personalities can distinguish. This is why, sometimes around high spiritual personalities, flower essences are recognized even by humans. These things, such as color and smell, are a science in themselves, and we are just beginning to touch on the subject.

The higher the spiritual personality, the more in control of one's self in all respects one needs to become. It is increasingly easier to take into account many wrongs suffered without justifying oneself, for one begins to realize that justification is not necessary and it is only pride that wishes to make itself correct. It is one thing to correct a person's wrong thinking. It is another thing to do it when it is either out of pride or not necessary. The line is so thin that it may take thousands and thousands of years to come to the place of accuracy. Higher spirituality is knowing the difference.

Spirituality is knowledge fused with wisdom and applied with experiential reality in the evolutionary worlds and above. It is applied existential and experiential reality in relation to God and to others of God's creation.

Higher spiritual personalities are social creatures. They are not isolationists. Solitude, although not only a temporal reality, can become a damaging thing when the spiritual personality begins to self-contemplate to the point of misaligning with higher authority or one's peers at any level. Social communication with colleagues within the same realm of spiritual ascension is medicine for the ovan soul.

It is within the union of souls that higher spirituality can be manifested and actualized by ascending beings. Higher spirituality in the company of one's elders knows when to voice an opinion and when not to, and higher spiritual teachers know when to ask of those individuals their opinions and when not to.

Higher spiritual personalities are ever so absolute. There is no question once they have presented their opinion based upon absolute reality as they know it. If question arises, it is in the misinterpretation of what the lower individual heard them say, and this is so throughout the ascension process. Truth is often misinterpreted, for it is heard at the level of one's own spirituality and no more.

The problem always arises, how does a higher ovan soul or being communicate with a lower one? Thus, spirituality is the ability to descend to a lower level and make one's self understood at that level of communication. For if you are not understood at any level, you have no value as a teacher of cosmic reality. You may do well in the solitude of the libraries of time and space, but in practical application to the rest of creation you could become a worthless individualist, and at the point where this begins to happen, the personality begins to default.

Always in these cases lack of patience is found in these individuals, and so it is increasingly important that the art of communication to lower-circle individuals be learned and acquired, and it begins in the personality when one begins to look at one's own impatience and inflexibility.

These tendencies are common to mortals of time and space void of the higher reception of the Holy Spirit, particularly in stronger Father-circuited personalities. In my own ascension to Paradise as a finaliter, it was one of my faults hardest to overcome. It is not in the text of this transmission to give the solutions to the preceding statement; I can only state the possible problem.

A person with higher spirituality is not envious or jealous of those who have acquired what he has not, either materially or nonmaterially. Envy and jealousy are two of the most difficult things to recognize in one's self. It can take thousands of years within the growth of an ovan soul before the degrees of envy and jealousy of an individual can be recognized. These faults of character are, again, lengthy in concept to describe.

These unfortunate traits were found in Lucifer, and we have found that it is ever so difficult to open the eyes of those who have followed in his footsteps and acquired these unfortunate traits. Justification of one's own jealousy and envy is quite a thing to measure on our side. There are volumes written on these subjects in the higher schools on the satellite worlds, so it is not a subject you just touch on.

One thing that we have found where envy and jealousy continue to exist in personalities is a decrease in their clairvoyant perceptions and of course the reception from their own Thought Adjuster, depending upon the spiritual acquiescence and other attributes of those individuals that determine the many things pertinent to their present reality and certain mandates given them. Mandates can be given to individuals who have traces of envy and jealousy, as mandates can be given to those with other bad habits.

It is true, God is the judge of these things; and it should be left to the Creator Son and personalities of Paradise origin to decide these things and contemplate upon them. We at lower levels can discuss these things and contemplate as to why mandates are given to the imperfect, but it is much easier for us to do so, for our memory circuits are more open at higher levels, and we remember our imperfect selves more clearly.

It is written that ascending mortals at times often think too highly of themselves. Spirituality and humility are siblings. They balance each other out and indeed are from the same parents. Humility cannot be known unless some form of spirituality exists, but spirituality can exist at a lower level where no humility at all exists. Spirituality comes first; humility follows, and grows, and grows, and grows. Throughout eternity humility is a learning process, which increases one's spirituality.

Spirituality is visionary. It is not crippled by fear. It is prophetic and finds its purpose in the recognition of the divine purposes of others as well as of oneself. The more one can recognize the function of others in the divine plan and can recognize another's individual placement in the timetable of the divine clock, the higher the spirituality within the personality.

Spirituality is adventurous. It begins to take risks because of increased faith, not only on the defaulted worlds of time and space but in relation to other unknowns of time and space that higher spirituality begins to build. It first learns to plant the seeds; then it learns to find the correct soils and what seeds to plant for the various beings of time and space. It learns the particular foods that need to be digested in body, mind, and spirit.

Spirituality does not always feel good to the individual, who learns to do what feels good to God and learns to recognize that one's own feelings may interfere with the perfect will of God. A person learns to separate one's likes and dislikes for the higher good of all.

Higher spirituality is not based upon always catering to your feelings. It discerns the will of God upon the combination of mind and heart fused with the mandated purposes of God as given first through the Thought Adjuster, Spirit of Truth, and Holy Spirit within, agreed upon then by Celestial Overcontrol at various levels, and on evolutionary worlds by mortal eldership.

Higher spirituality learns not only to listen to the inner self but to the inner selves of others who are their spiritual elders—human or celestial personalities—who are all together hearing the same divine mind. Higher spirituality understands the difference between rest and slothfulness and can discern the same in others and can make use of idle time for the purposes of God wherever it may find itself. Moment to moment, it is always useful to God, even in periods of rest and relaxation it is in divine will.

Higher spirituality does not overwork itself to the point of indifference to family, social, or union-of-soul responsibility. Whatever it does, its purpose is within the divine will, and it has learned to accept each moment as a gift of divine origin and looks upon the moment as a continuing learning experience.

The previous comments on spirituality are just a beginning of the comments that could be made and are not complete by any standard of time and space. They are presented here to clarify some misconceptions on Urantia of who and what is spiritual.

But before you can begin to understand any of this at the level necessary, I suggest that you turn your life over completely to God and request the Holy Spirit to make itself known within you, and this begins by accepting Christ Michael, your Universe Father, who became Jesus and left behind His Spirit of Truth for your education.

Begin your registration now at the University of Salvington so that your circuits can be opened to the capital of this universe of Nebadon, and align yourselves properly with the absolute truths, which are the foundation and stepping stones to Paradise. If you have not taken this first step, please do.

Some of the first century have met us in a number of ways: through the mail or Internet, in our former lives in the old order, at some public gathering, through acquaintances and friends. Some have actually come for a seminar or joined us for a period of time and left. Many others from various parts of the world cannot wait to get here. Those who left the community, for whatever reason, could not grasp fully what is taking place. I always know a little more about them than they know about themselves, because Paladin tells me. He gives me certain information about their past lives or their present one if necessary—something that I need to know, but they are not ready to know.

I have met several cosmic sons, for instance, who were not ready to hear that I am their cosmic father. Many sons and brothers do not want to humble themselves to the spiritual authority of an elder brother or elder sister, especially if in this life that elder is chronologically their same age or even younger. Few recognize the older soul inside the body—pride gets in the way. Some come half way, until something is said that goes against their opinions.

The opening of the memory circuits is a very slow process for ovan souls on Urantia at this time. It is God's reciprocation for the act of your submission to His will. It is the practice of humility. So you see, because we are so proud and arrogant, these past memories come gradually as we deserve the bits and pieces to the puzzle. We can compare humility to a complicated instrument, like a violin. The more you practice, the better you get. At some point, certain notes and chords become clear, pure, and true.

With each act of humility the character becomes more Godlike. Although at times it may come more naturally, you still have to use that free will and continue to practice or you will lose, perhaps, what you previously gained. After a season of applied experience you will begin to become a more accomplished student of virtue and perhaps one day even be recognized by others as a virtuoso. True humility is a treasure in the making.

CHAPTER 24

The Bright And Morning Star Walks In, And The Realities Of Community Life At The First Planetary Sacred Home

In early 1989 the Bright and Morning Star first came to speak to Niánn and me, along with three others who were close to us. We did not realize it at the time, but it takes five ascending sons or daughters of one cosmic family, together geographically, closely aligned to the purpose of God, to bring his presence through and enable interdimensional audio communications. To prepare me for this experience Paladin first fused with my body as I was hiking up Thumb Butte in Prescott while carrying one of the twins on my back. I was about ready to give up when he came in. The change in my body energy easily took me to the top. Celestial Overcontrol had been preparing me for his presence, saying to expect Paladin to fuse in the near future during daytime.

When these personalities first came to me, I could not open my eyes or make any movements. I progressed to where Paladin could actually drive the car. It was and still is fascinating. They can do anything in my body: eat, go to the bathroom, brush teeth, etc. Paladin would stay in for hours at a time. Those who say that beings come in and stay for months at a time and then another one takes over are not of the light forces, or more properly stated, of the loyal administration of Christ Michael. *The Cosmic Family, Volume I* begins to explain interdimensional communication in detail. Needless to say, much teaching is needed in this area.

One Friday evening the Bright and Morning Star came with more power, more fusion. It is hard to explain, but now I know it has to do with molecular and subatomic reality. He came in at 8:00 P.M. and taught for several hours, walking around the house. He was still in when I went to sleep, and Niánn was asked to sleep on the far side of the bed.

When I woke up around 5:00 A.M. (two hours earlier than usual), the Bright and Morning Star was still in. He first took me outside and walked around the property. He seemed to be blessing the land and giving orders to unseen entities. I know that he created some kind of vortex around the house. (Weeks later, I surrounded the house with quartz rock—no doubt he programmed me to do so that morning.) Next he took me into the bathroom and asked my permission to shave off my beard. I do not like my looks without my mustache and beard. I knew he had a good reason, so I complied.

When everyone woke up they met the Bright and Morning Star, who made breakfast for everyone. I usually have to be coaxed to do that. His other visitations had always been at night, so this was a new experience. He said he wanted to change the furnishings in the house to open it up. He created a sacred room in which we all ate, sitting on the floor, for the next nine months, until we moved to Sedona.

The Bright and Morning Star took Jonathan and me into town that day to buy cloth material for the sacred room and hallways. He took us into a retail store and the owner, a woman in her sixties, said to him, "Are you an angel?" He said, "It is written 'Never turn away a stranger for you never know when you might be entertaining an angel visitor.'" He invited her to his Sunday night visitations at our home, but she never came. She probably was told later by her husband, her pastor, or a friend that she was crazy and so lost faith in her own experience of truth. So often we are talked out of God's will by well-intentioned but ignorant loved ones.

We had been looking for some time for a wood cook stove. Prescott is full of antique shops and secondhand stores. The Bright and Morning Star gave us directions to drive to a certain one. The owner was just getting back from California with a shipment of goods. He still had the cook stove in the truck and was willing to trade for it. The next day we went back to pick it up.

That afternoon the Bright and Morning Star took all of us to our favorite Mexican restaurant. Outside the door we ran into a woman who was a proud and arrogant soul. When she looked at me she intuitively knew it was not me in the body and was very nervous. The Bright and Morning Star did not speak to her but smiled and moved us all inside quickly. I thought of Jesus' teaching to us, "Do not cast your pearls before swine." Then began the strangest ten minutes of my life. When we entered the restaurant, which was full to capacity, everyone suddenly stopped talking—an energy came into the room that was unmistakably not of this world. The four of us and the twins walked down the aisle together and sat near the front. Everyone began talking again after we were seated. They knew me there by my name, Gabriel.

The manager came up and whispered in my ear that I did not have any shoes on, a fact that I, as the human Gabriel, had not realized until that moment. The Bright and Morning Star did not like to wear anything on his feet. The manager informed the Bright and Morning Star that he would have to put on shoes or leave. He responded politely with a smile, "Sometimes we must obey God's rules above man's," and slowly and gently got up and motioned for us all to leave. Niánn, Evening Star, Jonathan, and the twins started walking out. However, the Bright and Morning Star, almost in slow motion, began walking backwards out of the restaurant, using his hands to bless everyone and saying out loud over and over again, "God bless you all, peace be unto you."

Again the whole restaurant was quiet and a divine energy came into the room until we all walked out of the restaurant, the Bright and Morning Star last. I fully expected to hear something about this incident in the next few days or even read about it in the newspaper, perhaps something like "Angel refused service at local Mexican restaurant," or "People become spellbound by an angel who likes Mexican food," but we never heard anything about it.

I now wonder if the event was blocked out of the minds of all who experienced it except we five who knew more of the reality that was taking place. When I asked Paladin he said, "I cannot give information on that incident." Needless to say, Niánn and I never went back to that restaurant. The Bright and Morning Star ate no meat and very little else. He wore only loose flowing clothes and a headband. Since that experience I feel lost without one. After three full days, the Bright and Morning Star (Gabriel of Salvington) left my body.

I began to connect more with my past lives, particularly those of royalty. I must confess, I began to feel the prince and king in me, not in any egotistical way, but in having a sense of responsibility for many beyond my immediate family. I had felt responsibility as a pastor, but this was different. I was just beginning to learn about the Mandate of the Bright and Morning Star and what it would mean to be his human reflection, his human audio fusion material complement. A new gentleness was a part of me. I even talked a little differently.

For the three days the Bright and Morning Star was in my body, Niánn and I of course could not be intimate, but even after he left, for many months I had little sexual desire. However, I began to love Niánn more purely. I realized I loved her spirit. I began to appreciate her more and see more of her godly quality. It was weeks before the Father circuits in my astral self balanced out the strong Mother circuitry of the Bright and Morning Star, and I was ready to grow back my beard. I was also told I had become stabilized on the second psychic circle. Peter the apostle, Francis the friar, and Gentle Eagle the Apache warrior, were becoming the more balanced ascending son, Gabriel of Urantia/TaliasVan of Tora.

I am still learning what it means to be a spiritual leader in the context of humans in Divine Administration. I feel God wants me to share some thoughts based on the experience of community relationships thus far, so that perhaps you who are reading this chapter and coming here in the future will not fall into some of these negative patterns. If anything, our experience should make it easier for those coming. We Elders and individual community members alike should be able to help others avoid the pitfalls of their lower natures and to function within the higher procedures of the divine mind and Divine Administration. Here I can only give in generalities what *The Cosmic Family* volumes teach in specifics.

- We are not just community members or cosmic family. We are all called by God to be representatives of the Divine Administration, which functions like the mechanism of a clock. Foremost, each of us is a vital working part of that clock. When one cog malfunctions, the whole clock either stops completely or loses time.

- Quite often some think they can do certain things better than the leader, that something should have been done this way or that way. Ten people could have ten different opinions about the same thing or procedure. The leader is damned if he does or damned if he does not. In short, people need to learn to acquiesce and trust the decisions of leadership, i.e. students to Second Assistants, Second Assistants to First Assistants, First Assistants to Elders, Elders to those over them, and up the administrative ladder. Honor must be given to those with overcontrol mandates. Some quality in them has earned them recognition by Christ Michael; can we do any less?

It takes at least a good year of being here at the First Planetary Sacred Home to really understand the reasons for certain procedures and how Celestial Overcontrol works with me and everyone else. If you become too quickly opinionated or critical without knowing all the facts, you do yourself harm by becoming disappointed in me, Celestial Overcontrol, other Elders, other mandated assistants or the whole process by not being here long enough to understand why I and others make certain decisions, teach certain things, or say certain things.

Patience can truly pay off in your own character growth and be a wonderful antidote to many of your own frustrations. Many of your perceptions need to be understood in the light of a spiritualized mind, which is one of the reasons you are a student at The Extension Schools of Melchizedek [a.k.a. Global

Community Communications Schools of Ascension Science & The Physics of Rebellion].

- Individuals can be blindly selfish, putting themselves first, or using their children in family quarrels, or taking their children out of school when the parents are mad at a teacher because of an interpersonal dispute that has nothing to do with education.

- Students must realize that Elders, particularly those more active in the process of bringing Continuing Fifth Epochal Revelation to Urantia, just cannot be a personal buddy to them. We are just too busy. If we spent our time socializing with all who want to, that is all we would be doing. I look forward to the future on our new planet when I can have more free time to just enjoy others. Right now on Urantia, I and others are quite busy helping to bring about that world.

- All must learn the law of reciprocation (as explained in Paper 202 of *The Cosmic Family, Volume I*) and give what they can of their time and finances. There is so much to do and little help or money with which to do it. Everyone wants to eat of the garden. Few want to work it. Also, you cannot be lukewarm[1] or serve two masters; you cannot serve God and the world.[2] As Paladin says "You must get off the cosmic fence. In all areas of your life you need to be in the perfect will of the Father."

- When you arrive in Divine Administration, after the romance period of being awed at the beauty of the area and new friendships, you begin to realize that the trials and tribulations of life will still occur. You must realize that you have need of growth. It may not be as easy as you think to change those old thought forms and habits. People need to own up to their own baggage. God is still using the circumstances of your reality to perfect you.

Many prophets today claim divine inspiration from God. For a few, on some level, this is true. But, Celestial Overcontrol states that, since December of 1989, I am the only vessel being used as the Audio Fusion Material Complement, though I am not the only one to whom God or His administration are talking in the various ways they do with mortals. Celestial Overcontrol has been working with me from a first-circle standpoint for many years now.[3]

It is written that judgment first starts in the household of God. This is the adjudication. Perhaps we here at the First Planetary Sacred Home who are older starseed—older souls with more ingrained wrong thought patterns—are the biggest hardheads. And they chose the biggest hardhead of all (me) to directly speak through. I certainly am not claiming to be better than anyone else in any way. The Mandate of the Bright and Morning Star is an awesome responsibility. For whatever reasons they chose me, I can think of other reasons why they should not have. All I can say is that I do seek to be perfect and try to own up to my shortcomings.

We ask people to come from all over the world and spend a few days with us to get to know us. If you cannot discern the fruits of the spirit functioning, particularly in us Elders, then I advise you to get away quickly. Those fruits of the spirit are: love, joy, peace, patience, kindness, temperance, honesty, and unselfishness—just to name a few. But if you do see them and in a marvelous way . . . wow! Perhaps this whole book and *The Cosmic Family* volumes of the Continuing Fifth Epochal Revelation are all true . . . wow! Wow! And Machiventa Melchizedek, the Planetary Prince and staff are really on the planet. Wow! Wow! Wow! And the head administrator of our local universe, Gabriel of Salvington, walks in his human audio fusion material complement periodically and teaches all of us. Wow! Wow! Wow! Wow! Wow! Jesus is coming back to this planet soon. Just like He said He would.

CHAPTER 25
Meeting Wallace Black Elk

One day while I was working down at my office table by the creek, I was just getting ready to go when a Celestial Overcontrol voice said, "Sit down and work some more." This happened several times, and I stayed at least one hour longer. Finally I saw a woman walking straight toward me, and I knew she was going to speak to me. She asked me my line of work, and when I told her she seemed to know and said that I should go over and introduce myself to a nearby Native American who was sitting just a few yards from me. I had only noticed the back of his head a few minutes before but still felt the power of his presence nearby. I knew immediately when she told me to go over that this meeting was pre-arranged by the midwayers. They had almost brought him to my table.

I introduced myself, and he took a long look at me before inviting me to sit down. I would have done the same. He began talking right away about the visions of Black Elk, who was his great uncle. His name was Wallace Black Elk. I had read *Black Elk Speaks* years ago. Wallace was a huge man but spoke with gentle authority. A lot of what he said for the next hour and a half sounded like Continuing Fifth Epochal Revelation in relation to the earth changes, and he mentioned how negative thoughts could actually trigger nuclear bombs anywhere in the world. He spoke of the fire coming from the earth.

Continuing Fifth Epochal Revelation teaches that lower-level pre-emergent energy created by negative Luciferic thought causes much distortion on the earth. I let him share the visions, which were a confirming of my own visions and Continuing Fifth Epochal Revelation. Much of what he said is written in this book.

I wish to elaborate on a different level of reality. First, I realized that our meeting was no accident and that part of the message to me was that the prophetic ministry of Wallace Black

Elk was now going to be replaced by my own and Continuing Fifth Epochal Revelation, i.e. the Mandate of the Bright and Morning Star—the old making way for the new.

After about forty-five minutes I began to send telepathic messages to Santeen to come join us at the creek. Santeen heard me amidst interactions with people in a New Age bookstore in uptown Sedona and came right down. Santeen's ability to be in the right place when he was needed was excellent. God used him greatly in many circumstances. Santeen, who usually had a lot to say, allowed Wallace Black Elk to continue to teach. Wallace liked him, and the three of us conversed for another forty minutes or so.

During this time, the real learning happened from what was going on around us. Walking by us were community members who were aligned with Divine Administration at various levels. Some glanced at us but probably did not realize who Santeen and I were talking to. One cosmic son, who was in a state of rebellion, walked by us. The funny thing was that he had paid to see Wallace Black Elk speak, while God sent Wallace to me where I was sitting and working.

This cosmic son looked at me and turned his eyes away. I believe he never saw Wallace Black Elk. I realized that this is what happens to rebellious souls. They miss their moments of higher destiny. If he had not been in rebellion, he probably would have noticed that I was talking to one of his favorite spiritual teachers. He missed meeting this great man because of his own erroneous thinking processes. I personally would have called him over to join us had he been more loyal to Christ Michael and the Universal Father.

Many millions of rebellious souls on Urantia have walked right past the moments of destiny that could have changed their whole life for the better. We were not even disturbed by tourists who usually come to take pictures in the very area where we were sitting. Our conversation of destiny was divinely guarded. I thought of another cosmic son in another state who first gave me the book *Black Elk Speaks*. If he had been with us, he too would have met Wallace Black Elk.

Higher love wishes to share with others all the best fruit, but others have not learned to be under the tree when the ripe fruit falls, so they miss out. The love and blessings of God can only be received by those who are in the perfect will of God, each moment, each day. They are under those trees catching the ripe gifts of God's moment-to-moment blessings. Many are blessed in a variety of ways—that is the nature of God. But so many miss all the other blessings that the Father is wanting to give His children. The reasons why are pointed out in this book and more specifically in *The Cosmic Family* volumes.

Naturally, I invited Wallace Black Elk to have a transmission with Paladin. It was one of the most powerful we ever had. The Apostles James and John (see Preface), the son of Peter of the first century (now Santeen), and Mary Magdalene (Delpheus) were all present. Niánn (Perpetua/Hannah/Peter's wife) typed while I (Gabriel/Peter) listened to Paladin/Sky Hawk. Paladin sometimes spoke the Lakota native tongue. Wallace Black Elk was a second-time Urantian and had been a son of Sitting Bull. He was being called to the First Planetary Sacred Home by the Wakan Tanka (Great Spirit) of Nebadon, Christ Michael. Onamonalonton, who is now on Urantia, was mentioned as wanting to work more closely with Wallace Black Elk. Up until his death, Wallace Black Elk was being called to be a Vicegerent First Ambassador to my mandate in the Melchizedek order.

After the transmission we took a picture together on my back porch with the great red rock vortex behind us. The middle of it looks distinctively like a Mohawk Indian facing east. Two years before this, God sent Great Bear, an Elder of the Seneca Nation, to our home, and we took the same picture. Great Bear had taken one look at the middle rock and immediately said, "He is looking for the great prophet to come out of the East." Onamonalonton came from the West, so I wondered who that could be. I did not realize until Wallace Black Elk and I took the picture that I was that prophet—born in Pennsylvania where the three rivers meet to form the Ohio River, now known as

Pittsburgh. This area was once sacred to many native tribes before the white man came.

I must say that when I was with Great Bear and Wallace Black Elk,[1] I relived many moments of my more recent past repersonalization as the Apache warrior Gentle Eagle. I felt the sorrow of the Earth Mother and her cry to give birth to her new children, spiritual children who would understand the beat of her heart and the feel of her skin, the soil. The Continuing Fifth Epochal Revelation is the Fifth World of the Hopi. It is the one language of the Iroquois and Seneca. The coming together of the cosmic families is the regathering of the Bird Tribes. It is the perfected government of the Lakota Sioux Indians.

The Continuing Fifth Epochal Revelation teaches the true meaning of the Kachinas of the Hopi, the starseed. The Native American way of the heart now must join with the mind. The Continuing Fifth Epochal Revelation calls it ascension science. The fusion of the heart and the knowledge of God and His creation with cosmic science, the wisdom of the grandfathers fusing with the evolutionary minds of their descendants, and the time of purification of the Hopi are happening now with the adjudication of the Bright and Morning Star versus Lucifer.

All the good truths of the old ways are now becoming one in spirit with higher truths. The four directions of the medicine wheel (which form the symbol of a solar cross) speak of the Creator of all the ancestors (Christ Michael). This planet—known in the universe of Nebadon as "the world of the cross" [*The URANTIA Book*, p. 229]—cries out for the return of the Creator Son, the Great Spirit of all the ancestors in Nebadon.

Wallace Black Elk was a young medicine man when he was at Wounded Knee with others whom God would send my way, and I would eventually spend time with Russell Means, Dennis Banks, and Clyde Bellecourt. They were all involved in the early beginnings of A.I.M. (the American Indian Movement). I also met Nancy Red Star, the author of *Star Ancestors*. She was the closest to understanding the concepts of Continuing Fifth Epochal Revelation and starseed and point of origin.

But to my disappointment, none of these Native American Elders and leaders ever came to the Fifth Epochal Revelation and Continuing. They seemed to be stuck in their traditions and very angry (justifiably so) with the white man's religions. I could not get it through any of their heads that *The URANTIA Book* and *The Cosmic Family* volumes did not teach of white man's religions but that the teachings were for all humanity and that they would understand their star knowledge teachings much better with this expanded revelation. This new revelation would give them Deo (God) power that they need to come into the new millennium and out of the bondage that the white man actually had placed upon them, for God-knowledge is Deo (God) power and, like the Native Americans of past history, they could have come into a higher understanding of the Great Spirit and His master universe.

CHAPTER 26

"If You See Me, You See The Father"

The Continuing Fifth Epochal Revelation is beautiful in that the word of truth becomes a living expression, right before your eyes. The message of Lucifer separated many families, and all had to fend for themselves. Life can be very cruel and lonely on your own, with no one to help you. Our work is calling those lost ones back home—first to God, then to the Creator Son, (Christ Michael), and then to their cosmic families. Here at the First Planetary Sacred Home the word of truth in revelation is constantly in front of you in the persons and circumstances of the cosmic families.

One such beautiful example is Santeen, my warrior cosmic son and son of Simon Peter. It is hard for me to express the love I feel for him. I have had many sons and daughters. I have had many brothers and sisters, some of whom have come to the First Planetary Sacred Home for a while and left. All I have loved and trusted. When this trust is betrayed, you cannot let that stop you from loving the next son or daughter, brother or sister. The degree of their alignment to God is the degree to which they become a great blessing—or a great heartbreak. There is no doubt in my mind that when you saw Santeen in this life, you saw Simon Peter as Peter was two thousand years ago. The good thing is that Santeen was like the Peter after the resurrection—the Peter of Pentecost, the Peter of the fire of baptism of the Holy Spirit.

After his transmission with Paladin, Santeen started bleeding in different areas of his body. Paladin told him that he must become the peaceful warrior. That, I am sure, was told to him in the first century. Finally, the Mother circuits were beginning to be truly activated in Simon Peter's son, which was Santeen. Perhaps, as a pre-Pentecost Peter, I was not a very good example for Santeen in the first century. I like to believe that he finally saw a reflection of the Father/Son/Mother balance in his cosmic father, Gabriel of Urantia/TaliasVan of Tora, that really means something to him. As Francis of Assisi, I also began to bleed when I became Mother-fused. Santeen helped me to understand the stigmata of Francis of Assisi by his continued bleeding in various spots on his body, for no apparent reason.

Santeen was as much a saint in these times as Francis was in the thirteenth century. Santeen's willingness to be what God wanted him to be is counted as perfect in God's eyes. When Peter—a powerful old soul discovering his God in a higher way and discovering his own balance between the Father/Mother circuits—walked with the Master, he often blundered. I believe the first-century Peter needed Jesus, like I need Paladin, a stronger voice of God-power authority over me. Santeen needed Gabriel of Urantia/TaliasVan of Tora, even as Gabriel/TaliasVan needed his loyal son, Santeen, and other loyal children.

It is an unfolding story that becomes more evident to me each day—the reflective mystery of our interdependency among the loyal sons and daughters of God. We all must know our individual place in the divine plan. When we do, envy and jealousy are things of the past. Divine cooperation takes its place and the plan of God is revealed in full to His most humble sons and daughters.

After Santeen read *The Cosmic Family, Volume I* and the first copy of *The Salvington Circuit*, he was off to meet us in Sedona. He needed to come and see us face to face, spirit to spirit. The truth of the book already was a breath of fresh air. Now he had to experience the dedicated souls of Christ Michael who helped bring this *Cosmic Family, Volume I* to Urantia. He came—he met us—he left to pack his bags and returned to Arizona two weeks later, leaving his beautiful beachside home in the San Juan Islands because he heard the call of God.

Santeen was my right arm, and I was his. I need my left arm son and all the other reflective parts of my seed. The Mandate of the Bright and Morning Star is a gift from Christ Michael to all. It is ever-expanding in scope. Now I know that my seed is the safety guard of future Urantia, the reflective right and left arms of all who need us. Men and women should aspire to the reflectivity of the Bright and Morning Star, the first-born son of Michael but know that for the evolutionary creature it is a long, difficult journey through time and space. With God or Deo power comes great responsibility.

Up the ascension ladder to God, all must love, honor, and obey their superiors. False pride, jealousy, or whatever the sin breaks the flow of God's blessings to you through your more ascended family members. This is the Divine Administration principle. In the world you must fight, worry, and even die to get what you need. In God's kingdom, you must give to get, love to get, honor to get, be loyal to get, and obey to get. By serving those above you in God, you serve God, and the highest leader is the servant to all.

I feel blessed to be a servant to all, but few understand who or what I really am or what it means. To give just a few examples, right now it is 70 degrees and sunny, and I would love to just go to the creek and be mindless, but this chapter would not get done, and I feel it will benefit many. Also, I just had to say something to three very close family members that probably no one else would have said to them. This is painful. I can trust my female complements, my brothers and sisters, my most faithful sons and daughters to speak openly with me. Love should pull no punches. Say what needs to be said without watering down the message.

With Santeen you never got a watered-down message. Jesus spoke for His Father. Santeen spoke for me. Individuals in the third dimension give people they trust the power of attorney. In the fourth dimension and up, we are just learning what this all means in terms of God's delegation of His authority to others of His creation all the way down the line to the human Mandate of the Bright and Morning Star, and my delegation of that Deo power to others under my authority.

Some of my cosmic sons and daughters have let me down tremendously. A cosmic brother who was put into a position of high authority completely misrepresented my mandate. I love and trusted all of them. Some day they will have to accept me as their elder brother and father, but for now false pride blinds them. We have to be reflective of our higher elder relatives, and as *The Cosmic Family, Volume II* states, we also must begin to reflect our angelic guides. When we reflect any true Deo power, we in turn represent God and the power of God. I could trust Santeen, my loyal son and mandated Liaison Minister, to always have my best interest at heart. Jesus said, "I and my Father are one."[1]

When a mandated soul acts within the will of God, all subordinates do not totally have to understand the how and why of the decision. Trust and obedience are necessary. Over a period of time those less ascended will come to understand that the mandated leader has God's best interest at heart. For all of us here at the First Planetary Sacred Home in the years to come, this will be an evolving, learning saga.

Some have had Deo power taken away because they wanted dio power. They did not truly understand the difference. I believe Deo power cannot be taught, it must be experienced. God is the only teacher here. In the third dimension, many who represent official authority abuse or misrepresent their position, such as some law enforcement officers or other government officials. They may get away with it in the third dimension, but even in the beginning stages of the fourth dimension and the Divine Administration, they will not last long because they have no real power.

God's Deo power operates in the laws of the first commandment, which is "Thou shalt love the Lord thy God with all thy heart, and with all thy soul, and with all thy mind,"[2] and therefore, leads to the second commandment, "Thou shalt love thy neighbor as thyself."[3] The bad seed will be separated in the adjudication because they will not reflect their elder father/brothers who are in Deo power positions over them. Therefore, not being true reflections of God, the motives of the heart/mind are worked out in the circumstances of your life. As *The URANTIA Book* says, "The act is ours; the consequences God's." [p. 556]

CHAPTER 27

A Visit To Titus
(One Of The Oldest Living Hopi Elders)
At The Time Of His Death

Paladin, the finaliter, told me that at some point in the future we would be meeting with Hopi Elders, and we would be sharing the Fifth Epochal Revelation with them. We were quite aware of the Hopi views about the times of purification and their understanding of the earth changes. We knew of their several trips to the United Nations to warn the governments of this world that they must change in relation to the people and the land in order for true peace and harmony to come once again to our planet. If that did not take place, our planet would self-destruct soon. We were aware that the Hopi elders thought that after their final trip to the United Nations the time of the purification had begun, and the earth changes would now become worse and worse.

Paladin told us that thousands of years ago extraterrestrials had made contact with the Hopi people and had given them information about the time of purification—the end of this Fourth World and the beginning of a new one. We believe the Fifth World, which is to come, is the Fifth Epochal Revelation and Continuing Fifth Epochal Revelation, which will be the new common language to all humanity—a language in the sense of a common conceptual understanding of spiritual reality, i.e. God and creation.

In early autumn of 1994 we were invited to one of the oldest living Hopi Elder's farm in Hopi land in northern Arizona. A sign at the entrance of his farm said, "Serving Under Creator's Law, One Mother, One Humanity." Under the words was a logo of a triangle with a circle inside of it and a solar cross inside the circle. This logo is similar to the original logo of Divine Administration, except the triangle is inside the circle on our logo. Obviously, the two logos imply the same message. In our terminology, the four directions symbolize the concept of the master universe, incorporating all of the universes. The triangle is a symbol of the Trinity at the center of the master universe, and the circle is the symbol of infinity, eternity, and the oneness of God.

With Niánn and me were Santeen, Kamon, Tarenta, Len'Mana, and Blue Evening Star. All of us are repersonalized starseed who had past Native American lives. All of us had Hopi lives, although as yet Celestial Overcontrol has not told us much about them. All we knew was that we had Hopi lives, and that we had been in contact at that time with extraterrestrial relatives, our ancestors from Avalon. We hoped that gradually, in the next few years as we became more involved with our Hopi brothers and sisters in Hopi land, more information would come from Celestial Overcontrol, as we mix our particle reality together, hand in hand and heart in heart.

It was late evening when we entered Titus' little hut. It was dark, and only a small lantern was lit. He was asleep, so we spoke to his adopted son who at the time was in his late fifties. Compared to Titus, who was around 106, his son is a young man. Titus' adopted son, Sacred Food Man, talked to us for several hours about eating the sacred food to nourish our bodies and about many things that we already understood in relation to the earth changes due to occur in the near future.

During this time I could not make eye contact with Titus, although he awoke for moments at a time and looked my way. I could not see his eyes because it was so dark, but I somehow felt his stare upon me, the same kind of feeling I experience sometimes when I know an angel, a midwayer, or the finaliter Paladin is nearby. I knew at that moment Titus was in touch with spirit beings, perhaps not in the way I was, but he definitely was in touch with them, and they began to enter the room. I think all of us that evening were taken back a few hundred, perhaps a few thousand, years to our past lives, and we heard the voices of our ancestors—our grandfathers and grandmothers—calling to us. Sacred Food Man told us to come back in the morning, and we would talk again with Titus.

The next morning, before we went back, we visited Sacred Prophecy Rock, which is considered by the Hopi as one of the most sacred spots on their land. There were various markings that depicted a chronology from creation to the future, and to what we would call the first stage of light and life and onward to outer space travel. Somehow I knew that I had been at this sacred spot before, perhaps thousands of years ago, and I and my relatives were the ones who had put this information on the rock. At that moment I felt that the past met the present to coordinate our destinies in the future—that the past is there upon that rock. Interestingly, in my lifetime as Peter, the Apostle, Jesus referred to me as "the rock."[1] Jesus knew that I would be a rock of faith and a prophet in succeeding lives of continued revelation.

Sacred Prophecy Rock on Hopi land confirmed the reality of what was happening to us—the extraterrestrial contact that I have in the Continuing Fifth Epochal Revelation and the Fifth World of the Hopi, and of our destiny to go out into the system of Satania and help adjudicate the other thirty-six fallen worlds of Satania. It was very clear that at the end of the earth trail, some of the Hopis would go into the skies. I knew what that meant, for Paladin had told us that the cosmic family consisted of all the tribes of the earth and three other universes who were the highest followers of God in His perfect will and who would ascend to help adjudicate the next fallen thirty-six worlds of Satania.

We left Sacred Prophecy Rock to go to see Titus. As we entered his farm now in the daylight, it again felt like we were taken back a thousand years or more. The simplicity of this land and the small hut gave me tremendous peace. It made me wish, in a sense, that I was him and had lived his life—the life of a farmer, the life of a teacher of the Massau'u (Great Spirit), a life of simplicity, oneness with the land and earth, and the sacredness of the food that he grew and ate. I knew, indeed, that I was going to visit my brother.

Sacred Food Man brought Titus outside and laid him on his couch, and all of us sat around in a circle as Sacred Food Man talked. Although Sacred Food Man taught many truths about proper eating, we thought that too much emphasis was put on the external rather than the internal purification of the spirit. We gave him a copy of *The URANTIA Book* and hoped that he would read it and become a student at The Starseed and Urantian Schools of Melchizedek [a.k.a. Global Community Communications Schools of Ascension Science & The Physics of Rebellion]. To this date, he has not.

Every so often during this talk Titus would awaken. He said nothing, but our eyes exchanged glances several times, sometimes for several moments at a time, and I felt him talking to my spirit. Some of the things that I felt he said to me were to keep the faith—the faith in the Great Spirit, faith in the future—to not be afraid of those who would come against the teaching of the truth, that this was the time of the return of the Great Spirit and the ancestors. He was telling me to believe in my destiny, to believe that peace would come to this planet, and that all men would again walk as brothers on the earth. His eyes kept on encouraging me not to lose heart.

Several times I got beside him and held his hand and embraced him. Because I have studied physics and Continuing Fifth Epochal Revelation, I knew at those moments his subatomic particles and mine were exchanging. I felt I was receiving much from him and that this interchange was "meant to be" by celestial beings who had set up this meeting for this physical particle interchange to happen before Titus transcended this earth by the death experience. It was an overwhelming feeling, this fusion between Titus and me. It was almost the same kind of fusion that I feel when Paladin or the Bright and Morning Star enters me.

It did not take long for me to realize that the finaliter, Paladin, was there, involved in this interchange. Then I knew that Paladin wished to come through and speak, and he did. He spoke directly to Titus and told the old Hopi elder that it was time for him to go on to the next world, that he no longer had to stay in this one, and that his ministry would be continued in an even higher way by this group of souls who sat around him. He told Titus that his work was over, that he no longer had to hang on, and that he could do more good now on the other side. Basically, Paladin very audibly confirmed to Titus that he could move on to the spirit world and join his ancestors.

What we all saw next was one of the greatest serendipities that I have ever seen in my life. Titus became alive, and lit up like a fire was under him, his eyes bright and shining. He began to sing and chant in his Hopi language, raising his hand in prayer. I think at that moment, and for the resulting few minutes afterwards, Titus saw many spirit beings surrounding him. It was quite a sight to behold.

I knew that I had received some kind of subatomic transference from Titus's body to mine and that I would now hold within my molecular reality some kind of mandate from this Hopi Elder—some kind of responsibility that he wanted me to carry on, some kind of responsibility that he wanted me to fulfill for his people. At the time of this writing, I am not quite sure what all that is, but I know that it will all unfold. I made a promise to Titus and to God, the Great Spirit, that I will not let them down, and I will do what I can to fulfill Titus' wishes for the Hopi people.

When I knew it was time to leave, I looked at Titus' eyes closely one more time, and he said good-bye and then closed his eyes and smiled. (We learned several weeks later that Titus had transcended the planet.)

Paladin came through again and spoke to Sacred Food Man and told him some things about who he was, and where he came from, and a brief message about his destiny. Then we got into the van and went to First Mesa. I knew that we were to go there. Paladin told us that we had some other Hopi people of importance to meet.

I did not know it at the time, but we were to acquire a touring company called Dorian Tours, which would be renamed "Spirit Steps Tours." Spirit Steps Tours would be a link in bringing past repersonalized Hopi ancestors back to visit Hopi land, to be around their descendants once again, to learn and experience the old ways, and to be taught Continuing Fifth

Epochal Revelation (the language of the Fifth World) by our tour guides of Global Community Communications Alliance. Again Celestial Overcontrol was setting the stage to bring the past into the present to help create the future.

We met some beautiful Hopi people, which eventually led to Spirit Steps Tours receiving permission to visit First Mesa under the blessing of that mesa's Eldership. We looked forward to a possible future relationship between Global Community Communications Alliance and Spirit Steps Tours, the Hopi Elders, and the people of Hopi land. We know that these people of peace are a sacred people, a beautiful people. Now I am one with them, and our cosmic family is one with them. I know that I and this community are to help them, and as time goes on, I will know how. It will be revealed.

We have much to learn about "unity without uniformity." On this planet, throughout the ages of the past, when the true God of the universe of universes brought revelation to the pristine lands and people of the new world, all too often that message of the cosmic God was distorted in the consciousness of colonialism as it tried to conform all peoples to its viewpoint of God and culture.

The challenge for teachers of higher truth is to help all of the peoples of the planet to understand that cosmic God—who is the God not only of this planet but of trillions of other inhabited planets—and that somehow all these planets and all the various tribes of these planets can keep their individuality but be united in the oneness of that God who is eternal truth. This is a challenge that I will try to meet with respect to all peoples, their ways and cultures. Our oneness has to go beyond ourselves to a greater unity. I believe sincerely that the concepts of the Fifth Epochal Revelation and Continuing Epochal Revelation are the cosmic unity that is found throughout all the master universe.

I, myself, being a very multi-dimensional being, like to dress sometimes like a Native American, sometimes like an Egyptian, and at other times like an Israeli. Sometimes, I prefer to go barefoot. My outward self may change, but my inward understanding of God remains constant. Too often people judge from the outside. They do not look any further than how a person is dressed. Sometimes it is good to bring some tradition into the present, to beat the drum, to chant the chant, and to dance. Today thousands of young Americans are finding the Native American way, and in the understanding of the old ways, they themselves have become new. They have found a new oneness with Mother Earth and the Great Spirit.

We of Global Community Communications Alliance know that the Native Americans have to take another step—they have to learn the dance of the cosmos, to understand the cosmic God. They have to fuse mind with heart, and expand their minds with cosmic revelation, and come to understand that the concept of the Great Spirit incorporates God the Absolute, God the Qualified and Unqualified, God the Ultimate, and God the Supreme. In their higher understanding of the cosmic God and in the greater fusion of the truth of the old ways with continuing revelation, they will then not just be at one with the earth and their ancestors, but they can also begin to be at one with their own destinies and be able to manifest that which will actualize their connection to the ancestors they know about who are now living on other worlds of time and space.

Continuing Fifth Epochal Revelation is that link to them, not only to the past, but a link to where they are now. It is not only a connection of mind and heart, but from planet to planet, system to system, universe to universe, and the past to the present and future. It is a higher union with God and is the link that will bring this planet into the Fifth World, the first stage of light and life and that first millennium of peace that all of us want so badly for our beloved Urantia/Earth.

Since my meeting with Titus, I have met many Native American Elders who basically came to me to be speakers at our venue, Future Studios, including Clyde Bellecourt, Dennis Banks, and Russell Means who were all co-founders of A.I.M. (American Indian Movement), and there have been others. As I said in an earlier chapter, to my deep disappointment, none have embraced the Fifth Epochal Revelation or Continuing. They have a very difficult time seeing any white man as their elder, even though they often asked for my and Santeen's help in business matters. They continue to refuse to accept a higher revelation of the cosmology of the natural and spiritual universe.

Eco-tours in hybrid vehicles

Toll-free (866) 508-0094
e-mail: info@spiritsteps.org
www.spiritsteps.org

Visit us at our three locations:

Tubac, Arizona
29 Tubac Plaza • (520) 398-2655
P.O. Box 1951, Tubac, AZ 85646 USA

Sedona, Arizona
2140 West Hwy 89A • (928) 282-4562
P.O. Box 3151, Sedona, AZ 86340 USA

Tucson, Arizona
630 N. Fourth Avenue, Tucson, AZ 85705 USA
(520) 398-2655

A Synopsis Of Ancient Hopi Prophecy Correlated With Fifth And Continuing Fifth Epochal Revelation

[Everything in square brackets is the corresponding Fifth Epochal Revelation terminology.]

The Hopi understanding of creation, simply stated, is that there is one Creator of all things—Massau'u [the Universal Father]. Their God created a Nephew [Creator Son] and Daughter [Universe Mother Spirit] to carry out His creative plan of the life in the universes of time and space.

After the creation of the Hopi First World [First Epochal Revelation, which was the arrival of the Planetary Prince 500,000 years ago] there came "the Talker" [Lucifer, the System Sovereign, and Caligastia, the Planetary Prince, who rebelled with Lucifer] who spread confusion throughout the world and segregated the people with his thoughts and words [the Lucifer Rebellion, which occurred 200,000 years ago]. As a result of the chaos instigated by the Talker, every world of the Hopi has gone through a purification process [an epochal revelation] to cleanse the planet of the harm caused by inappropriate thought and deed.

In each world, those walking the highest path and hearing from the Creator [Creator Son, Christ Michael], were allowed to continue their journeys and begin again on each new world [each new epochal revelation]. The destruction of each world [the default or human misappropriation of the epochal revelations] came about because the group consciousness had reached a point where the majority were no longer hearing from God and choosing His will over their own.

Today, in the Fourth World of the Hopi, the world will be destroyed by earth changes, disease, nuclear holocaust, and uncontrollable crime [the adjudication or tribulation] because of man's choices to do his will over the Creator's. Only those good and peaceful "Hopi" people [cosmic family aligned with Divine

Administration]—whether they be yellow, red, black, or white—will be spared, and their homeland will be preserved as a safe haven where refugees will flee to [the First Planetary Sacred Home, primary and secondary protected areas].

Bomb shelters, digging in, moving back to the land, and raising food are futile for those "non-Hopi" who do not adhere to the revelation of God. This is a spiritual battle being fought on material ground. We of the cosmic family are at the front lines. Those who are at peace with their Creator are already in the great shelter of life [stabilized third psychic circlers]. There is no shelter for evil.

The Fourth World with its materialism [the third dimension] will be destroyed and the Hopi Fifth World [the fourth and fifth dimensions of the Fifth Epochal Revelation and Continuing Fifth Epochal Revelation] will be created—one world, one nation, under one power: the power of the Creator [Jesus/Christ Michael].

The Hopi believe that the time is near for the emergence of the Fifth World [the Fifth Epochal Revelation (*The URANTIA Book*) and Continuing Fifth Epochal Revelation (*The Cosmic Family* volumes)]. It is being brought about by many people of many nations who have the courage and humility to follow the "song" of the Creator. All must accept a higher level of perception that will lead into a divine new Fifth World [the Divine New Order of light and life].

*CosmoArt rendition of the 7 sectors of Urantia (Earth)
with the New Jerusalem approaching*

Color prints of original art available for sale.
Call CosmoArt Studio (520) 490-2554 or email info@cosmoart.org

Part III

Moving Into The New Millennium

The next five chapters—28 through 32—were written after the Second Edition of this book in 1995. These five chapters are new to the Third Edition and deal with events from 1996 to present day, Summer 2013.

CHAPTER 28

The Continuing Story: Van Or Nod?
(See Preface)

On March 3, 1996, during a community transmission, Paladin gave the astounding information that I was either Van or Nod. Those of us who know these personalities from *The URANTIA Book* understand the significance of that statement. Nod, the fallen supermortal of the staff of Caligastia, led the fallen sixty supermortals who all became mortal due to their choices for rebellion against Michael of Nebadon.

Van was the steadfast leader of forty loyal staff members of the Caligastia One Hundred, who along with the loyal Urantian, Amadon, stood against the fallen Planetary Prince. As leaders of those who did not fall in the Lucifer Rebellion, they had extended lives on Urantia due to having access to the Tree of Life. (You can read about Van and Amadon in Paper 67 of *The URANTIA Book*, which gives a more-than-excellent depiction of these heroes of the Rebellion.)

Because in this life Niánn and I are the parents of the beautiful Amadon, the loyal human leader who did not take part in the Rebellion, I went through much inner turmoil contemplating myself once being his enemy. Since I had been told that I was involved in many renaissances on this planet, if I was Nod I figured that I must have repented before, in my past life as Abraham when I was with Machiventa Melchizedek as his student.

As a little boy, Amadon would ask me about Van, as if he once knew him. He would say, "When is my brother Van coming?" Since they were together for approximately 462,000 years, it is easy to see why Amadon referred to Van as his brother, even though Van was a supermortal from Avalon. How could I be this supermortal leader? My own humility can be my worst enemy. It was actually easier to see myself as the fallen Nod, so I was more than willing to accept the possible fact that I had once been the leader of the fallen "Caligastia Sixty" supermortals. All of this false humility (and that is what it is) was a great lesson for me when it was eventually (more than seven months later) confirmed by Paladin that I was indeed Van.

The world desperately needs new leaders, spiritual leaders of higher consciousness. Many people are searching for signs of the reality of God and a bigger world than just Earth. They see the apparitions of the Virgin Mary in many countries, including here in America. They join UFO groups and proclaim abduction by them. People are looking for something supernatural outside of their mundane lives. They follow false prophets who proclaim divinity and walk in purposeful fake humility. My humility contributed to my inability to accept who I am. The error for me was in not accepting it as OK to know who we of the cosmic family once were and to be proud of those lives when we were servants of humankind and God.

Paladin had said that if I was Nod and at some point in my past history on Urantia had repented, what a beautiful act of forgiveness of Christ Michael to mandate me to be the human leader in the correction of the Rebellion! If I was Van, how noble of me to choose to return to Urantia as a human mortal in order to experience the effects of the Rebellion and know what error, sin, and iniquity were from firsthand, painful, lifetime-after-lifetime experiences.

I was shocked to hear that I could have been Van. How could this be? For more than seven months I went through much introspection until the answer came in a Sunday night transmission on October 27, 1996 revealing I was Van and John was Nod. Paladin went on to reveal more of my soul's repersonalizations in the lives of Moses, Lao-Tse, and many other spiritual renaissance leaders. I was humbled to discover my soul had dwelt in all these special personalities in history.

Years before, Celestial Overcontrol told us that Sananda (who used this name but should not have)[1] and White Cloud should use their first-century names for a while, as that was a higher Deo life for both of them. So we began to call them John (instead of Sananda) and James (instead of White Cloud). For me, and others who knew them in the first century, it was natural, and it helped to open up many memory circuits and emotional astral feelings. I saw myself as Peter interacting with both of them many times. I believe this helped James to reach higher levels of his consciousness and move out of John's influence. John on the other hand, as he did in the first century, referred to himself as "the Beloved Disciple" or "the one whom Jesus loved." These, of course, were John's own words about himself in the book of John in the New Testament and quite appropriate for his arrogance.

That John was Nod made much sense, since I already knew that we had bouts in history as opponents, such as with Saul and David and with Pope Leo X and Martin Luther. Now I was told my soul indwelt Moses. John could be no other than Ramses II. Moses was chosen to free Israel from the Pharaoh who was impressed with his own dio (evil) power and unwilling to release the seekers of the one God. How perfect Christ Michael's plan—for these two mortal souls to continue the battle between good and evil, lifetime after lifetime!

I knew from reading *The URANTIA Book* that I left Urantia as Van when Adam and Eve came. What I did not know until this revelation from the finaliter, Paladin, was that both Van and his complement, Niánn, would return. We chose to return. We wanted to return to the fallen world and confront Caligastia and Nod. We were with Amadon on Urantia for 462,000 years and now felt very Urantian. We wanted to experience the various results of the Rebellion in the different consciousnesses of the evolution of the planet as evolutionary mortals in material form, rather than supermortals, lifetime after lifetime, era after era. Now it all became clear.

The dio experiences in those beginning years between Sananda/John/Nod and the community became a learning curve, first for Niánn and me, and then for all here in Divine Administration. These types of experiences are explained in very technical terms in *The Cosmic Family, Volume I*. For the benefit of all who read this, Nod—the name he became known by due to direction from Celestial Overcontrol—agreed that I share my private impressions of situations that have involved him. His willingness to disclose this information was indicative of his soul growth and his continuing process of repentance. However, sadly Nod would eventually default and go to the local Sedona newspapers with slanderous lies.

When I first met the contemporary Nod in 1991, though he was very charming and we all saw his good points, I also saw that he was the epitome of individual rebellion. To discern his dio manipulation in action was to observe a master of deceit who continually tried to exalt himself. To try to stop the results of his iniquity seemed impossible. My best efforts were to try to lessen the effects of his evil upon others. One can read *White Robe, Black Robe*, by Charles L. Mee, to see the soul of Nod (Pope Leo X) working schemes of deceit in the sixteenth century. The Nod of these contemporary times was more adept in deception. When confronted, he cast blame on us. He had difficulty seeing, let alone admitting, a wrongdoing or sin. He claimed he "never fell in the Rebellion."

After he learned he was John the Apostle, his ego got the best of him. He compiled all the positive quotes about John into a booklet and sent it to selected individuals. He attempted to exalt himself and gain some kind of favor with new students and community members. This behavior was consistent with his first-century attitude of thinking of himself as "the beloved of Christ." He was a good study for the physics of rebellion, a concept introduced in *The Cosmic Family, Volume I*. I began to see Nod's interactions produce the negative results of rebellion on others.

He became the "pied piper of rebellion" for those in the community who were in error, sin, or iniquity. He was their ally, their confidant, their dio associate. Before some members moved to our First Planetary Sacred Home, he would send letters and telephone them. He chose the young first-time Urantians, the new souls. He chose those who he could easily control. He wove a web with the dio expertise his 200,000 years of experience had taught him in rebellion to God (excluding years of being in a sleep state, which is unrevealed as of this writing).

Many left the community and Divine Administration who may have stayed had he spoken up for the decisions and the procedures that Celestial Overcontrol and human Eldership had established. White Cloud/James/Rafeel stood beside Sananda/John/Nod during those early years, which made it all the more difficult to confront Nod. Rafeel truly was deceived himself. Nod was knowingly divisive, approaching others as if they were victims of Divine Administration. His habitual dio thinking carefully planned every move to gain allies.

When he sent me little gifts, he made sure they were seen by others. Like Caligastia, he would speak to others with words of acknowledgment of me in some areas, as he dropped words conveying his disappointment of me and my decisions in other areas. Nod's continual undermining of my authority probably accounted for at least two dozen people leaving the community/Divine Administration in the early years. However, Nod believed the number to be under a dozen.

Dio rebel forces are tactful in mixing some truth with lies to deceive. Much metaphysical and channeled information is structured in this fashion. Sometimes a whole article or transmission will have much truth, and then the dio bombshell is delivered. This bombshell may make Jesus the same as any other prophet, or say that all roads lead to God, or that there is no evil. Eventually, all roads do lead to God, but I wouldn't want to spend most of my life miserable, unactualized, uncomplemented, and following a lesser path.

So people would leave Nod's "tea parties" with the seed planted to convey I was not quite right, but he "put up with me anyway." This of course would leave people to pick and choose what they wanted to accept from my counsel and administrative community procedures. This went on for several years until Nod's mandate as an Elder and Vicegerent First Ambassador was removed.

Celestial Overcontrol asked Rafeel to move from under the roof of Nod's control. Rafeel was Raphael at the time of Pope Leo X. It seems Leo X emotionally abused the great painter then. This was a repeat from what happened in the first century when they were brothers as James and John Zebedee. In this present repersonalization Rafeel and Nod were in a homosexual relationship when they first arrived at our First Planetary Sacred Home but agreed to separate when asked by Celestial Overcontrol. Nod did, however, retain control over Rafeel, and it was a very slow process for Rafeel to see Nod for who he is. It took many years for Rafeel to overcome Nod's passive control, and up to Rafeel's death in August 2010, he was still in the process of healing psychospiritually from the results of lifetimes of Nod's dio influence on him.

Nod was extremely jealous of my musical talent and would not publicly acknowledge my musical ability. (He played the organ and liked to perform for individuals.) This confused community members. When I felt led by Christ Michael many years ago to form The Bright & Morning Star Band and record my vocal spiritual music for the people of the planet, Nod did not want anyone supporting that cause.

I have often wondered how long this single act delayed the production of our first CD, *Holy City*. Once during a seminar when I sang one of my songs, his pride was so intense that he actually got up and went outside until the song was over. This was very painful because of my previous experience in Hollywood where artists struggle for recognition, and jealous people in positions of power want to own and operate you.

Only recently have I understood completely events with Sananda (Nod) in his home in Santa Fe in December of 1989 and August 18, 1990. He claimed that Caligastia had visited him personally on those days and that he had confronted Caligastia. I often wondered how Caligastia could have been in the same room with John, a former apostle of Christ. The answer is that Nod was for many centuries the dio material complement of Caligastia himself. A scary thought indeed.

If Celestial Overcontrol had told me this truth in the beginning of our meeting in this life, I most likely would not have accepted the then Sananda (Nod) in my life. I would have missed much valuable experience in discerning error, sin, and iniquity in a soul bent on division and self-exaltation. However, in this life, since the time *The URANTIA Book* came to Sananda (Nod) in the early sixties, he began to change in his dio ways and recognize Caligastia as his enemy and the rebel against Christ Michael that Caligastia is.

Nod did not realize how much dio needed to be removed and how long it would take. Nod stated: "I emphatically requested this confrontation, which was granted. During this long meeting I repeatedly pleaded with Caligastia to surrender to Christ Michael and to bring no more harm or suffering to the planet or souls upon it."

The truth of the matter is that Nod could never stay in his higher self, and he fluctuated from the seventh to the fourth psychic circle all in one day. He was so accustomed to manipulation of people that he did it by habit, which was also part of his thinking that we learned, later in Continuing Fifth Epochal Revelation terminology, to be termed as dio thade thinking or dio thade thought.

✥✥✥✥✥✥

If one studies the history of the two souls of Van and Nod—as repersonalized in Joseph of Jacob and the Pharaoh who "knew not Joseph," Moses and Ramses II, David and Saul, Luther and Pope Leo X, and Cromwell and King Charles I—one could easily see the battle between the forces of Michael of Nebadon and Caligastia's rebellion continued throughout history.

Machiventa Melchizedek was indeed the new Planetary Prince of Urantia. Nod was not in any way then Machiventa Melchizedek's First Ambassador. By the mercy and grace of

Christ Michael, Celestial Overcontrol mandated Nod *in potential* and gave him every opportunity to uplift the Mandate of the Bright and Morning Star held by Niánn Emerson Chase and myself. Instead Nod continually planted seeds of discord in community members' minds. When I confronted Nod with these dio acts of disloyalty against the Mandate, he denied everything and became indignant that we would accuse him of such things. Niánn and I were at a loss as to what to do. There were only four Elders at this time, and Sananda/John/Nod and White Cloud/James/Rafeel were the other two. We prayed for supernatural help.

Santeen showed up in God's perfect timing. He told us that twenty years earlier he had met Sananda (Nod) in the hills of California, teaching *The URANTIA Book*. Many in the Urantia movement thought that Sananda claimed to be Machiventa Melchizedek. However, Nod says he never believed he was Machiventa Melchizedek. When Nod met Santeen again in Sedona, Nod began to realize that he needed to seriously look at his own mistakes and opinions of me and realize that Christ Michael was sending me talented individuals to help me and the Mandate of the Bright and Morning Star. But Nod did not give up his patterns easily nor completely.

We lost many first-century souls whom the midwayers worked so hard to guide to us in Sedona. Nod even allowed his own cosmic children, who loved him, to default rather than give their loyalty to me, his rival Van, and to the Mandate of the Bright and Morning Star. Santeen completed the First Triad, consisting of Niánn, Santeen, and myself. We represented the Continuing Fifth Epochal Revelation concept of divine Trinity administration functioning on a human level in the highest way—the most ascended cosmic father, cosmic mother, and cosmic son on Urantia.

On December 21, 1996, a most significant meeting took place between Nod, Marayeh (our morontia counselor), Niánn, and myself. Nod said he wanted to confess his sins personally to Niánn and me and ask our forgiveness for the many lifetimes of pain he caused us and all humanity. For many months Paladin had made it very clear that Nod had to do this in a sincere way and be very specific about his error, sin, and iniquity. Nod had never been able to get specific in the past when he was confronted with his dio actions here in Divine Administration, even before we knew he was Nod.

It was August of 1990 that Caligastia had come to the then Sananda, his human complement, in Santa Fe. At this same time Niánn and I and our three children—SanSkritA (Alcyone), DeleVan (Sonta-an), and Amadon, all in diapers—were living in a tent in a campground in Sedona, attempting to purchase our first home within the First Radius. More than six years had passed since that 1990 visit from Caligastia to Nod in Santa Fe. Perhaps Nod's soul had experienced the tribulation that he, as John, had written about in the book of Revelation two thousand years ago during his highest ascended life on Urantia.

Nod was no longer the leader of the fallen staff of the Planetary Prince, nor leader of the Nodites, nor Pharaoh of Egypt, nor Pope of Rome, nor guru—now he was reduced to one being adjudicated and revealed. His identity as Nod was first revealed to all the Elders and mandated Assistants, and then to all the students in the community. Now even the young souls and students knew who he was and were cautious of his patterns. He had finally lost most of his dio power. We had prayed for him for some time that he would truly repent. Now the cage he had built for himself over the centuries, which jailed his soul, was ready to be opened.

Listening to Nod on the winter's solstice in 1996, I wanted with all my heart to believe his words of repentance. He was still unable to get specific as to persons he affected and the methodical ways in which he accomplished his dio actions of self-assertion and division. He admitted to being prideful and "not knowing or realizing his divisive behavior." He owned up to the sins of past lives but not of this life. He did not want to recognize he was being so divisive and rebellious in this present repersonalization.

Chapter 28

The following is written by a second-time Urantian and student of The Starseed and Urantian Schools of Melchizedek [a.k.a. Global Community Communications Schools of Ascension Science & The Physics of Rebellion]—who had read *The URANTIA Book* for fifteen years before he came to Divine Administration—evaluating the two weeks following the announcement that I was Van and John was Nod.

When Gabriel said 'I am Van,' this changed everything in the community. We already knew that he was Van, but it needed to be confirmed. For those of us who have been studying The URANTIA Book for a few years, this statement had a tremendous impact on our relationship with Gabriel.

Gabriel being a Melfax Prince on another planet in another universe had tremendous impact; now, when Gabriel reveals himself as Van, this statement shows the repersonalization plan in a light that was unrevealed until now. This repersonalization plan (rehabilitation plan) was developed and in place it seems before rebellion ever began in the system of Satania. It's almost eerie to think about, but our Creator Son, Christ Michael, seems to have known about what was brewing in Lucifer's mind long before any hint of rebellion began to appear in manifestation. Van, who was rebellion-tested, and Nod, who had been rehabilitated twice before, were both on the staff of the Caligastia One Hundred. The profundity, which these statements seem to imply, is that rebellion happens more frequently than what The URANTIA Book indicates.

The utilization of the repersonalization plan and the use of rebellion-tested starseed to rehabilitate a rebellion-torn planet, by keeping the truth alive in succeeding generations, are beyond the imagination. Urantia had many opportunities to repent and accept the light. Adam and Eve's mission could have been successful. Christ Michael could have been accepted when He was here as Jesus. Christ Michael knew though that the odds were against that happening. The truth became so buried in Luciferic thinking that to bring it into the light only brought greater resistance to the highest truth. Keeping the truth alive was what these repersonalizations have been succeeding in doing.

"Awesome" is my word for being allowed to be here at our First Planetary Sacred Home. Grow up fast and get on with my destiny. The depth of the revelation of Gabriel being Van and of the needed repentance of Nod rocks my soul to the depths. I have yet to assimilate much of what has been revealed. I recognize that if Nod is able to rehabilitate through repentance, then this act will possibly bring many in rebellion back to Christ Michael's fold. The change point for me is happening right now.

These changes have affected me in that I have changed my perspective completely about how I need to rearrange my thinking. I need to accept at a greater level of depth what we are capable of doing here in Divine Administration. I realize that this sounds rather shallow, but when Gabriel became Van, this changed everything inside of me. I know now that we, with Gabriel, can do what is necessary as change agents and Cosmic and Urantian Reservists to bring about a human change point. Before it was all on faith. Now the reality of what can be accomplished is a fact.

Respectfully
Ah'Nuit [2]

I give others the benefit of the doubt when they ask forgiveness or profess loyalty to the Mandate of the Bright and Morning Star. Trust has to be earned and loyalty proven. Celestial Overcontrol provided many opportunities for Nod to prove himself to the Universal Father, Christ Michael, and the Mandate of the Bright and Morning Star. Our prayers continue to be with Nod and all those who are in rebellion on Urantia. Unfortunately, Nod chose to default from his highest destiny in Divine Administration in September of 2004, eight years after his winter's solstice confession and repentance to Niánn, Marayeh, and me.

Not only was Nod not be able to be reinstated as a mandated minister those many years, he could not remain committed to his higher calling in Divine Administration, basically due to his self-centeredness, many selfish demands, and refusal to submit to any spiritual authority over him. When Nod left, his only service to Divine Administration was pasting routing forms on intracommunity mail envelopes. Because of his chronological age and his continued rebellious attitude, I do not think he will reach his higher calling from Christ Michael as a First Ambassador for Divine Administration and the Mandate of the Bright and Morning Star.

I believe that the majority of higher-consciousness individuals in the Urantia movement are truly in error—in error for not accepting the Continuing Fifth Epochal Revelation as presented in *The Cosmic Family* volumes. They deny thousands of starseed in the Urantia movement opportunity to find their higher selves, to come into their cosmic mind, to come back into their point-of-origin reconstruction, and to become Destiny Reservists, Cosmic or Urantian. Millions of Christians, who have a personal relationship with Jesus at some level and love their Lord with all their heart, need to also realize their error and embrace Jesus as Christ Michael, as presented in *The URANTIA Book* and *The Cosmic Family* volumes.

Christianity and the Urantia movement need to unite in one common movement to bring the true teachings of Jesus to the rest of the people of this planet. Can leaders in these two representations of Jesus' teachings recognize the truth of Divine Administration? Can they, like John the Baptist, realize they need to decrease and let the teachers at The Starseed and Urantian Schools of Melchizedek [a.k.a. Global Community Communications Schools of Ascension Science & The Physics of Rebellion] increase? Can they submit in true humility to their soul elders and to more ascended, higher psychic-circled brothers and sisters? Or will they continue to try to teach and lead in old wineskins?

We all pray for the return of Jesus, Christ Michael, to Urantia. Many of us are united in belief that He will return and establish His true kingdom on Earth. His Divine Administration is beginning now on Urantia. Even if He does return tomorrow, the more of us who can understand the procedures of this administration, the faster the first stage of light and life will come. The longer it takes Christianity and the Urantia movement to accept continued revelation, the longer our other brothers and sisters on this planet will suffer. We must come together and join all godly resources, material and nonmaterial, for the sake of all God's children on Urantia.

All must forgive and forget past differences and hurts. Great teachers and teachings, laws of Jesus, Christ Michael, are all here at Planetary Headquarters. This is Christ Michael's true church government in every sense, for a divine church government (that represents His laws) receives and functions in continued revelation of His administrative procedures in a planetary Divine Administration based on the higher consciousness (or higher psychic circles).

True spiritual ascension and Divine Administration encompasses all the diversified people on the planet. It administers justice and equality to people at all consciousness levels. We are truly at the dawn of the Age of Aquarius, the beginning of the new millennium, the first stage of light and life. Together we can come out of the chaos and disorder of spiritual misunderstanding and come into the cosmic insight and individual actualization of harmonic love of the Divine New Order of the twenty-first century. It begins with those who join the Spiritualution[SM] movement for Urantia.

CHAPTER 29

The Interuniversal Marriage Triads And Trimonads.[1]
The Intrauniversal Birth Of Ellanora Of Panoptia.

When I first saw TiyiEndea I knew she was my complement—a single mother with two children of two former marriages. She had a twelve-year old girl—a second-time Urantian, now given her cosmic name of Anwyn—and a six-year old boy—a starseed, whose cosmic name is Eyinel. I sensed that TiyiEndea, like most single parents, had struggled for many years trying to raise these children alone.

TiyiEndea had a strength about her that went beyond her struggle to survive in this life with her precious two children. She also was very emotionally tired of traveling and looking to find her place in this world, and she expressed that she had given up on finding the right man. After being with Global Community Communications Alliance for a few days and meeting me and other community members, she was ready to "run" again. Even though she knew that Divine Administration was for real, she also realized that she had romantic feelings for me and that I was already with Niánn.

I, of course, realized much more than she did but knew that she would have to align with Divine Administration and the work here completely and be at a certain ascension level before I could even make any decision to have her with me as a complement. I knew that the first triad unit was destined to happen. At this time I had no understanding of trimonad relationships. Celestial Overcontrol had said that a former complement, whoever she was, would give birth to Ellanora of Panoptia. I wondered if this complement might be Tenache, a former wife of an Apache repersonalization.[2] Later I learned TiyiEndea was Four Robes, a second wife of Sitting Bull.

That I felt very responsible for this little family was certainly in my consciousness, as God put this concern immediately there. So when TiyiEndea was packed and ready to leave after being here only a few days, I prayed extra hard that God stop her in some way. My prayer was answered when her twelve-year-old daughter told her mother to turn around and go back because she needed to learn about God from Gabriel and others in the community. I did not know at the time that this child was my cosmic daughter from the Martin Luther life and that her last name in this life was Luther.

I learned from Paladin that I had rejected TiyiEndea publicly in other past lives, and both TiyiEndea and Anwyn were rejected by me publicly in the Luther life. Even as Bathsheba, a wife of David and mother of Solomon, she was rejected by the people who looked upon Abigail (Niánn) as their queen. "And when the servants of David were come to Abigail to Carmel, they spake unto her, saying, 'David sent us unto thee, to take thee to him to wife'."[3] "And David said to Abigail, 'Blessed be the Lord God of Israel, which sent thee this day to meet me'."[4]

TiyiEndea was also Hagar, the handmaiden of Sarai (Niánn), given to Abraham to give birth to Ishmael. Both Hagar and Ishmael were eventually cast away alone to fend for themselves in the desert. "Now Sarai, Abram's wife, bare him no children: and she had an handmaid, an Egyptian, whose name was Hagar."[5] "And Sarai, Abram's wife, took Hagar, her maid the Egyptian, after Abram had dwelt ten years in the land of Canaan, and gave her to her husband Abram to be his wife."[6]

Not being allowed by me to be my complement or princess actually goes back to TiyiEndea's universe of origin, Fanoving, located in what is called Centaurus by earth astronomers. In another book I am writing, called *The Fall From The Bright Star*, I explain in detail all about her and this interuniversal mission of myself as TaliasVan, a Prince Melfax, who went from Avalon to her world in another universe to intermarry and procreate in order to upstep the genetics of the races there—much like the mission of the Material Son and Daughter of Nebadon, Adam and Eve. This was the beginning of TiyiEndea not being allowed to be by my side as a princess, as my native planet of Tora would not accept a daughter of Fanoving as their princess, even though triad relationships (interuniversal marriages/polyfidelity) had for many centuries been the reality on this very old planet of Avalon.

Eyinel, her son in this current life, is my cosmic son from Tora. Although not as old a soul as Amadon, you can recognize similar genetic characteristics in both of them. Eyinel is chronologically one year older than Amadon in this life. They look like brothers from the same seed, and that is because I am the cosmic father of Eyinel and the father of Amadon in this life. It is obvious that these two young men have the same genetic source from me.

Of course I was with Amadon in his first life for so many hundreds of thousands of years, and he was encoded with Avalon genetics (from Tora). Both he and I ate of the Tree of Life with the system's life-sustainable energies.

After she was in the community for six months, I felt TiyiEndea becoming very restless and frustrated. I knew, and she knew, that there was no other ascending son on the planet able to handle her strong will or reach her heart enough to counsel her and be her spiritual complement leader and husband guide. I felt that if she left, her precious little family was in danger of getting lost in the world that could be so cruel to single mothers. So I reached out to her, offering my heart. This is what she needed, and I was the only soul on the planet who could give her the love and spiritual support she needed.

I knew this was the Father's perfect will. Niánn also knew, but it was not easy for her to share my love with another woman, even though Niánn knew that Ellanora was going to come through another complement. Niánn had our three beautiful children in her forties. We had decided that her health was in danger to try to have another child.

In 1989 Celestial Overcontrol had first told us about Ellanora coming through me, and on April 22, 1993 (two years before TiyiEndea joined Divine Administration), a special transmission had came through from Paladin, Paper 275 of *The Cosmic Family, Volume III*, that spoke again of the coming of Ellanora of Panoptia. *"Hundreds of thousands of knowing ovan souls, . . . such as Ellanora, mentioned in* The URANTIA Book, *who like her are in high loyalty to their respective Creator Sons and Universe Fathers, are awaiting repersonalization to be born as babes . . . .*" So, Niánn encouraged me to cultivate my love for TiyiEndea and reach out to her. This only increased my love for Niánn, and my heart was in turmoil.

> The Lucifer Rebellion was system wide. Thirty-seven seceding Planetary Princes swung their world administrations largely to the side of the archrebel. Only on Panoptia did the Planetary Prince fail to carry his people with him. On this world, under the guidance of the Melchizedeks, the people rallied to the support of Michael. Ellanora, a young woman of that mortal realm, grasped the leadership of the human races, and not a single soul on that strife-torn world enlisted under the Lucifer banner. And ever since have these loyal Panoptians served on the seventh Jerusem transition world as the caretakers and builders on the Father's sphere and its surrounding seven detention worlds. The Panoptians not only act as the literal custodians of these worlds, but they also execute the personal orders of Michael for the embellishment of these spheres for some future and unknown use. They do this work as they tarry en route to Edentia. [*The URANTIA Book,* p. 607]

I felt responsible to Michael of Nebadon, our local universe Creator Son, to bring to this planet the loyal daughter of Panoptia, yet knew that this decision would be ridiculed by many in the Urantia movement as well as the Christian world. We already took the brunt of their anger for concepts that they did not accept, like repersonalization and Continuing Fifth Epochal Revelation. I knew that my decision would have to be the Father's perfect will.

What if TiyiEndea got pregnant and did not bring through a girl baby? Celestial Overcontrol had made it very clear to the whole community that Ellanora of Panoptia [now called DesManae] would be the next child of my seed. My faith in the reality of my contact with these beings was continually tested.

Niánn encouraged TiyiEndea and me to give birth to Ellanora. I began to feel more at ease when I saw that all seventy-five adults in the community at that time accepted my decision. I was made to feel comfortable by all the other Elders, reminding me of Celestial Overcontrol's promise to bring Ellanora through my seed.

At this time TiyiEndea was not pregnant. When she became pregnant we all knew who was on the way from the mansion worlds of Satania. This would be the first repersonalization of a child of Nebadon from a higher world (the mansion worlds) to a fallen world that was not her own native world (or point of origin) for a special intrauniversal function. Amadon was from Urantia, but Ellanora was not a native Urantian. (There have also been in the past history of Urantia sixth- and seventh-mansion-world progressors who have returned to Urantia for ministry functions, as well as sixth-stage finaliters.)

On October 11, 1997, at 4:44 A.M. a beautiful baby girl, Ellanora of the planet Panoptia of Nebadon, was born. We became a very happy family with Amadon, SanSkritA (Alcyone), and DeleVan (Sonta-an) accepting Ellanora as their baby sister. TiyiEndea had already been accepted into the family and was considered their second mommy. Our children understand interuniversal culturalistic marriages and other universal realities, as we foster their memory circuits to tap into their past.

Niánn and I had decided to no longer be sexually intimate when we accepted TiyiEndea as my complement and wife. We three became a trimonad relationship and did not feel the need to share our sexual intimacies with the children or, for that matter, the world at large. However, our family has felt the sting of ridicule by insinuations of a secret affair between TiyiEndea and me, which of course was never the case.

In a trimonad relationship, the male is only intimate sexually with the wife with whom he is to bring children into the world. TiyiEndea's and my relationship did not change the fact that Niánn was my highest spiritual complement, who co-shared the Mandate of the Bright and Morning Star. My love for Niánn has only increased, as well as my admiration for her loyalty to God, her total dedication to our Heavenly Father and His perfect will. Niánn, like Mary the mother of Jesus, is truly blessed. Niánn is named so perfectly "the cosmic woman of grace."

On some higher ascended planets where trimonad relationships exist—with sex only between the male and one of the females[7]—the celibate female is considered "married" to the male as a spiritual complement and may be the highest complement spiritually. In America today many marriages end because the pressures of raising a family create tension between husband and wife and dulls the sex life. Divorce does not have to be the answer. The two can live a happy life together through their trials and rekindle that beginning romance. Love and marriage between a man and woman does not always have to include sex. Companionship and spiritual union mean so much more than sex, though sex may be a part of the relationship. Do elderly people lose their love for each other when their sex life is over?

Without any sexual intimacy, supermortals of the staff of the Caligastia One Hundred gave birth to primary midwayers approximately 500,000 years ago.[8] I believe the nonsexual unions of some of the supermortals of the Caligastia staff and their birthing of invisible midwayer babies is the origin of the virgin birth legends on Urantia.

Niánn, TiyiEndea, and I are the only trimonad unit in our community. As this interuniversal-soul community matures, we expect that other triads or trimonads will evolve. Continuing Fifth Epochal Revelation is bringing forth God's cosmic reality and the terminology for new family relationships for the twenty-first century. We foresee interuniversal family relationships developing.

All of these cosmic relationships and cosmic families are part of the future of this planet. They are the answers to divorce, separation, loneliness, and the breakdown of families on this planet. They are the answers that higher planets once came to after millions of years of evolution. They are the answers that the starseed once lived and understood to be their truth and way of life. They are the answers that hundreds of millions of starseed are looking for. They are spiritual answers of relationships and family life of interuniversal cultures that involve higher spiritual maturity of the parents, for the common good of all—the interuniversal children, as well as all the native children of the planet, starseed and Urantian.

CHAPTER 30

Divine Administration Moving Into The Twenty-First Century And The State Of The Planet

Our beloved Liaison Minister and Niánn's and my cosmic son, Santeen, passed to the mansion worlds in January 2005. I believe that by coming to Divine Administration his life was extended for more than ten years, and he served faithfully while with us. He did not take good care of his body before he came to Divine Administration, and he had already developed many symptoms of the illness that finally took his life. His father had been an alcoholic, and at times, Santeen turned to drink instead of being able to pull through the many disappointments that he had to overcome in fighting evil as a Liaison Minister. The abuse of his liver finally led to his death. He had warning after warning from Celestial Overcontrol through Paladin.

I speak so frankly about my dear, dear, cosmic son and Liaison Minister because I am a man of truth. If I did not tell it like it is here, readers would think that the rest of the book was untrue. I also hope that any alcoholic can learn from reading this, that no matter how much they love God, they have to prove it by loving God more than that next drink. I am sure Santeen would want me to write about this. I know that he is terribly lonely without us and that his present sojourn on the mansion worlds is quite painful without those of his cosmic family who are still on Urantia/Earth.

So we had to continue on without Santeen. While it seemed the whole world was beginning to fall apart—with the tsunami in Indonesia (which killed 300,000 people in one day), the 7.6 earthquake in Pakistan (which killed more than 90,000 people and displaced millions), the 2005 hurricane (Katrina) in New Orleans, and so many other catastrophes all over the world, including wars—the loss of Santeen somehow made life even more difficult for those of us trying to make real a difference for the world.

Because of the attack on me and Global Community Communications Alliance from the media that included many falsehoods about us from embittered ex-community members and hate sites on the Internet, our work became even more difficult, for people who would have possibly joined us to help implement Divine Administration on this world were influenced by the media misrepresentation. In a way, I felt it was the same for the first true followers of Jesus, who became outcasts and were often crucified or thrown to the lions in the arenas of Rome.

Many, who at first thought they wanted to join us, quickly disassociated themselves from Divine Administration as soon as some pressure came upon them from parents or friends or as soon as they realized they too might be stigmatized. To this day, I still do not have the answer as to how we can overcome such insurmountable obstacles.

I met several Hollywood movie stars and producers in Sedona, but quite frankly they don't deserve to be mentioned in this book. One, however, who I feel honored to meet was Nick Nolte. While still living in Sedona we had our house up for sale and for vacation rental, when I got a call one day that Nick Nolte wanted to see my home for a possible four-month rental because his home in Malibu was badly damaged by fire. He brought his wife Clytie and toddler daughter to our home, and we decided to spend the day together, so we took them to sacred Avalon Gardens and then had lunch together at my home.

Celestial Overcontrol had told me before he even arrived that he was either my cosmic son or brother and that we had had other lives together. So, when I first met him in person and saw his rugged face, I looked him in the eyes and said, "Sure took you a long time to get here!" Of course, I meant a whole lifetime, as Nick was in his seventies. I don't know how he took it. He probably thought I meant the drive. To this day Celestial

Overcontrol has never confirmed his cosmic relationship to me, because Nick was very caught up in his Hollywood career and had little or no time for higher revelation or to accept the concept of me being his spiritual advisor. I did encourage him to try to make more spiritual movies, like the one he made called *Peaceful Warrior*. I pray for Nick and his family often.

When I met many of these Hollywood people, I noticed that some of them used my original terminology but never knew that it was me who brought it to the planet. When I asked them where they got it, they said that they read it in such-and-such book or heard it from so-and-so on the radio or television.

For many years, I have continued to listen to the paranormal shows on radio that reach millions, and I hear the concepts that came through me (beginning in the late 1980s) being used by guests on the shows without giving any credit to where they got it—basically from Continuing Fifth Epochal Revelation and *The Cosmic Family, Volume I* (which was first published in 1993). But Niánn and I in the late 1980s began to send out literature all over the world with these Continuing-Fifth-Epochal-Revelation concepts. I had to ask myself the reason for being upset dozens of times when I heard someone use these concepts. Was it because I wanted recognition or because of the way these individuals were presenting the concepts as twisted and half-truths? I think being a spiritual leader does not necessarily make one exempt from wanting to be recognized for one's work. I definitely think Christ should have been recognized as a spiritual leader and not just as a carpenter.

Over the years, I listened in great distress when so-called "experts" on *The URANTIA Book* spoke on these paranormal radio shows. They left out the most important thing that *The URANTIA Book* had to say, which the whole end of the book was written about: The Jesus Papers, and who Jesus Christ actually was—that He was a Michael Son and what this means to Urantia/Earth. I do not mean to sound like a fundamentalist, but until all humankind understands who Christ Michael is, we as a divided humankind, will continue to argue and war over the very one thing that can save us all: God.

This is why we change agents in Divine Administration from five continents diligently continue to try to bring the Fifth Epochal Revelation and Continuing Fifth Epochal Revelation to Urantia, because humankind desperately needs a common denominator of God, a common language of divine understanding.

The Lucifer Rebellion is alive and well on Urantia. In Christianity people continue to play church. They, as well as individuals in the New Age, refuse to find true spiritual Elders and submit to them. They refuse to come under any true spiritual authority. What sells is superficial spirituality—the "love, love, love" reality. However, on a fallen world often love has to be very tough to individuals who have chosen so many other things over the perfect will of God, and true spiritual elders who point this out do not get their voices on national radio or television.

Instead, we hear about the coming catastrophes and doom-and-gloom from the remote viewers and the false psychics. We get the "eat-this; don't-eat-that" healers as the answers to humankind's problems. We hear the false psychics supposedly communicating with your lost loved ones. We get time-travelers who are just as lost in their time when they come back to tell us that we are lost in ours! We get the wisdom of the indigenous, whose cultures are the poorest in the world. We get the false shamans and gurus, who claim to heal you with their magic potions if you pay their price.

Granted, we are living in perilous times, but two of the worst problems to befall humankind are individual selfishness and apathy. In the first book of the Bible, Genesis, the teaching to humankind is that we are to be our brothers' and sisters' keeper. The fallen evolutionary consciousness has become more self-oriented, more narcissistic. The iconoclastic tendencies to destroy the sacred are en vogue.

People who say that they are on spiritual paths have no idea what true spirituality is. Instead, they practice a form of quasi-spirituality, which borderlines sophisticated evil. The sophistries of manipulation are rampant in modern spirituality, and millions are fooled by false prophets, false healers, and false spiritual teachers.

I would like to close this chapter with a quote from *The URANTIA Book*, which I feel speaks of Divine Administration, which began as a celestial experiment on Urantia in 1989.

> But paganized and socialized Christianity stands in need of new contact with the uncompromised teachings of Jesus; it languishes for lack of a new vision of the Master's life on earth. A new and fuller revelation of the religion of Jesus is destined to conquer an empire of materialistic secularism and to overthrow a world sway of mechanistic naturalism. Urantia is now quivering on the very brink of one of its most amazing and enthralling epochs of social readjustment, moral quickening, and spiritual enlightenment.
>
> The teachings of Jesus, even though greatly modified, survived the mystery cults of their birthtime, the ignorance and superstition of the dark ages, and are even now slowly triumphing over the materialism, mechanism, and secularism of the twentieth century. And such times of great testing and threatened defeat are always times of great revelation.
>
> Religion does need new leaders, spiritual men and women who will dare to depend solely on Jesus and his incomparable teachings. If Christianity persists in neglecting its spiritual mission while it continues to busy itself with social and material problems, the spiritual renaissance must await the coming of these new teachers of Jesus' religion who will be exclusively devoted to the spiritual regeneration of men. And then will these spirit-born souls quickly supply the leadership and inspiration requisite for the social, moral, economic, and political reorganization of the world.
>
> The modern age will refuse to accept a religion that is inconsistent with facts and out of harmony with its highest conceptions of truth, beauty, and goodness. The hour is striking for a rediscovery of the true and original foundations of present-day distorted and compromised Christianity—the real life and teachings of Jesus. [*The URANTIA Book*, pp. 2082–2083]

CHAPTER 31

Moving From Sedona To Another First Planetary Sacred Home Area
Written in January 2007

When Santeen was still alive several years ago, I started to hear from Celestial Overcontrol about the possibility of moving Divine Administration to another location becoming more imminent. Niánn and I were told by Celestial Overcontrol from the very beginning, starting in 1989, that if overdevelopment was not stopped in Sedona, Arizona, Divine Administration would have to move, as the quantity of lower-psychic-circle souls would overcome the quantity and quality of souls in Divine Administration. There are more than 20,000 residents in the Sedona area and only about 90 adults in Divine Administration. Millions visit each year to see the red rocks. The majority would rather take a commercial Jeep tour than our Spirit Steps Tours to receive spiritual information about the area.

What makes an area protected is the quality of the spiritual people living there, not the mountains or the rivers. We were told by Celestial Overcontrol that the protection of Divine Administration is wherever we are located. So, when we leave, so will thousands of celestial beings in the fifth and above dimensions, for they are only here to help Divine Administration, not vice versa. I wrote in 1989 that "Sedona is the spiritual Mecca of Western civilization." This will become true of the new area that we did relocate to. Sedona will continue to destroy itself by its greed, prosperity message, and anti-God philosophy of the New Age.

When the word "spirit" is mentioned it should be synonymous with divine personality. And if there is no relationship with God as a personality, the use of the word "spirit" means nothing. God the Father needs to be able to guide our lives. The use of the words "spirit" or "universe" often mean a nebulous and ambiguous definition of a quasi-force, who does not direct one's life.

Sedona, Arizona continues to draw people with financial excess, and a greedy environment does not make an area sacred by any means. The beauty of the physical mountains is often masked by the greedy people who you run into in the business establishments and the public places of Sedona. The media of Sedona—its radio stations and newspaper—as well as the city and county governments are controlled by over-development principles. Our enemies say that we were chased out of Sedona by continuous newspaper negative coverage. But that is not the case. We outgrew the 15+ acres and had difficulty building under the county codes there.

Even the beautiful Oak Creek is becoming polluted and often is not safe to swim in. The vortices of Sedona have now become dead energies and no longer have their spiritual powers because the beings who were once transported from extraterrestrial and interdimensional locations moved with Divine Administration.

Divine Administration while in Sedona fought very hard for the environment and other social issues. Unfortunately, when we were attacked by local media and jealous and hateful Sedona residents, very few people came to our defense. The words of Martin Luther King, Jr. became very real for us: "In the end, we will remember not the words of our enemies, but the silence of our friends."

Along with the knowing that we would have to move also came the knowing that we would have to change our name, as we outgrew both Sedona and our name. In the beginning, it was hoped by Celestial Overcontrol that term "Aquarian Concepts" would reach fourth-order starseed souls in the New Age. But as the years passed, it became obvious that the New Age did not want a God-centered philosophy. It would be more advantageous for us spiritually to be in a geographic area where the majority of people are Catholic or Christian and not New Age.

It is still our mission to bring alternative and new thought ideas of spirituality to the Christian world and to bring a personal God to the New Age. The New Age has many Aquarian concepts—concepts of the Aquarian Age of cooperation and unity—but is unable to unify those teachings with holistic alternative health teachings that can benefit the Christian world. It is the mission of Divine Administration to unite the truth of Christianity with the truth of the New Age.

As we began webcasting internationally, the community's new name evolved as well as my new name: Global Community Communications Alliance and Gabriel of Urantia/ TaliasVan of Tora. *Global* because we are global in our outreach; *Community* because we are both an active EcoVillage and an intentional community of global citizens; *Communications* because we dedicatedly bring continued revelation to the world; and *Alliance* because people who are searching for truth all over the world and beginning to understand the teachings of Continuing Fifth Epochal Revelation are forming an alliance by aligning in some way with us. We already have people here with us from five continents.[1]

Although we do not accept all of the doctrines of Christianity, we feel we are certainly Christ-centered, as we believe that Jesus Christ Michael is the Son of God, being a Michael Son whose origin is Paradise and the sovereign of His local universe of Nebadon. We believe that we are followers of the true teachings of Jesus Christ and that much of Christian doctrine is not what Jesus Christ taught. This is why Jesus Christ Michael allowed that bringing through of the Fifth Epochal Revelation (*The URANTIA Book*) and Continuing Fifth Epochal Revelation (*The Cosmic Family* volumes) to the world, through His created beings—human and nonhuman.

The battle between good and evil continues in every walk of life, and God is more concerned about us doing the right thing than He is about us knowing the cosmology of the master universe. So in understanding this truth, one realizes that millions of souls who pass from this world in all religions will go directly to the first mansion world and will continue on in their ascension process—not because they so much called God "Christ" or did not, but because they lent a helping hand to someone who needed it whenever they could, and not because they claimed to be washed in the blood of Christ, but because they did not malign another person by their words or deeds.

In some mysterious way someday people of this planet will no longer call themselves Christians, Jews, Hindus, Moslems, Buddhists, New Agers, or whatever. They will only identify themselves as ascending sons and daughters of God and brothers and sisters created by the One Father/Mother God. I began to teach the concept of radical unity and coined the phrase, "One God, One Planetary Family."

In 2010, I developed the Be Aware Proclamation. These are spiritual, social, environmental, and political points that all Americans and, indeed, the rest of the world need to "be aware" of.[2] "One God, One Planetary Family" and "Be Aware" are the themes for my concerts wherever I go, with the intention of bringing this message of hope to the entire world.

September 12, 2012 Addendum

After I performed at the May 2010 Be Aware Festival in Tumacácori, Arizona, I collapsed and went to a doctor in Tucson, a nephrology specialist, who said that my kidneys were both chronic and acute, which means my kidneys had totally failed me. I was taken to the emergency room at the hospital, and they put me immediately on dialysis. This began an eight-month nightmare on dialysis and with the medical field that I wrote about in a book called *The Sharp End Of The Needle. Dealing With Diabetes, Dialysis And Transplant*.

In July of 2011, I was well enough for The Bright & Morning Star Band to go on the road with a tour that we planned for four states and five cities, starting out in Arizona with our Be Aware Festival and then Durango, Colorado. The arts and entertainment editor for *The Durango Herald* unfortunately had been contacted by the "negative network" that triggered him to send Mycenay (the booking agent) a very hateful letter, actually threatening my and the band members' lives. He also indicated that he would do everything he could to make the concert a failure.

We had a 700-seat auditorium and only a few people showed up. It was devastating for my musicians and me to perform to just a few people, with all those empty seats glaring at us. Of course we all were concerned for our safety, especially for my life. I figured the same person or persons of the "negative network" would probably do the same thing in Denver (the next scheduled stop) as well as in Santa Fe (the third stop on this trip), so I decided to cancel both concerts.

We left Arizona with great expectations and joy but returned greatly discouraged. I was in total shock that people would be so evil to do something like this, and that others were so easily influenced by hearsay and hatred. I also cancelled concerts in Tempe, Arizona at The Center of Arts and a beautiful amphitheater in Vista, California.

Since this incident in Durango, my health has been gradually deteriorating from the stress and emotional damage I feel this has done to my musical career. My one good eye seems to be getting worse and my legs (which suffer from neuropathy) weaker. I now struggle with the tendency to overeat (which is not good for my new kidney) to compensate for the empty feeling of unfulfillment I am experiencing.

Music ministry has meant a lot to me all of my life because it is another way in which I can bring hope and healing to people, through my music. To not be able to perform in music ministry, as I have been doing for forty-two years now, is devastating to my emotional health, which translates to my body. The dream of going on tour cannot be a possibility until this negative network is stopped. So we are seeking legal process to do just this.[3]

The following is a song I wrote about this experience.

I'm Still Trying to Regain

by
TaliasVan

I'm still trying to regain.
The dreams I lost that day
When I seemed to lose the Way
When I seemed to lose the Way

The Way, the Way the Way

When my soul just flew astray
Another sad melee, the devil's holiday.
When I lost the will to pray
When I lost the cosmic say.
When pain overwhelmed me.
Pain overwhelmed me.

Now I'm struggling to fight on
To believe the Spirit is strong
Stronger than the evil world.
Than the evil world.

'Cause I seemed to lose the Way.
Who caused this mad betray
In destiny's delay
A very sad dismay
Lost the holy door-Way

The Way The Way The Way The Way

Oh to find myself anew
To find myself in You
To feel Your strength again
To sing the holy Amen — Amen

So hello, to all my unseen friends
I know that you're there
I know that you care
I know He hasn't forsaken me
Forsaken me

I just seemed to lose the Way.
Darkness won that day
In the magic Prince ballet
Just seemed to lose the Way.
Just seemed to lose the Way.

The Way, the Way, the Way.

© 2011 Global Community Communications Alliance
All rights administered by Global Change Multi-Media,
P.O. Box 1613, Tubac, AZ 85646 USA
All Rights Reserved.

I have my ideas about who could have misrepresented me. Two of the people who come to mind are two men who consider themselves "cult experts" and make their living off of their so-called expertise. Neither one of these men have ever met me or come to our community to find out anything about us personally, because they do not really care. They receive huge sums of money from "concerned" parents and other family members and friends by feeding these people's fear and ignorance with misinformation about alternative groups or, what these "experts" refer to as, "cults." These two men, Rick Ross and Stephen Hassan, exploit people's personal agendas of wanting their adult family member out of the alternative lifestyle and back into the family control and mindset. Ross and Hassan use clever tactics to convince family members that the individuals they are "concerned about" are in dangerous cults, no matter what the actual facts and truth are.

Others involved in the negative network are some ex-community members who could not live up to our moral standards, or jealous musicians, or wanna-be spiritual leaders who try to build their name on my coattail. And then there are those who thrive on cyber-attacks on others who rock their ideological boats. Another is a newspaper in Sedona that misrepresented me for many weeks with front-page headlines and articles because the publisher (owner) had "interests" in a certain pending development that I and members of the community joined with other concerned citizens to stop because of this particular development's unethical and unsustainable tactics that were causing environmental rape of the land.

When we first moved to Tumacácori, this same negative network contacted neighbors and also fed them a plethora of lies about me and our community. We were written negatively about in the *Nogales International* and the *Arizona Daily Star*, and many neighbors surrounding us choose to believe these lies because it fits their agendas. These same neighbors came against us with the Santa Cruz County planning and zoning department, trying to stop us from building our church. We took them to court and won the case, but as of this writing, we have

Chapter 31

been slowed down for more than a year in building our worship center.

At every turn, these particular neighbors try to harm us by calling county, state, and even federal agencies to stop us in our building projects and costing us tens of thousands of dollars for attorneys—money that could have been used instead to help humanity through our many service ministries. Without getting into a lot of detail, we are an EcoVillage. We live a sustainable lifestyle. And everything we build—in Sedona and now in Tumacácori at Avalon Organic Gardens & EcoVillage—is beautiful and flows in harmony with the earth. These neighbors act like we are going to build a typical mega-church because our plans state that our building project is 17,000 square feet, which consists of not just a worship center but a library, children's and adult schools, and a music and rehearsal studio. We actually are only asking for a worship center that would house approximately 250 people.

They also wrongly presumed that we are going to build a big church steeple. A church steeple is the last thing in the world we would build; we are not "steeple people." These neighbors lied about the amount of car parking spaces we were asking for (which was only sixty spaces and they said hundreds), and they lied about the place where the parking would be, saying that it was at a major road where it would be eyesores to the neighbors. This parking area is planned to be well into our property, out of any neighbor's eyesight.

At the county meeting these particular neighbors acted like a vigilante mob. They were not there to listen to reasoning or our side of the picture, which was to present the facts. Evil never does listen to the light. That is how Jesus got crucified. That is why He did not even try to defend Himself. He knew His accusers were not looking for justice. They all had their own agendas.

It always baffles me that evil people have no fear of God and have no idea or do not care that they will have to stand before the Ancients of Days and Jesus Christ Michael one day and be judged for their evil deeds. As of this writing, in the few short years we have been here, we have made our 185 acres a little paradise on Earth. We have built Earth Harmony homes made of sandbags that look like homes from *The Lord Of The Rings* movie where the hobbits lived. They are magical. We have remodeled homes to make them more "green," sustainable, and nontoxic. We use bricks made of recycled paper, called papercrete, for some of our building projects. We are building what we call Trinity Domes, which are three dome structures with a community center in the middle that will house comfortably and privately new agricultural workers and students and some of our people, including families and children.

We are building fish ponds and hatcheries. And we have a Community Supported Agriculture (CSA) program, blessing many supportive neighbors with fresh local organic vegetables and fruits. We have goats and make our own goat cheese and milk. We have our own chickens for eggs and meat and graze our own organic grass-fed beef. We have an agricultural internship program and work with many local organizations in agriculture, sustainability, permaculture, and food-for-the-hungry programs.

So despite the constant harassment and evil deeds of evil people and people who may not be evil but are just not very open to anything alternative, we continue to prosper and go forward with the hope of a new world to come—the first stage of light and life as mentioned in *The URANTIA Book*—a Divine New Order. We believe that the Promised One will return to Urantia/Earth and bring peace and justice to all of the peoples of the earth. We pray for Jesus Christ Michael's return every Wednesday at 11:11 A.M. We ask that others join with us, from all over the world.

January 30, 2013 Addendum

Since the last writing in this book, in the United States hundreds of tornadoes, floods, and fires have hit including the superstorm Sandy on the East Coast, which displaced tens of thousands and affected millions all up and down the coast. The sun is not normal. Its rays are sometimes blinding to the eyes, and if you are in the sun too long, it will cause skin cancer faster. The corporate news is very quiet about the effects of the changing sun, as the news is very quiet about most of the dangers to humankind.

One thing that is certain to me, and to all who have eyes to see, is that evil people are getting more evil and the good seed is being separated from the bad seed—just as Jesus spoke of in the first century, that that would happen in the last days prior to His coming. We in Divine Administration continue to "circle the wagons" and try to get off the grid completely.

On January 27, 2013 the Bright and Morning Star came in at 6:06 A.M. and then gave a transmission to the whole community that evening, giving some clarifying information that I have long felt uneasy about. During the transmission discussion the next day, others shared they had felt uneasy about the information too. The clarifying information that he gave was that Nod was not the Apostle John, Rafeel was not the Apostle James, "Matthew" was not the Apostle Matthew, "Luke" was not the Apostle Luke, and "Phillip" was not the Apostle Phillip. The Bright and Morning Star identified who actually was Paul of the first century. (Please refer to the Preface for details.)

Celestial Overcontrol allowed these seeming "errors" to occur so that I could observe the dio in these individuals and Overcontrol could come in and write technical transmissions about what I observed, using Continuing Fifth Epochal Revelation terms and incorporating contemporary scientific physics. Thus, we have the term "the physics of rebellion." I am relieved that these individuals were not the apostles of the first century.

The individuals who actually were the Apostles John and Paul—who I met in Tucson, Arizona in 1977—were truly saints. In knowing these men as a young minister in my early thirties, I was able to see what a true man of God was and follow their example. The repersonalized Paul's birth name was Fred Brown, and he was a second-time Urantian. The repersonalized John's birth name was David Strickland, and he was a higher order of starseed.

Divine Administration continues to go forward and grow, both in the physical and nonphysical, despite the enemies of Divine Administration, who try to block the outworking of God's will through us. At the end of 2012 we acquired a beautiful sacred building in Tucson, Arizona, that we are calling The Sea Of Glass℠ (named after the Sea of Glass in *The URANTIA Book*), which will be a center for the arts and include a farm-to-table restaurant featuring plant-based foods, called Food For Ascension℠ Café. To acquire this outreach in Tucson was a direct command of the Bright and Morning Star, and he also gave the name for it. All in Divine Administration are excited about this.

We also continue to build our housing. We most recently completed the "Patience House" and have begun construction on the "Trinity Domes." At some point in the near future, it is our hope to start building the Global Communications Center, which Celestial Overcontrol said will manifest people to come for higher spiritual instruction from all over the world. To God be the glory!

CHAPTER 32

Miracle of Miracles: 630 N. 4th Avenue, Tucson
A House Of Destiny With God And Me

In 1976, again on a step of faith, I moved to Tucson, Arizona—from Pittsburgh (where I had returned for about a year)—to work as a faith Minister in the 4th Avenue area. I went there upon request by a young Christian man named Mike who was taking in the homeless but didn't really want to start an official full-time ministry as he had a full-time cooler installation business and needed assistance of someone who had street experience, which I had, and would make it into a real ministry. He lived at a house at 630 N. 4th Avenue and told me that though he had no more room at that location, he would try to have a place for me by the time I arrived at the airport.

When I did arrive, he informed me that he was getting married the next week, sooner than expected, and that I could stay with him on the floor for a week until he moved out. Then I could have his room and take over the leadership of the group of street people, runaways, alcoholics, and drug addicts whom he, with a group of other young Christians were living there with, but not really having the time to minister to these homeless. With Mike's business repairing coolers, ministry was not his first calling. However, he did love the Lord, and at one point in my new ministry there, he gave me his old 1964 Volkswagen bus.

At the time of my arrival, there was by no means any form of an organized ministry at 630 N. 4th Avenue. The young Christian men were completely disorganized and scattered, but their hearts were in the right place. I began to bring order and implemented a ministry with principles that I had learned from Nicky Cruz and other Christian ministries that I had worked with, like Youth With A Mission.

Within weeks, God sent me a middle-aged man named Scotty, who at one time had been a street person himself, to help me because most of the other young Christian men went on to do other things and had no real calling to work with the homeless, drug addicts, mentally ill, and other disenfranchised people for any length of time.

About six months later, the owner of the property, George Mehl (now deceased), a very successful contractor in Tucson who built major shopping malls, had his secretary call me and said to come to his on-site office-trailer the next morning. I of course thought that he was going to throw me out of the house because I was bringing in many more street people.

When I arrived, there was a line of about 50 men with white hats and blue hats waiting to meet with the contractor. I went to the end of the line and a few minutes later, a secretary came out and said, "Is Reverend Anthony Delevin here?" I yelled from the back of the line, "Yes I'm here." She said, "Come up." All the men stared with interest at me, thinking, "I wonder who this dude is?"

At the time, I had no idea that George Mehl was a multi-millionaire who hired hundreds of people for his many construction projects. He called me into his office and had me sit down. I thought he was going to say, "I appreciate that you're a minister, but I don't like what you're doing with my house" and ask me to leave. To my delight and surprise, instead he said, "I've been praying for someone like you who knew what they were doing to come along and start a real ministry there. I understand you have a background of working with Nicky Cruz halfway houses and come from the inner city of Pittsburgh." He obviously had done his homework.

He then proceeded to say, "So I've decided to give you the property with all the equity that I have in it so far and to continue making the mortgage payments until your ministry can get on its feet to pay the little balance that is left on it." (It took me four short years to pay off the balance.) George continued, "You need to start a nonprofit organization for your ministry there on 4th Avenue."

In the Preface of this book I describe how around this same time I met David Strickland (the soul of the Apostle John) who was the one who helped me in forming the nonprofit ministry that I called Son Light Ministries. The first sign that I put up at 630 N. 4th Avenue included this quote from Acts 2:44–47:

> And all those who had believed were together and had all things in common; and they began selling their property and possessions and were sharing them with all, as anyone might have need. Day by day continuing with one mind in the temple, and breaking bread from house to house, they were taking their meals together with gladness and sincerity of heart, praising God and having favor with all the people. And the Lord was adding to their number day by day those who were being saved.[1]

(Little did I know that my work with this first community of social outcasts and young ministers, who came to help me, would one day lead to the spiritual community and EcoVillage that I have today.)

From that point on, many miracles happened in my life. First, meeting and later marrying Jerri, who quit college in order to be part of the ministry and who also wanted to have a job in order to help the young ministry financially. She first lived in the guest house in the back, which I now have found out was built as an addition in 1946 (the year that I was born). Although we are no longer together, due to the pressure of the ministry and our youth, I love her to this day and always will.

During those early years of ministry on 4th Avenue, I was given many donations serendipitously, one of which was a baby grand piano. Often I would discover in the mailbox envelopes with money in them, anonymously given. I began to learn how within the laws of God the needs of those who walk by faith and serve others are taken care of.

About a year after Jerri and I separated, I left this house and ministry in 1982 because the memories of my life with Jerri there were too much for me to take, and I had to get on with my life. I had always wanted to start a coffee house there, called The Holy Ghost Filling Station, but I had had no money for lumber for beams and posts and could not hire a carpenter to do the work. But in that last year there, I took a sledgehammer and knocked a wall out (to enlarge the front room) as a step of faith to see what God would do next, because I wanted this coffee house to happen and knew that if I began to knock the wall out, God would take the next step.

The day after I knocked out the wall, a young man from Montana by the name of Bob knocked on the door and, low and behold, said, "I need housing, and I heard you have a ministry here. I'm a carpenter, and I'll do whatever work you want me to do." A day or two later, a construction contractor called me, saying that he had these extra beams and posts and could I use them. We went down immediately and got them. And I never sent out any message to anyone of what I was planning to do!

One day, when we were just about done with the construction and bringing the old wood floors back from the years of linoleum and layers of tar, I was driving up University Boulevard and saw a train engine made of wood sitting on the curb outside someone's house, like they were going to throw it away. So I stopped my car, walked up to the house, and asked the woman if I could have it and told her what I was naming my coffee house. She said, "Yes, of course." It sat in the front yard for as long as I had the coffee house open. I myself was too emotionally broken from my separation with Jerri to run it, so I chose two Christian friends to manage it for me.

A Miracle Happens Again At 630 N. 4th Avenue

Now, 33 years later, I have acquired 630 N. 4th Avenue back, to begin another form of ministry there, called Spirit Steps Tours, which we started in Sedona, Arizona to bring higher spiritual consciousness to tourists from all over the world. Again, in the acquisition of this property have been other serendipities, all too numerous to mention.

One I would like to share about is that one morning I asked a real estate agent from our church to look for property on 4th Avenue. In the afternoon of that same day, he said, "You won't believe this but your old place has just come up on the market today." (I had often mentioned this property in my public sermons about the serendipities that had occurred there for me many years before.) I heard God's voice say to me, "Proceed to obtain it, as I have plans for you there again."

So, as of July 1, 2013 escrow will close on 630 N. 4th Avenue, and Global Community Communications Alliance will own this property. Another use of this property will be as a place for musicians to stay a night or two, coming to town from all over the United States and world, who will be playing at The Sea Of Glass—Center For The Arts℠ that we also just purchased on 7th Street, a few blocks away.

It is very hard to express this, but I feel that my real spiritual self began to come into maturation there at 630 N. 4th Avenue more than three decades ago. Now, in the last seasons of my life, I have it back to do God's perfect will there for this particular house and property, which has been through many transitions since I sold it in 1982. The last use of it was a hair salon. I never thought that I would consider purchasing this property again, but I had the thought every time I drove by it that I was sorry I sold it, because I could see its value as a perfect spot for a ministry for God. I cannot wait to make this old historic house look even better than it looked in 1938, when it was first built.

Though more than thirty years ago my little train engine in front of the Holy Ghost Filling Station did not have its own tracks, now, right outside of 630 N. 4th Avenue are tracks with a trolley stop for the new antique-looking trolley cars (reminiscent of the old trolley that ran through 4th Avenue for more than seventy-five years) that go from the university through 4th Avenue to downtown Tucson. When they stop outside of 630 N. 4th Avenue, they will see Spirit Steps Tours, and I'm sure many of them will be tourists and hopefully want to take a tour of Tucson with a touch of "spirit." They may also want to take a tour of this historic home in which I first applied for historic zoning.

I'm sure that the serendipities with acquiring 630 N. 4th Avenue back will continue. All that I can say at this point is it is so exciting to see how the hand of God works in a person's life who dedicates himself or herself to the purposes of God.

NOTES

Statement By The Author

[1] The editors would like to stress the difference between a "channel" and an audio fusion material complement. For definitions see the Glossary. We strongly advise your further study by reading Paper 209 in *The Cosmic Family, Volume I*.

Chapter 3

[1] Myers-Briggs Type Indicator is a measure of personality dispositions and interests based on Jung's theory of types. It provides four bipolar scales: Introversion/Extroversion, Sensing/Intuition, Thinking/Feeling, and Judging/Perceiving. Scores are reported by a four-letter type code.

[2] Acronyms from the Myers-Briggs Type Indicator of psychological preferences. INFP = Introversion, iNtuition, Feeling, Perception and ENFP = Extraversion, iNtuition, Feeling, Perception

Chapter 4

[1] The publishers want to make it quite clear that this was an extraordinary event. Contrary to popular belief, the souls of deceased relatives do not as a rule make contact with their loved ones here on Earth. However, because of the urgency of the times and the extraordinary Mandate of the Bright and Morning Star, which Gabriel of Urantia/TaliasVan of Tora had earned over many lifetimes, our Universe Sovereign, Christ Michael, allowed Gabriel's grandmother to make contact with him in a morontia body on some type of space transport to help awaken him to his destiny.

Chapter 5

[1] "Where the three rivers meet" in Pittsburgh, Pennsylvania was the home of several Native American nations that extended to Canada at the time of the French and English wars in the New World. The five Iroquois Nations came together to develop a common spiritual language. This was a precursor to the Fifth Epochal Revelation. There is an energy reflective circuit "where the three rivers meet." Gabriel of Urantia/TaliasVan of Tora was born in this area. In 1992 an elder from the Iroquois Nation, Great Bear, met with Gabriel/TaliasVan in Sedona, Arizona. He was told of the ancient Iroquois prophecy about a prophet who would come from the East at the end times. Gabriel/TaliasVan is that prophet.

Chapter 6

[1] Throughout this book, some people's names have been changed to respect the privacy of individuals mentioned from my past.

Chapter 7

[1] Hebrews 9:27 (KJV)

[2] Matthew 22:14 (KJV)

Chapter 9

[1] Paladin was made Chief of Finaliters on Urantia in January 1992, basically because of the ascension of Gabriel of Urantia/TaliasVan of Tora (his cosmic son) and other of his seed. This is technically explained in Paper 226 of *The Cosmic Family, Volume I*.

[2] Dalamatia was the name of the location—near what is now the Middle East—where the world's first celestial Planetary Prince (named Caligastia) and his staff of other celestials (including his second in command, Dalagastia) and 100 supermortals set up the first Planetary Headquarters on Urantia/Earth, nearly 500,000 years ago.

[3] The author is not implying that at this time pluralistic relationships should be practiced on Urantia. Usually most pluralistic relationships today, in all cultures on Urantia, are based on sexual lust rather than genuine committed love and respect. Even though members of Global Community Communications Alliance are aware of other modalities on other worlds, it takes a high level of spiritual maturity, which people of this planet are not yet ready for. Global Community Communications Alliance's religious order members have been and are celibate until they are in a committed monogamous relationship.

[4] At the time of the editing of this Third Edition (Summer 2013), it is not recommended that pluralistic relationships should be the case on Urantia. The members of Global Community Communications Alliance religious order choose to be celibate until monogamous committed relationship or marriage. Though members are aware of these other relationship modalities on other planets (and some souls have experienced these realities on other worlds), it is realized that it takes a high level of spiritual maturity to achieve these types of complex relationships within divine pattern.

At this time, the vast majority of people on Urantia (Earth) are not yet ready for any type of pluralistic reality, especially those outside of Divine Administration where these concepts within divine pattern are just beginning to be explored. Those pluralistic relationships that have occurred and continue to occur in third-dimensional reality are usually painful and based upon dishonesty and/or coercion as well as lust rather than genuine lasting love and long-term loyal commitment.

Chapter 12

[1] This man, referred to as Judas here, is not to be confused with the first-century apostle of Jesus, also named Judas, who was a different soul.

[2] Matthew 5:9 (KJV)

Chapter 16

[1] This transmission became Paper 213 of *The Cosmic Family, Volume I*, entitled "The Adjudication Of The Bright and Morning Star Versus Lucifer, The Establishment Of The Administration Of The Planetary Prince Using Human Personalities, And The Announcement Of Machiventa Melchizedek As That Planetary Prince Of Urantia."

[2] This transmission became Paper 214 of *The Cosmic Family, Volume I*, entitled "Hologram Appearance Of Machiventa Melchizedek To One Of His Potential Material Complements And Potential Vicegerent Ambassadors, With The Announcement Of His Elevation To The Office Of Planetary Prince Of Urantia; Clarification Of The Title Of The Planetary Prince; Warning To Caligastia Regarding Protection And Safe Passage For All Those Called To The Extension Schools of Melchizedek At The First Planetary Sacred Home In Tubac/Tumacácori, Arizona, USA."

[3] As of January 10, 2001 Celestial Overcontrol, under the authority of Christ Michael, has completely disbanded the mandate of transfiguration on Urantia until the first stage of light and life is a reality on Urantia.

[4] Before December 1989 certain prospective Reservists and Vicegerent First Ambassadors were contacted by the Midwayer Commission and Machiventa Melchizedek in Toronto, Ontario, Canada, and other energy reflective circuits.

[5] At the time of editing the Third Edition [of *The Cosmic Family, Volume I*], Spring 2011, there are no Vicegerent First Ambassadors. Santeen (now deceased), who had a higher mandate as a Liaison Minister, was the only example of the office of Vicegerent First Ambassador functioning the way it should under the Mandate of the Bright and Morning Star.

Chapter 17

¹Although there has not been a direct attack as of yet on the United States by China, they have certainly given us quite an economic blow, as we are in debt to them for trillions of dollars. Also just recently, in 2013, Russia, China, Iran, and Syria are planning a joint military alliance.

Chapter 19

¹It should be understood that before the printing of this book, all responsible mandated personalities—from Liaison Ministers to Vicegerent Second Assistants and all nonmandated community members—knew that the democratic vote was not always the best way or divine way. The trust that those aligned in Divine Administration had in Gabriel of Urantia/TaliasVan of Tora and Niánn Emerson Chase was well earned.

² Currently in 2013 in Global Community Communications Alliance the term "soul watcher" is an administrative title for individual household coordinators who also do much ministry and counseling within community homes.

Chapter 21

¹ Ecclesiastes 1:2 (KJV)

²On this side of the Celestial Divine Administration, as human mortals with the Mandate of the Bright and Morning Star of Salvington, Gabriel of Urantia/TaliasVan of Tora and Niánn Emerson Chase had to grow into the reality that they were to become—the human versions of Planetary Prince and Princess of Urantia—a function of responsibility they were being trained for for thousands of years, as will be explained in the next chapter.

Chapter 22

¹Since this chapter was written, the identity of one of these warrior souls was revealed by Machiventa Melchizedek in Paper 291 of *The Cosmic Family, Volume III*, which was published in the November/December 1993 issue of *The Salvington Circuit*.

²You can read what *The URANTIA Book* says about Ikhnaton (Akhenaten) on page 1047.

Chapter 23

[1] From Paper 210 (February 6, 1992) in *The Cosmic Family, Volume I*, Global Community Communications Publishing, Tubac/Tumacácori, Arizona, 3rd ed., 2011

Chapter 24

[1] Refer to Revelations 3:16

[2] Refer to Matthew 6:24

[3] To better understand the psychic circles, read the section on psychic circles on pages 1209–1212 of *The URANTIA Book*, and for more explanation of an audio fusion material complement read Paper 209 of *The Cosmic Family, Volume I*.

Chapter 25

[1] Wallace Black Elk went to the other side on January 25, 2004.

Chapter 26

[1] John 10:30 (KJV)

[2] Matthew 22:37 (KJV)

[3] Matthew 22:39 (KJV)

Chapter 27

[1] Matthew 16:18 (KJV) "...thou art Peter, and upon this rock I will build my church..." Footnote in *The New Oxford Annotated Bible* states: The Greek text involves a play on two words, Petros (Peter) and Petra (rock). Palestinian Aramaic, which Jesus usually spoke, used the same word for both proper name and common noun "Kepha" and "kepha." Page 24 NT

Chapter 28

[1] See Chapter 16 for more information on the term "Sananda."

[2] As of May 13, 2011, Ah'Nuit is a mandated minister of Divine Administration

Chapter 29

[1] The author is not implying that at this time pluralistic relationships should be practiced on Urantia. Usually most pluralistic relationships today, in all cultures on Urantia, are based on sexual lust rather than genuine committed love and respect. Even though members of Global Community Communications Alliance are aware of other modalities on other worlds, it takes a high level of spiritual maturity, which people of this planet are not yet ready for. Global Community Communications Alliance's religious order members have been and are celibate until they are in a committed monogamous relationship.

[2] On March 28, 2013 it was confirmed TiyiEndea was Tenache.

[3] I Samuel 25:40 (KJV)

[4] I Samuel 25:32 (KJV)

[5] Genesis 16:1 (KJV)

[6] Genesis 16:3 (KJV)

[7] For more information, see Paper 313, *The Cosmic Family, Volume IV*

[8] The account of this fact can be read in *The URANTIA Book* on page 745.

Chapter 31

[1] We have formed many alliances since we have been here in the last five years. For more detail see "Alliance Organizations" in the back of this edition.

[2] Visit beawareproclamation.org

[3] As of this date (July 2013) and tens of thousands of dollars in legal fees later, we have not heard from the courts as to if they are even going to properly allow our case in court, which will then cost tens of thousands of dollars more, without any assurance that we will win.

Chapter 32

[1] Acts 2:44–47 (NASB)

GLOSSARY

"Although these definitions are as exact as they can be in relation to the students who are studying this revelation, updated information can change the definition to some degree. The content of the meaning will still be there. We are limited, based upon language from our side to yours, and hindered by your own inability to understand such a massive volume of information of specific details. Sometimes a definition has many meanings or two terms are very similar. Whenever we can we will try to introduce them but often are not able to clearly differentiate the terms at the time. If you can somewhat begin to understand 10% of these definitions in total, we can expand on them and go from there. It could take years to completely comprehend these very cosmic technical terms in ascension science until it becomes second nature to you. Two-brained types such as are now on Urantia, both native and ovan soul, have the ability of complete comprehension at some point in their future evolution."

Paladin,
Chief of Finaliters on Urantia

Acting Governor General See Governor General of Urantia.

Adam and Eve The Material Son and Daughter, father and mother of the violet race, who came to our planet almost 38,000 years ago to biologically uplift the evolutionary races.

adjudication of the Bright and Morning Star versus Lucifer The combined celestial and mortal judicial process, led by the Bright and Morning Star (Gabriel of Salvington), representing the final determinations and conclusion of the Lucifer Rebellion throughout the planetary system of Satania.

agondonter An evolutionary will creature "who can believe without seeing, persevere when isolated, and triumph over insuperable difficulties even when alone." [*The URANTIA Book*, p. 579]

Amadon A native Urantian who belonged to one of the highest strains of the evolutionary Andonite race, 500,000 years ago. He was the associate of Van, the head of the loyalists in the Rebellion. Both remained on the planet until the arrival of Adam and Eve. Amadon became the human hero of the Lucifer Rebellion. He remained loyal to Christ Michael and has now repersonalized during the final phase of the adjudication of the Bright and Morning Star versus Lucifer.

Ambassadors (First and Second, including Vicegerents) Mandated to serve as ambassadors to the world, representing Machiventa Melchizedek's Administration within the human Divine Administration under the Mandate of the Bright and Morning Star.

Ancients of Days Trinity-origin beings who rule a superuniverse and, as Trinity representatives, are the judges of all personalities of origin in that superuniverse. There are three Ancients of Days in every superuniverse.

antahkarana A New-Age term for the central channel in the body connecting the chakras according to the ancient Tibetans.

apostles The first-century apostles (including Matthias, Luke, and Paul) who have repersonalized in the twentieth century. They are a mixed group of starseed and second-time Urantians. An apostle is one who is in full-time spiritual ministry in contrast to a disciple who is in part-time ministry.

archangels They are a high order of local universe personalities created by the Creator Son and Universe Mother Spirit. They are an order separate from angels. They are dedicated to the work of creature survival and to the furtherance of the ascending career of the mortals of time and space. In recent times a divisional headquarters of the archangels has been maintained on Urantia and is presently located at the First Planetary Sacred Home in Tubac/Tumacácori, Arizona, USA. There are no archangels communicating with humans at present.

ascension science A universe spiritual science that fuses the spiritual with the scientific.

Ashtar Command The various celestial and ascending mortal beings in spaceships assigned to Urantia for various duties in relation to the adjudication of Urantia, including physical evacuation by spaceship, and the coordination of activities relating to interdimensional changes, under the command of Ashtar, a finaliter, who has assumed a seventh-stage morontia body to work in the physical realm.

Assistants Mandated First and Second Assistants to Gabriel of Urantia/TaliasVan of Tora and Niánn Emerson Chase, under the Mandate of the Bright and Morning Star of Salvington functioning in various aspects of reflectivity of Celestial Overcontrol.

astral body A composite of the bodies a personality has existed in before at any point in time and space. Each existence has a separate body connected to it. The astral body in the present is ever growing, that of the past is an inactive completed form, yet is not separate from the present physical body. The astral body of a second-time Urantian does not begin to form until death.

audio fusion material complement A term describing a fusion between a celestial being and a mortal, a fusion of one entity with another in the complete aonic-to-cellular reality of the lower being. The fusion takes place within the particle reality of the life force of the existing soul. They co-exist within the life force, and the existing soul does not leave. It is a gradual process over many years, and the higher the virtue of the chosen vessel, the higher the fusion, the higher the being, and the higher the level of revelation that can be brought through. Gabriel of Urantia/TaliasVan of Tora is the only Audio Fusion Material Complement on Urantia. Paladin, Chief of Finaliters, fuses with Gabriel/TaliasVan daily.

auhter energy The higher force-energy synergetic field resultant from cosmic nuclear fusion created by the joining or rejoining of spiritual cosmic families or groups based upon the personality bestowal of the Universal Father and each individual's acquiescence to his or her personality, and the group consciousness in relation to Celestial Overcontrol. This auhter energy creates a measurable light that is visible light-years away.

Avalon Name of a neighboring universe. Most of the starseed in the First Cosmic Family come from Avalon. Some of the Caligastia One Hundred were morontia progressors originally from that universe and, because of a different Avalon ascension scheme, were on assignments in this universe of Nebadon.

Bright and Morning Star The Bright and Morning Star of Salvington is the Chief Administrator of the universe of Nebadon and the first-born personality creation of Christ Michael and the Universe Mother Spirit. The Bright and Morning Star visits Urantia in overcontrol of the adjudication by the Bright and Morning Star versus Lucifer and speaks through his mandated Audio Fusion Material Complement,

Gabriel of Urantia/TaliasVan of Tora, and manifests in reflectivity through this vessel

Caligastia The former Planetary Prince who arrived on Urantia 500,000 years ago with a staff of 100 rematerialized ascending sons and daughters (the Caligastia One Hundred) to bring the First Epochal Revelation to Urantia. His headquarters was the city of Dalamatia. Many of the legends about Atlantis go back to the times of Dalamatia. Caligastia followed Lucifer in a rebellion 200,000 years ago. Although shorn of all administrative powers, Caligastia has been allowed to remain on the planet until his adjudication is over. The "devil" is none other than Caligastia.

Caligastia One Hundred The physical mortal staff of ascenders from three other universes who came to Urantia 500,000 years ago with Caligastia and Daligastia to bring the First Epochal Revelation to Urantia. They were 50 males and 50 females, referred to as the Caligastia One Hundred, who had been transported by seraphic transport from the system capital, Jerusem, and had been rematerialized to be Caligastia's administrative staff on the physical level. Dalamatia was their headquarters, and they were organized for service in ten councils of ten members each. For 300,000 years they taught the evolutionary races on this planet and remained undying by being in the perfect will of the Father and partaking of the fruit of the Tree of Life. During the Lucifer Rebellion forty remained loyal and sixty fell. The rebellious ones mated with the evolutionary races and created the Nodite race, named after their leader Nod. Some Urantians have their interuniversal genetics.

Caligastia Sixty The sixty supermortal members of Caligastia's staff who fell in the Lucifer Rebellion with Caligastia.

Celestial Overcontrol A term designating orders of beings who function on higher levels of universe administration guiding and overseeing the human mandated personalities on a planetary level functioning in cooperation with the Planetary Prince, who is the final authority of planetary affairs.

chakras The seven energy centers of the human body that are wheel-like vortexes that are considered sources of energy for psychic or spiritual power, known in Continuing Fifth Epochal Revelation as circuits.

change agent A Continuing Fifth Epochal Revelation term for an apostle in full-time spiritual ministry, who is aligned and functioning under the Mandate of the Bright and Morning Star.

change point See final change point.

Chief of Seraphim A primary supernaphim from Paradise stationed at the First Planetary Sacred Home on Urantia and in command of the twelve corps of Master Seraphim of Planetary Supervision and the seraphic hosts. The Chief of Seraphim first arrived on Urantia at the time of Pentecost, accompanying the first Governor General.

Christ Michael The Universe Father, Sovereign, and Creator Son of this universe of Nebadon. He earned His sovereignty by bestowing Himself seven times in the likeness of seven different orders of personalities in His own universe, reflecting the seven aspects of the Paradise Trinity. In His last bestowal, He came to Urantia to portray the nature of the Universal Father. He fulfilled the Fourth Epochal Revelation to this planet 2,000 years ago in the life of Jesus of Nazareth. Among the 700,000 Creator Sons in the grand universe, Christ Michael was the only Creator Son that was put to death by His own creatures. After His seventh bestowal He poured out the Spirit of Truth for the benefit of His entire universe. Continuing Fifth Epochal Revelation teaches that He is expected to soon return to this planet as He promised.

circles See psychic circles.

circuits Of or relating to the various Paradise circuits of both upper and nether Paradise that connect, via the Salvington circuit of the Nebadon headquarters world of Christ Michael, to human mortals through the various circuits within the body, the main ones being previously known as chakras in lower teachings. The reopening of these Paradise circuits to evolutionary mortals is Continuing Fifth Epochal Revelation.

complementary polarities Personalities of similar spiritual status who function in pairs, usually male and female, but in some cases can be two males or two females.

Constellation Fathers Name for those Vorondadek Sons (local universe Sons of God) who rule the constellation governments of the universes. There are one million Vorondadeks in our local universe of Nebadon. Our constellation, Norlatiadek, is ruled by twelve Vorondadek Sons.

Continuing Fifth Epochal Revelation The continuation of the Fifth Epochal Revelation (*The URANTIA Book* is only one-tenth of it), which is now coming through the Audio Fusion Material Complement Gabriel of Urantia/TaliasVan of Tora.

cosmic brothers/sisters Males and females who had the same cosmic father or cosmic mother, or both cosmic parents, in a former life.

cosmic children See cosmic sons/daughters

cosmic family A genetically related family of ascending sons and daughters. They are generally of origin in universes outside Nebadon but include Urantians with extraplanetary genetics, usually related to a finaliter. At present there are seven cosmic families on Urantia coming from four different universes.

cosmic name A new and more spiritually potent name attributed to an ascending soul by a qualified cosmic ancestor, such as the finaliter Paladin or his son Gabriel of Urantia/TaliasVan of Tora. The new name can open the consciousness of the benefactor and significant others to a higher state of ascension in a former life or to a higher destiny purpose in the present life or both. There are very distinct characteristics carried in the sounds, accents, and syllables of the spoken cosmic name including personality bestowal, genetic heritage, and cosmic family relationships.

cosmic parents The parents a soul has in his or her very first life, whether originating on this planet or on another world.

cosmic relatives Cosmic family members linked through their interuniversal genetics from various Creator Sons, Material Sons and Daughters, and finaliters.

Cosmic Reserve Corps of Destiny A group of ovan souls on Urantia who function under the guidance of various entities, such as midwayers and seraphim, to bring cosmic consciousness to the planet and are called to serve in the Machiventa Melchizedek Administration in various capacities in order to fulfill their destiny purpose. These souls are members of one of the seven cosmic families presently sojourning on Urantia. All Cosmic Reservists are called to the First Planetary Sacred Home for further training.

cosmic son or daughter The children that one has been the biological parent of in their very first life, whether on this planet or in another universe.

CosmoPop® TaliasVan's unique form of Global Change Music performed with his Bright & Morning Star Band. CosmoPop® is universally hip, popular spiritual vocal music that addresses soul ascension and global humanitarian issues. CosmoPop® includes various styles such as CosmoRock™, CosmoCeltic™, CosmoFolk™, CosmoJazz™, and CosmoMystic™. His vocal style is a mystical experience. The music incorporates various modern rhythms and moods with future expressions. It opens the memory circuits of starseed.

Creator Son A personality of Paradise origin, created by the Universal Father and the Eternal Son, belonging to the order of Michael. Together with a Creative Daughter, a Creator Son is the creator of a local universe of time and space. There are 700,000 local universes. To gain full sovereignty over His universe, a Creator Son bestows Himself seven times in the likeness of the created personalities on various levels in His own creation, reflecting one of the aspects of the Paradise Trinity, after which He earns the title of "Master Son." A Creator Son does not live the life of a mortal man to die for humankind's sins but to reveal the loving nature of the Paradise Father.

Dalamatians The inhabitants of the original Planetary Headquarters city founded by Caligastia, Urantia's first Planetary Prince, 500,000 years ago, on a peninsula since submerged in the Persian Gulf. Dalamatia was named after Daligastia, Caligastia's assistant. The many legends about Atlantis and the sons of God mating with the daughters of men go back to the time of Dalamatia.

Deo Good; godly; of God.

Deo-atomic A term designating atomic structure in alignment with God, as in Deo-atomic cells (which are cells aligned with Paradise absolutes and are the cells of the morontia or light body).

Deo-atomic reflectivity Manifestible and negotiable features of God the Father, God the Son, and God the Spirit that are transmissible through the divine mind circuits of the Infinite Spirit to all beings concerned in the outworkings of the vast scheme of universal divine mind intelligence. One of the miraculous thrills of Deo-atomic reflectivity coming of age on a world entering light and life is the power of lower universe creatures becoming reflective of the nature, and to some extent the presence, of the higher divine orders of being.

Deo function A function in administration based upon one's virtue and desire to serve. The value of the Deo function and the Deo power within that function depends upon experience, wisdom, and higher ascension as well as the Deo function power of those in authority above one.

Deo power Power used within divine mandates and administration in accordance with the character and will of God.

dio Erroneous; evil; ungodly; not of God; out of divine pattern.

dio power The power of self-assertion, self-exaltation, greed, and other rebellious attitudes.

diotribes A Continuing Fifth Epochal Revelation term referring to negative or harmful particles in the human body due to wrong thinking induced by the individual's acquiescence to Luciferic thought patterns. They are the cause of disease in the human body.

Divine Administration Personal and authoritative outreach of God and His laws to all His creation and creatures via a vast and marvelous hierarchy of divine and celestial beings. Divine Administration begins in the perfect relationships within the Paradise Trinity and the divine family of beings, is coordinated on Paradise, and directed outwards to the created universes. It is the ministry of Paradise love, regard, and guidance poured out upon Havona, superuniverse, local universe, constellation, planetary system, and even planetary levels. With the appointment of Machiventa Melchizedek as Planetary Prince, Urantia now has the unique opportunity of implementing human representative government in reflectivity to, and coordination with, Divine Administration.

divine mind The mind of God the Father, the First Source and Center. All beings, spirit and mortal, derive their mind from the divine mind. Within the divine mind there is always the perfect plan for the unfolding master universe and all will creatures.

Divine New Order communities Communities of ascending sons and daughters spiritually aligned with the Divine Administration of Machiventa Melchizedek on Urantia and functioning within the seven sacred/protected areas being established as administrative sectors of the planet.

divine Trinity administration A pattern of overcontrol on material, mindal, and spiritual levels that is established and implemented on Paradise with the three Paradise Deities—the Universal Father, the Eternal Son, and the Infinite Spirit—that is then practiced throughout the grand universe, which includes the central universe of Havona, the seven superuniverses of time and space, and the outer space levels. Though this pattern is adapted to each situation within the grand universe, there is always the foundation of God's administration of love, mercy, and justice that is used in the divine administration principles and practices that are applied in each situation.

Eldership Hierarchy of human leadership on Urantia under the authority of the Bright and Morning Star and the human overcontrol of Gabriel of Urantia/TaliasVan of Tora and Niánn Emerson Chase, including the Liaison Ministers at the top, then those titled as Elders, First Assistants, and Vicegerent First Ambassadors.

encoded To be encoded means a special genetic infusion by Celestial Overcontrol at birth of some extraordinary trait that goes well beyond the soul's astral ability to have or know. An example would be a musical or scientific skill.

energy reflective circuits A Continuing Fifth Epochal Revelation term designating energy fields on a planet that allow for interdimensional communication and transportation. Also known in lower-level terminology as vortexes.

epochal revelation A revelation designed for the uplifting of an entire planet as distinguished from revelation to specific individuals or groups. There have been only five epochal revelations on Urantia to date, all having to do with the sorting and censuring of the successive religions of evolution, each ever-expanding and more enlightening.

— The First Epochal Revelation was inaugurated 500,000 years ago when the Planetary Prince, Caligastia, established Dalamatia, the first Planetary Headquarters on Urantia.
— The Second Epochal Revelation occurred thirty-eight thousand years ago with the advent of Adam and Eve.
— The Third Epochal Revelation came approximately at the time of Abraham with the arrival of Machiventa Melchizedek.
— The Fourth Epochal Revelation was fulfilled when the Creator Son of our local universe, Christ Michael, bestowed Himself as a human mortal, Jesus of Nazareth, to portray the nature of His Paradise Father.
— *The URANTIA Book* is the first one-tenth of the Fifth Epochal Revelation to the evolving races of Urantia. Continuing Fifth Epochal Revelation (the other nine-tenths) is now in progress through the Audio Fusion Material Complement, Gabriel of Urantia/TaliasVan of Tora.

Eternal Son The second person of the Paradise Trinity, co-creator with the Universal Father and Infinite Spirit. Not to be confused with a Creator Son of a local universe

existential reality Relating to God eternal, without beginning or ending. There is no time that He did not exist and He has full knowledge without experience.

experiential reality Relating to that part of God that grows through experience. This includes the experiences of all personalities in time and space. The Supreme Being is the personalization of all universe experience.

experimental planet One planet in ten is used by the Life Carriers for experimental purposes to produce new and improved variations in the evolutionary life plasm. Also called a decimal planet. Urantia is a decimal, experimental planet.

Continuing Fifth Epochal Revelation teaches that Urantia is unique in having humans who are being trained in Divine Administration.

Fanoving Name of a neighboring universe. Some of the fourth-order starseed come from Fanoving where they fell for the sophistries of the Lucifer Rebellion. Many have repersonalized on Urantia over the centuries and are here now for the adjudication.

Father-circuited An entity who is encircuited in and manifests the essence of the Universal Father. In humans, both males and females have Father circuitry, but the normal male is more Father-circuited.

fifth dimension See third dimension, fourth dimension, fifth dimension.

Fifth Epochal Revelation *The URANTIA Book* is the first one-tenth of the Fifth Epochal Revelation to the evolving races of Urantia. Continuing Fifth Epochal Revelation (as found in *The Cosmic Family* volumes) is now in progress through the Audio Fusion Material Complement, Gabriel of Urantia/TaliasVan of Tora. The living revelation is revealed and actualized in the lives of the ascending sons and daughters who have aligned with the Divine Administration of the Planetary Prince, Machiventa Melchizedek, under the Mandate of the Bright and Morning Star of Salvington, and are trying to walk in the perfect will of God on a moment-to-moment basis.

final change point The instant of time in which Urantia moves from the third to the fourth dimension completely. Only the First to Third Radii of Planetary Headquarters reflect fourth-dimensional reality to some degree. After the change point, only those personalities who have also manifested fourth-dimensional bodies will be able to return to and remain on Urantia.

finaliters Ascending mortal or nonmortal sons or daughters who have ascended from their planet of origin through the local universe, the superuniverse, the central universe of Havona, and have reached Paradise. After having been embraced by the three Paradise Trinity personalities, these ascenders have been mustered into the Mortal Corps of the Finality. Finaliters are sent off on assignments in the superuniverses of time and space and are always involved when a planet is about to move into the first stage of light and life. Paladin became Chief of Finaliters on Urantia in January 1992. He is the head of the First Cosmic Family.

First Ambassadors See Ambassadors.

First Assistants See Assistants.

First Cosmic Family A family of ascending sons and daughters, mostly of origin in the Pleiades, but containing interrelated members from the other six cosmic families presently on Urantia. The First Cosmic Family is the most closely involved with planetary administration and is responsible for gathering the other six cosmic families. The First Cosmic Family is headquartered at the First Planetary Sacred Home in Tubac/Tumacácori, Arizona, USA. The finaliter Paladin is the head of the First Cosmic Family.

First Epochal Revelation The first of five epochal (planetary) revelations to Urantia. Occurred beginning 500,000 years ago when the first Planetary Prince of Urantia, Caligastia, arrived with his staff of 100 ascendant Jerusem citizens and established Planetary Headquarters in Dalamatia. For 300,000 years the planetary staff, which included a large number of angelic cooperators and a host of other celestial beings, worked to advance the interests and promote the welfare of the human races. This revelation to the primitive people centered on the First Source and Center (God the Father) and was promulgated until the Lucifer Rebellion broke out.

First Planetary Sacred Home Planetary Headquarters of the celestial Divine Administration. The first of these headquarters on Urantia was Dalamatia at the time of Caligastia's arrival 500,000 years ago. The second planetary headquarters was the Garden of Eden at the time of Adam and Eve 38,000 years ago. The third was the schools of Salem at the time of Machiventa Melchizedek approximately 4,000 years ago. The fourth was wherever Jesus was 2,000 years ago. At present, it is located where the Planetary Prince, Machiventa Melchizedek, resides in Arizona, USA.

first stage of light and life The first of seven successive stages of an inhabited, evolutionary world becoming progressively more settled in spiritual attainments and refined existence levels reflecting divine pattern in all ways.

first-time Urantian A new soul whose planet of origin is Urantia and whose present life is the very first existence of that soul. Most people on this planet are first-time Urantians.

fourth dimension See third dimension, fourth dimension, fifth dimension.

Fragment of the Father An actual fragment of the Universal Father that indwells the mind of every mortal with a normal mind. It is the spirit nucleus that, with the cooperation of that mind, creates the soul. It is the destiny of the soul to fuse with the Fragment of the Father and ascend to Paradise.

fusion Merging of diverse essences, entities, phenomena, or elements into a unified whole. In the ascension process, there can be a soul-spirit fusion between an evolutionary mortal and a higher celestial being or a personality fusion between an ascender and a Thought Adjuster. It can involve a fusion of the past and the present in relationship to the experiential reality or a fusion of semi-spirit and spirit reality in relationship to inter-dimensional reality, both material and non-material.

Gabriel of Salvington First-born son of Christ Michael and the Universe Mother Spirit, also called the Bright and Morning Star. It was Gabriel of Salvington who appeared to Mary to announce she had been chosen to become the human mother of Jesus.

Gabriel of Urantia/TaliasVan of Tora Co-founder and leader of Divine Administration (Global Community Communications Alliance and its affiliates), mortal head of the First Cosmic Family on Urantia, and holder, with his complement Niánn Emerson Chase, of the highest mandate of God for mortals on the planet, the Mandate of the Bright and Morning Star. He is the only audio fusion material complement on Urantia.

Gabron and Niánn Primary midwayers on the present staff of Machiventa Melchizedek assisting in the implementation of the Divine Administration in and through human personalities.

Garden of Eden The site of the second Planetary Headquarters on Urantia, founded nearly 38,000 years ago by Adam and Eve, the Material Son and Daughter, on a since-submerged peninsula extending into the Mediterranean Sea from the area of present-day Lebanon. After the default of Adam and Eve, a second Garden of Eden was established in Mesopotamia, between the Tigris and Euphrates rivers. Now a third Garden of Eden is developing at the First Planetary Sacred Home in Tubac/Tumacácori, Arizona, USA.

Global Change Music[TM] Global Change Music lyrics speak of a Spiritualution[SM] — Justice to the People concept of a spiritual revolution (where spirituality means social action, not pious, hypocritical religiosity). The lyrics speak of taking action against any form of those injustices where the people are oppressed. Global Change Music promotes sustainable living, which includes growing your own organic food, building green, permaculture, sharing services and goods (trade and barter), and having a protective environmental consciousness. The music itself can be any genre, however, the musicians must live their message of national and international radical changes.

Global Community Communications Schools Formerly called the Extension Schools of Melchizedek and later The Starseed and Urantian Schools of Melchizedek, these schools focus on Divine Administration principles reflective of the self-governing taught by the Melchizedeks. Adult courses incorporate the highest truths from many world religions as well as continuing epochal revelation. The two school programs for teens and children are a home school cooperative and a parochial school.

Global Community Communications Alliance See section titled "Global Community Communications Alliance and Divine Administration" at the back of this book.

Governor General of Urantia A formerly rotating one-hundred-year assignment amongst the Council of Twenty-four (prior to December 1989 when Machiventa Melchizedek was officially inaugurated as Planetary Prince of Urantia) wherein the designated council member served as the mortal coordinator of all superhuman planetary affairs, acting more as a fatherly advisor than a technical ruler.

grand universe The inhabited part of the master universe, which includes the eternal central universe of Havona of one billion unique and perfect worlds and the seven evolutionary superuniverses of time and space, which include 700,000 local universes, created by the Creator Sons and Creative Daughters.

Havona The name of the central universe surrounding Paradise, which functions as the pattern for the time–space universes. Havona consists of one billion unique and perfect worlds. It is part of the destiny of mortals to go through all these billion perfect worlds before reaching Paradise.

heart circuit The circuit within the body that is connected to Christ Michael and where the Spirit of Truth is first activated. Students at The Starseed and Urantian Schools of Melchizedek [a.k.a. Global Community Communications Schools of

Ascension Science & The Physics of Rebellion] are given more information about this and other circuits.

highest complementary polarities A mortal male and female pair who have reached the highest spiritual relationship (sometimes called twin flames) usually leading to procreation of higher starseed children. For ovan souls these mates may be on another planet. Usually there is only one highest complement but not always.

Holy Spirit The ministering spirit circuit of the Universe Mother Spirit, not to be confused with the third person of the Paradise Deities (the Infinite Spirit) or the Spirit of Truth poured out at Pentecost (which is the Spirit of the Creator Son, Christ Michael).

Hopi Fifth World The Native American Hopi people believe that the present Fourth World of materialism will be destroyed by disease, crime, nuclear holocaust, and cataclysms, and the Fifth World will be created by good and peaceful "Hopis"—one world, one nation, under the power of the Massau'u (Creator of All). The Hopis believe that the emergence of the Fifth World has begun with the appearance of people all over the world (the cosmic families), who with courage and humility follow the "song" of the Creator, and that all must come to a higher perception of truth to lead us into a Divine New Order.

Infinite Spirit Third person of the Paradise Trinity, not to be confused with Holy Spirit, which is the spirit circuit of the Universe Mother Spirit of a local universe. The Infinite Spirit is the Mother aspect of God.

interplanetary receiver A being in the spiritual chain of command who receives interplanetary and interdimensional messages and transmits them to the people on the planet.

interuniversal marriage / polyfidelity A triad marriage relationship between one ascending son and two ascending daughters of different universes, where there is fidelity between him and each woman. He may or may not have sexual intimacy with one of these women, as in any normal marriage relationship. This is a higher form of spiritual relationships within long-term, committed loving relations, not based on fleeting and sexual desires. On Urantia, there have not been successful interuniversal marriages with polyfidelity, as the spiritual maturity required has not been attained by the individuals involved or the masses.

Jesus The man of Nazareth, Son of Man, incarnated Creator Son Christ Michael of Nebadon, who bestowed Himself upon Urantia 2,000 years ago to earn His sovereignty and to portray the nature of the Universal Father, fulfilling the Fourth Epochal Revelation to this planet. And it is also literally true that this Paradise Creator Son of God, when He was Jesus of Nazareth, promised that He would someday return to Urantia.

John the Baptist The forerunner of Michael's mission on Urantia and, in the flesh, distant cousin of the Son of Man. John was the extraordinary Jewish preacher and prophet of the first century who dressed like Elijah of old and thundered admonitions for all to repent and make ready for the end of the age, proclaiming that the kingdom of heaven was at hand. After the death of John the Baptist, Jesus began His public work. John the Baptist along with Elijah and Enoch are members of the Twenty-four Counselors on Jerusem who are now resident at the First Planetary Sacred Home on Urantia.

ley lines Grid lines of energy between energy reflective circuits used for communication and transportation.

Liaison Ministers Those holding the second highest Mandate of the Bright and Morning Star in reflectivity to Brilliant Evening Stars, who act as liaison officers in human overcontrol between the Bright and Morning Star Mandate and the Machiventa Melchizedek mandated personalities. The Liaison Ministers also function as Elders on the Inner Board of Divine Administration.

Life Carriers Local universe Sons of God who implant and foster life on the evolutionary worlds. They are created by the Creator Son, Universe Mother Spirit, and one Ancient of Days.

light and life One of the marvelous successive ages of physical security, intellectual expansion, and spiritual achievement for evolutionary worlds to be settled in as the inhabitants achieve more heavenly values and relationships in God. There are typically seven stages of light and life that an evolutionary world evolves through; our world Urantia is currently in the pre-stages of light and life.

light body See morontia body.

Lucifer A Lanonandek Son, the fallen System Sovereign of Satania, who led a rebellion against his Creator Father, Christ Michael, which involved thirty-seven planets in the system of Satania, including Urantia. Lucifer's Manifesto was about unbridled personal liberty, rejection of universe allegiance, and disregard of fraternal obligations and cosmic relationships. Since the bestowal of Christ Michael on Urantia as Jesus of Nazareth 2,000 years ago, Lucifer has been imprisoned and awaits his final adjudication. Although many of today's currently-accepted teachings contain some truth, they are sprinkled with very deceptive Luciferic lies.

Lucifer Rebellion A rebellion led by Lucifer 200,000 years ago in Satania. Thirty-seven of the 619 inhabited worlds in the system participated. It involved many personalities of various celestial orders as well as mortals. On Urantia an adjudication by the Bright and Morning Star began early in the twentieth century and is expected to be completed in the twenty-first century. Many fallen starseed had to repersonalize on Urantia at the present time for this adjudication.

Machiventa Melchizedek Planetary Prince of Urantia since December 1989. This same Melchizedek, who belongs to a high order of local universe Sons, incarnated in the likeness of mortal flesh and lived on Urantia for ninety-four years during the time of Abraham and was known as the Prince of Salem. Machiventa Melchizedek came on an emergency mission when the spiritual light on Urantia was almost extinguished and taught the one-God concept. He brought the Third Epochal Revelation to this world. He established a school where missionaries were trained who later brought his teachings to all parts of the world. Now The Starseed and Urantian Schools of Melchizedek [a.k.a. Global Community Communications Schools of Ascension Science & The Physics of Rebellion] at the First Planetary Sacred Home in Tubac/Tumacácori, Arizona, USA, are again training teachers to bring the Fifth and Continuing Fifth Epochal Revelation to the rest of the planet.

mandate An authorization to act, given to a representative. In Continuing Fifth Epochal Revelation this refers particularly to human personalities authorized to represent Divine Administration authority on the planet.

Mandate of the Bright and Morning Star The universe directive from Christ Michael, Creator and Sovereign of the universe of Nebadon, authorizing His Chief Administrator, Gabriel (the Bright and Morning Star of Salvington) to adjudicate the Lucifer Rebellion, beginning with our planet Urantia. Under this mandate is the authority to reinstate Divine Administration on Urantia through the highest complementary-polarity couple on the planet—the Audio Fusion Material Complement Gabriel of Urantia/TaliasVan of Tora and Niánn Emerson Chase—in cooperation with the present Planetary Prince, Machiventa Melchizedek, and the human representatives of the seven cosmic families. This mandate includes bringing through Continuing Fifth Epochal Revelation, healing of the various bodies, and the authority to train and mandate humans to administrative positions in Divine Administration to help all humanity meet their God-given destinies.

Gabriel of Urantia/TaliasVan of Tora is the repersonalization/ incarnation of the soul of Van of *The URANTIA Book*, Peter the Apostle, Francis of Assisi, and other souls of history who have created renaissances, regathered separated tribes into one people, and seeded the beginning of higher social service to the citizens of many nations. Other apostles and other special souls called Destiny Reservists, who are new souls and older souls with a specific life-mission to accomplish, have come to Divine Administration from five continents to help in the global change of this planet. This information is given to help you find your highest destiny in God so that you can become a higher servant to humanity.

mansion worlds Morontia training worlds in the system of Satania that souls normally go to sometime after their physical death. They are situated near the system capital and have been provided to overcome mortal deficiencies. After the final change point, Urantia will function as another mansion world.

master universe The universe of universes, including the eternal central universe of Havona, the seven evolutionary superuniverses of time and space, plus the presently mobilizing but uninhabited four outer space levels.

material complement The highest order of interplanetary and interdimensional receiver of communication. They also function as conduits of universal energies transmitted to them by higher celestial personalities. One mandated in reflectivity to a celestial personality.

Material Sons and Daughters The highest type of sex-reproducing beings in a local universe, the Adams and Eves, who are the biological uplifters of the evolutionary races, physically present in administrative capacity under a Planetary Prince. They are the founders of the violet race. Usually only the progeny of the Material Sons and Daughters procreate with mortals.

mediumship The lowest and least accurate form of interdimensional communication, which, since 1989, is entirely limited to contacts with fallen entities.

Melchizedeks A high order of local universe Sons. They function in many capacities but mainly as teachers and emergency ministers. Ever since the Lucifer Rebellion and the Caligastia betrayal, twelve Melchizedeks have been guarding the spiritual evolution on our planet. In 1989 one of these twelve Melchizedeks, Machiventa Melchizedek, became our new Planetary Prince.

memory circuits Pathways of the mental processing system that registers, modifies, stores, and retrieves that which is being, or has been, experienced or learned.

Michael The order of Michael is an order of Paradise Creator Sons (created by the Universal Father and the Eternal Son) who, in cooperation with the local Universe Mother Spirits, create the 700,000 evolutionary universes of time and space.

Midwayer Commission A delegation of twelve midwayers from the Brotherhood of the United Midwayers of Urantia, who were officially assigned to portray the life and teachings of Jesus (Part IV of *The URANTIA Book*). Now they are working in cooperation with Celestial Overcontrol to help bring through the Continuing Fifth Epochal Revelation.

midwayers Unique beings about midway between mortals and angels. They are the permanent citizens of an evolutionary world. Primary midwayers are the offspring of the rematerialized staff of the former Planetary Prince, Caligastia. Secondary midwayers on Urantia are descendants of Adamson (firstborn of Adam and Eve) and Ratta (pure-line descendant of the Caligastia One Hundred). During the time of the Lucifer Rebellion the majority of the primary midwayers went into sin. Many of the secondary midwayers also failed to align with the rule of Michael of Nebadon.

At the time of Pentecost they were interned and held into custody, but since 1989 and the arrival of Machiventa Melchizedek as the new Planetary Prince, they have been freed and given another chance to align with the Divine Administration. Unfortunately not all have done so, and many are still communicating with lower channels, teaching Luciferic concepts in a very deceptive way, causing much confusion even among some *URANTIA Book* readers, who refuse to align themselves with the Machiventa Melchizedek Administration. They are soon to be adjudicated.

Mighty Messengers A class of perfected mortals who have been rebellion tested or otherwise equally proven as to their personal loyalty; all have passed through a definite test of universe loyalty. After having ascended to Paradise and having been embraced by the Paradise Trinity, they are sent out on assignments of all phases of universe activities. Several papers of *The URANTIA Book* were authored by a Mighty Messenger.

mind Organized consciousness that can be classified as physical, mindal, or spiritual. In human life, the adjutant mind spirits and celestial beings associate with the mindal mind, the Thought Adjuster associates with the spiritual mind, while the physical mind is involved in the physical aspects of life. It is in the physical mind that the power of choice has developed.

morontia A level of local universe reality between the material and spiritual levels of creature existence. The human soul is an experiential acquirement that is created by a creature choosing to do the will of the Father in heaven. This new reality that is created by the cooperation of the mortal mind with the divine spirit is a morontia reality that is destined to survive mortal death and begin the Paradise ascension.

morontia body The various body forms of the 570 ascending morontia levels of creature existence an ascending soul uses within the local universe. It is also known on Urantia as the light body. While souls usually receive a morontia body after death, it is possible to construct one by moving into Deo-atomic reality while living at Planetary Headquarters, being aligned with the Divine Government of the present Planetary Prince, Machiventa Melchizedek, and living in the perfect will of God moment-to-moment. Many variables are needed in order to attain a morontia body without passing through the death experience.

Morontia Companions Children of the local Universe Mother Spirit who have been created especially to serve as friends and associates of all who live the ascending morontia life after death. These companions are touchingly affectionate and charmingly social beings.

morontia counseling A form of counseling that is concerned with spiritual progression, fulfillment of destiny purpose, and personality actualization of an ascending mortal, especially important to ovan souls during this time of adjudication to bring them back to their spiritual proficiency prior to their fall.

morontia progressors Ascending souls on any of the 570 levels of morontia life before they become full-fledged spirits. The morontia career actually begins on the planet of origin, and in the Nebadon ascension scheme there are 8 morontia body changes in the planetary system, 71 in the constellation, and 491 during the sojourn on the spheres of Salvington. All along the way, these souls are becoming more spiritual and less material in their natures.

Moses Hebrew prophet, lawgiver, and liberator of the Israelites from Egypt who lived approximately 1000 B.C. and is considered one of the greatest historical characters between Melchizedek and Jesus. The greatness of Moses lies in his wisdom and sagacity. Other men have had greater concepts of God, but no one man was ever so successful in inducing large numbers of people to adopt such advanced beliefs.

Mother-circuited Encircuited in and exhibiting the characteristics of the Universe Mother Spirit. In humans, both males and females have Mother circuitry, but the normal female is more Mother-circuited.

Nebadon The name of our local universe, the creation of Christ Michael, Universe Sovereign, and the Universe Mother Spirit. Salvington is its headquarters.

New Jerusalem A triune particle city that will also be the planetary headquarters of Urantia when the planet enters the first stage of light and life. Although the arrival of the New Jerusalem must await the whole planet's entrance into the settled age of light and life, implementation of the architectural design for the triune particle city is already in motion and will be realized at the First Planetary Sacred Home within the Machiventa Melchizedek Administration sometime after the final change point.

Niánn Emerson Chase Co-founder of Global Community Communications Alliance who shares the Mandate of the Bright and Morning Star with her complement Gabriel of Urantia/TaliasVan of Tora. Just as the highest Son/Mother representation and ministry in the local universe of Nebadon is that of the Bright and Morning Star of Salvington bonded with the highest Evening Star, so is the highest dual ministry of administrative divine power on Urantia reflected in the complementary polarity of Gabriel of Urantia/TaliasVan of Tora bonded with Niánn Emerson Chase.

Onamonalonton A leader of the red race in the distant past who advocated veneration of the Great Spirit and who subsequently become one of the Twenty-four Counselors on Jerusem.

Orvonton The name of the superuniverse in which our local universe of Nebadon exists. It is superuniverse #7 of the seven superuniverses included in the grand universe and is roughly equivalent to what Urantia astronomers call the Milky Way galaxy. Uversa is its headquarters. Orvonton is ruled by three Ancients of Days. Orvonton is destined to reflect the nature and wills of the three Paradise Deities. Because it is more difficult to do this, Orvonton has had more rebellions than any other superuniverse and has been called "the superuniverse of mercy."

ovan souls Souls who have survived the initial experience of mortal planetary existence and who have attained the morontia consciousness equivalent of the first mansion world and the realization of Paradise circuitry in a morontia body.

Paladin A finaliter who became Chief of Finaliters on Urantia in January 1992. He is the head of the First Cosmic Family and the cosmic father of Gabriel of Urantia/TaliasVan of Tora. Paladin, who fuses with and speaks through Gabriel/TaliasVan, is the chief spokesperson for celestial personalities bringing Continuing Fifth Epochal Revelation to Urantia. Paladin first introduced himself to Gabriel/TaliasVan as Sky Hawk because Gabriel/TaliasVan has had several repersonalizations on Urantia as a Native American.

Paradise The abiding place of the Universal Father, Eternal Son, and Infinite Spirit. This eternal Isle is the absolute source of the physical universes—past, present, and future. It is the universal headquarters of all personality activities and the source-center of all force-space and energy manifestations. It is the geographic center of infinity and the only stationary thing in the master universe. It is the goal of all ascending sons and daughters to ascend to Paradise.

personality The presence of the Universal Father in His personality circuitry that is destined to have an endless love affair with Deity and which, like Deity, is characterized by volition and unity. As unifiers, Deity and personality each act at the level of the total. Deity always seeks manifestation as personality, and it does this on the levels of the prepersonal, personal, and superpersonal, all of which manifest phases of volition. While personality strives to unify the physical, mindal, and spiritual realities within the realm of its influence, Deity endeavors to join the personality of its association with other Deity-associated personalities and with itself.

physics of rebellion An aspect of the science and study of rebellion from God and divine pattern as expressed in physics. There is literally a measurable scientific set of equations and phenomena associated with the outworking of rebellion in souls and their bodies as well as the worlds they inhabit.

Planetary Prince The spiritual ruler of an inhabited world in time and space. The first Planetary Prince of Urantia, Caligastia, arrived approximately 500,000 years ago with his assistant Daligastia. Their headquarters was Dalamatia in the Persian Gulf region. The Planetary staff included a large number of angelic cooperators and a host of other celestial beings assigned to advance the interests and promote the welfare of the human races. He also had a corporeal staff of one hundred. Unfortunately Caligastia chose the side of Lucifer during the Rebellion. In A.D. 1989 Machiventa Melchizedek became Planetary Prince and has his headquarters in Tubac/Tumacácori, Arizona, USA. Christ Michael also earned the title of Planetary Prince of Urantia after His seventh bestowal 2,000 years ago, during which He lived the life of the human mortal Jesus of Nazareth.

Pleiades A cluster of stars in the constellation of Taurus. Continuing Fifth Epochal Revelation teaches that they are not stars but planets settled in light and life. Most of the First Cosmic Family come originally from the Pleiades or have Pleiadian genetics.

psychic circles The seven levels of personality realization on a material world. Entry on the seventh circle marks the beginning of true human personality function. Completion of the first circle denotes the relative maturity of the mortal being. Destiny Reservists at the First Planetary Sacred Home who are on the third psychic circle receive an angel of enlightenment.

reflectivity The reflection in mandated humans of the personality virtues of nondivine celestial counterparts, such as the Bright and Morning Star, Brilliant Evening Stars, Melchizedeks, seraphim, etc.

rematerialization One of several techniques providing a physical body for a personality of another dimension. The Caligastia One Hundred were rematerialized when they arrived from the system capital 500,000 years ago as the staff of the now former Planetary Prince Caligastia.

repersonalization A term used in Continuing Fifth Epochal Revelation to describe the transfer of ascending mortal ovan souls back into third-dimensional reality through the birthing technique for specific destiny purposes. Some members of the Cosmic Reserve Corps of Destiny have repersonalized on this planet in all of the major spiritual renaissances. Gabriel of Urantia/TaliasVan of Tora writes about some of these in this book. With the exception of about two thousand second-time Urantians, who for undisclosed reasons have for the first time been allowed to repersonalize, these souls come originally from other universes where the ascension schemes are different from that of this universe. In Nebadon souls, as a rule, do not return to their planet of origin. Not to be confused with the erroneous earthly concepts of reincarnation.

Reserve Corps of Destiny A corps of living men and women who have been admitted to the special service of the superhuman administration mainly to assure against breakdown of evolutionary progress. There are Cosmic Reservists (starseed from other worlds) and Urantian Reservists (natives of this world). Since the coming of the new Planetary Prince, Machiventa Melchizedek, all Destiny Reservists are called to the First Planetary Sacred Home in Tubac/Tumacácori, Arizona, USA, to receive further training in Divine Administration at Global Community Communications Schools of Ascension Science & The Physics of Rebellion.

sacred/protected areas These are areas of the planet near major energy reflective circuits set up by people who are aligned with the Machiventa Melchizedek Administration. There will be only seven major protected areas on the planet. Some secondary areas will also have a certain degree of protection. The degree of protection depends upon a person's level of alignment and virtue.

Salvington Salvington is the headquarters sphere of the universe of Nebadon, home of Christ Michael and the Universe Mother Spirit. Salvington was the first completed act of physical creation in Nebadon and took a little more than one billion years to complete. It is situated at the exact energy-mass center of the local universe. It is the destiny of ascending sons and daughters to sojourn on Salvington as part of their training and Paradise ascension. When a soul leaves Salvington he or she is a fully-fledged spirit.

Sananda The term "Sananda" is a title (but not name) for a highly respected spiritual teacher or master. It was the title of Christ Michael on another planet when He bestowed Himself as a Lanonandek Son and took the office of Planetary Prince. It is not the name of Christ Michael and never has been, not on this planet or any other. It is a title given to Machiventa Melchizedek, who became Planetary Prince of Urantia in 1989. People on Urantia who call themselves Sananda have no true connection to the Divine Administration of the Planetary Prince, Machiventa Melchizedek.

Satan First assistant to Lucifer, Satan was an able and brilliant primary Lanonandek Son. Both Lucifer and Satan had reigned on Jerusem for 500,000 years when they fell into rebellion against the Universal Father and His Son, Michael of Nebadon. Satan was sent by Lucifer to advocate the cause of the Rebellion on our planet. Satan was imprisoned after Michael's bestowal on Urantia and is awaiting his adjudication.

Satania The local system of inhabited worlds in which our planet Urantia is number 606. It was named after Satan,

Lucifer's assistant, long before they both went into rebellion 200,000 years ago.

Second Assistants See Assistants.

second-time Urantians A unique group of Urantians who were sleeping survivors and who—for the first time in the history of Urantia by decree of Christ Michael—have for undisclosed reasons been allowed to repersonalize on Urantia since the beginning of the twentieth century. Some of the first-century apostles have repersonalized and are second-time Urantians.

sector An administrative headquarters area and on Urantia a protected area in which a Divine New Order community is or will be established before and/or after the final change point. There will be seven sectors on this planet coordinated with the seven cosmic families of Urantia.

seraphic transport "All groups of ministering spirits have their transport corps, angelic orders dedicated to the ministry of transporting those personalities who are unable, of themselves, to journey from one sphere to another." [*The URANTIA Book*, p. 430] "The angels cannot transport combustion bodies—flesh and blood—such as you now have, but they can transport all others, from the lowest morontia to the higher spirit forms." [*The URANTIA Book*, p. 431] When enseraphimed, you go to sleep for a specified time, and you will awake at the designated moment. The Caligastia One Hundred came to Urantia 500,000 years ago by seraphic transport, after which their physical bodies were rematerialized. As material bodies cannot be transported by seraphic transport, they must be evacuated by dematerialization or spacecraft when a planet is no longer safe to live on.

seraphim Local universe angels who are of origin in the Universe Mother Spirit and are designated Ministering Spirits of the local universe. Seraphim are created slightly above the mortal level. Those assigned to the watchcare of ascending mortals are called Seraphic Guardians of Destiny. An angel of enlightenment can also serve as a destiny guardian.

sixth- and seventh-mansion-world progressors Ascending mortals sojourning on the higher of the seven mansion worlds, which are the beginning stages of morontia progression after leaving an evolutionary world. In Continuing Fifth Epochal Revelation, those who are called "ascended masters" by metaphysical and religious groups are in reality ovan souls who have in the past come from the sixth or seventh mansion world to Urantia for specific assignments.

soul A growing formulation of identity between the physical and the spiritual, also known as character, which is contactable by other souls but cannot be discovered by exclusive physical or spiritual testing. Growth of the soul (development of spiritual character) comes from the conscious attempt to follow the leading of the Thought Adjuster. Survival comes as personality relocates its seat of identity from the physical mind to the soul.

soul mates A New-Age term for complementary personalities who serve together harmoniously in some capacity.

Soul Watcher A Divine New Order community member who functions as household coordinator and watches over the overall well-being of his or her household.

spirit Supernatural extension of God's presence such as the indwelling Father Fragment that adjusts the human mind to progressively divine attitudes, along with the everywhere-active presence of the divine spirit of the Eternal Son. All pure unfragmented spirit and all spiritual beings and values are responsive to the infinite drawing power of the Eternal Son. Although all divine beings can be referred to as spirits, in the Infinite Spirit's functional family, the term 'spirit' is confined to the seven Supreme Spirit groups and the Ministering Spirits of Time. In general, spiritual beings occupy spirit space charged by spirit potency and inhabit spirit form made of spirit substance, carrying out numerous spirit activities, but they also inhabit material spheres and exist in relationship to physical space.

Spirit of Truth The spirit of Christ Michael bestowed on Urantia at Pentecost. It is experienced in human consciousness as the conviction of truth and needs to be continually activated by soul growth through a relationship with God and His will (not man's wishes) as opposed to religious doctrine. The Spirit of Truth should override false interpretations of any written scripture or text, be it the Bible, *The URANTIA Book*, or *The Cosmic Family* volumes. The Universe Mother Spirit acts as the universe focus and center of the Spirit of Truth as well as Her own personal influence, the Holy Spirit.

spiritualized mind The totality of experience in absolute truths pertinent to the decision-making process and relating to circumstantial reality at any point or sojourn in time and space. It takes into account all lives lived, genetic inheritance, and interuniversal genetics.

Spiritualution[SM] **— Justice To The People** A global spiritual-revolution, designed to inspire and influence millions to come out of the system of greed and organized and antiquated religions, and join communities, and grow their own food near a good water source, as Gabriel of Urantia/TaliasVan of Tora believes in the prophecies of the Hopis, Mayans, Nostradamus, the Prophets of the Old Testament, and the Book of Revelation that speak of the purification of the Earth Mother through drastic climate changes, which he believes are now happening and will continue to worsen.

star children Souls from other planets in other universes who repersonalize on Urantia or on other planets as part of their ascension career. Also called starseed.

starseed A term generally used on Urantia to designate mortals, originally from another universe, born of human parents through the repersonalization technique. There are seven orders of starseed. Much of the understanding of starseed in New-Age circles—in relation to "walk-ins," soul transference, space visitors, etc. who are presently on Urantia referred to as starseed—is Caligastia's confusion.

Starseed and Urantian Schools of Melchizedek See Global Community Communications Schools.

superuniverse One of the seven primary divisions of time and space in the grand universe, which contains 100,000 local universes comprising one trillion inhabited worlds and is presided over by three Ancients of Days. Every superuniverse is divided into ten major sectors. The name of our major sector is Splandon. Each major sector is divided into 100 minor sectors. The name of our minor sector is Ensa. Each minor sector is made up of 100 local universes. The name of our local universe is Nebadon.

system (generic grouping) A consistent and complex whole made up of correlated and interdependent parts. For example, a biological system can be the entire organism, a complex of structures anatomically and physiologically related, or a member or group within a species.

system (planetary grouping) An administrative grouping of evolutionary planets within time and space. A system ultimately will have 1,000 inhabited worlds settled in light and life. Each system is ruled by a System Sovereign, usually of the order of Lanonandek Sons. There are 100 local systems in a constellation. Jerusem is the headquarters world of our system, Satania, which is system number 24 in the constellation Norlatiadek. Sandmatia, Assuntia, Porogia, Sortoria, Rantulia, and Glantonia are six planetary systems in the neighborhood of Satania whose System Sovereigns are working closely with Lanaforge, System Sovereign of Satania, for the implementation of the first stages of light and life for our planet Urantia.

System Sovereign A primary Lanonandek Son who is the administrative head of a local system of 1,000 inhabited worlds. Although brilliant administrators, Lanonandeks have been prone to rebellion. Our System Sovereign in Satania is Lanaforge, who replaced Lucifer after his fall 200,000 years ago.

TaliasVan of Tora See Gabriel of Urantia/TaliasVan of Tora.

third dimension, fourth dimension, and fifth dimension Three currently available and contemporary levels of individual and mass consciousness in the fusion between mind and spirit, which can be clearly differentiated today as Urantia moves from the pre-stages of light and life into higher planetary dispensations.

— The third dimension is the time-present level of self-consciousness in growing comprehension of breadth, height, and depth of mathematical and logical coordination; the pre-mind dominated time-and-space orientation.
— The fourth dimension is the time-coordinate level of group-consciousness that merges mathematics and logic with morality and brotherhood; mind-spirit directed space-time orientation.
— The fifth dimension is the time-transcending level of spirit awareness that integrates the spirit and non-spirit mind into organic and inorganic coordinate purpose; spirit-mind and body fusion within causal design. Even though Continuing Fifth Epochal Revelation can bring fourth-, fifth-, sixth-, and higher dimensional reality to ascenders on Urantia, one cannot formulate a higher body on any level until one begins to spiritualize in some form of three-dimensional thought.

Third Garden of Eden Geographic location of the present First Planetary Sacred Home, wherein complementary polarities of higher ascension status function near one another on a daily basis tapping into Paradise circuitry coming out from Paradise to create a new reality in which ascending mortals on Urantia can achieve kinetic fusion with higher dimensional reality and higher celestial beings and settle into the first stages of light and life.

The First Garden of Eden was prepared by Van (TaliasVan of Tora) and his associates as the place of abode for the arriving Material Son and Daughter (Adam and Eve), biological uplifters, to begin their sojourn and work on evolutionary Urantia. The Second Eden was the cradle of civilization for almost 30,000 years. The Third Eden, founded by Gabriel of Urantia/TaliasVan of Tora and Niánn Emerson Chase, is the regathering site for all seven cosmic families of Urantia wherein personalities within the higher circles of attainment can come to understand each other at a fourth-dimensional and higher level, thereby stabilizing their personalities within the mind circuit for the opening of memory circuits, the activation of certain abilities, and the recovering of certain talents for the good of all in the system of Satania.

Thought Adjusters Prepersonal fragments of the Universal Father that indwell normal minds of human mortals. It is through the Thought Adjusters that the Universal Father has personal communion with mortal beings. Fusion with the Thought Adjuster guarantees eternal survival. Also called Mystery Monitors.

Tora The third planet from Alcyone in the Pleiades and the point of origin, at least in the superuniverse of Orvonton, of the finaliter Paladin and certain members of the First Cosmic Family on Urantia.

Tree of Life Originally a shrub of Edentia (the capital of our constellation Norlatiadek) sent to Urantia by the Most Highs with the arrival of the Caligastia One Hundred. The fruit of this tree provided indefinite life to otherwise material bodies via the system's life-sustainable energies and currents.

Triad-Unit I A complementary relationship between an ascending son and two ascending daughters in which the ascending son has children with both.

Triad-Unit II The same thing as Triad-Unit I, without children with one or both.

trimonad family A relationship between a husband and wife living together but celibate with each other. The husband still will be having children with another wife. In this case Niánn Emerson Chase is Gabriel of Urantia/TaliasVan of Tora's highest spiritual complement and co-shares the Mandate of the Bright and Morning Star with him.

trimonad unit A complementary relationship between an ascending son and two ascending daughters in which the ascending son is not sexually involved with one of the ascending daughters.

Trinity Teacher Sons Paradise Sons of Trinity origin who appear on an evolutionary world when the time is ripe to initiate a spiritual age. They are the exalted teachers of all spirit personalities.

tron therapist Mandated therapist who will use a psychospiritual therapy that will restore broken circuitry within the body, remove diotribes, and will be a touch therapy destined to replace surgery. It will be done only in conjunction with psychospiritual counseling and will involve the permanent healing of all bodies—the astral, etheric, and physical—for those who are in alignment with their God. Tron therapy will be available only at the First Planetary Sacred Home through mandated therapists.

twin flames New-Age term for complementary polarities.

Union of Days Trinity-origin Sons of God who represent the Paradise Trinity as advisors to the Creator Sons of the local universes of time and space. The Union of Days associated with Christ Michael of Nebadon is named Immanuel.

union of souls A group consciousness reflecting the ideals and status of ethical relationships and functioning in the realm of harmonious teamwork. Also a descriptive name of a group of ministering spirits of the order of secondary seconaphim, the Union of Souls.

Universal Father The first person of the Paradise Trinity; Creator, Controller, and Upholder of all creation. The Universal Father desires to have communion with mortals through the prepersonal fragments of Himself, the Thought Adjusters, who indwell the normal human mind. He also has reserved the prerogative to bestow personality and maintains personal contact with His creatures through the personality circuit.

universe The creation of a Creator Son and Creative Daughter. There are 700,000 local universes in the grand universe. Each universe is subdivided into 100 constellations. Each constellation is divided into 100 local systems. Each system is destined to have 1,000 inhabited evolutionary planets. Our local universe of Nebadon is a relatively young universe and is far from finished. Urantia has seven cosmic families from four different universes: Nebadon, Avalon, Wolvering, and Fanoving.

Universe Father A Creator Son of a local universe. Christ Michael of Nebadon is our Universe Father and was created by the Universal Father and the Eternal Son on Paradise.

Universe Mother Spirit A Creative Daughter, created by the Infinite Spirit. A Universe Mother Spirit is a co-creator of a local universe and complementary polarity to a Creator Son.

universe supervisors See Celestial Overcontrol.

Urantia The cosmic name of our planet. Urantia is planet number 606 in the system of Satania, in the constellation of Norlatiadek, in the universe of Nebadon, in the superuniverse of Orvonton. Urantia is the planet that Michael of Nebadon chose among all the planets in His universe for His seventh bestowal as a human mortal.

Urantia movement A term designating variously organized readers of *The URANTIA Book*.

Urantians Ascending sons and daughters whose planet of origin is Urantia. Most people on this planet fall into this category and are souls who are experiencing their very first life. There is also a group of Urantians who are here for the second time.

Vicegerent First Ambassadors See Ambassadors.

Vicegerent First Assistants See Assistants.

Vicegerent Second Assistants See Assistants.

vortex A New-Age term for energy reflective circuit.

walk-in In New-Age understanding, a walk-in is a soul who takes over the body completely and the previous soul leaves. Since 1989 no soul ever really leaves a body, even if a fallen or rebellious entity comes in whose sole purpose is to teach false teachings mixed with just enough truth to deceive, if possible, even the very elect of God. No beings of light have spoken through anyone but Gabriel of Urantia/TaliasVan of Tora since 1989.

Wolvering Name of a neighboring universe. Some of the fourth-order starseed on Urantia are repersonalized starseed who partook in the Lucifer Rebellion but are originally from Wolvering and are here for the adjudication.

About The
Audio Fusion Material Complement
Gabriel of Urantia / TaliasVan of Tora

Gabriel of Urantia/TaliasVan of Tora has been an ardent student of metaphysical/spiritual truth for more than thirty years. Born in Pittsburgh, Pennsylvania, he studied theology at Duquesne University and became one of the first students involved in the charismatic renewal of the Catholic Church, exploring priesthood in Benedictine and Franciscan monasteries in three states.

He has worked as an ordained minister and counselor at various spiritual communities across the United States, including the Nicky Cruz/Teen Challenge organization and Youth with a Mission in Hollywood, California. On the campus of the University of Arizona, he founded a student spiritual organization and became a volunteer chaplain of the Pima County Sheriff's Department in southern Arizona. For eleven years he worked with the homeless and destitute by providing shelter and counseling. He has explored the writings of all major religions, denominations, and metaphysical sects. After becoming a Reiki Master, he progressed on to *The URANTIA Book* and became the vessel to bring through the Continuing Fifth Epochal Revelation (*The Cosmic Family* volumes).

Gabriel of Urantia/TaliasVan of Tora was a human Planetary Prince of several worlds in other universes, with the title Melfax. His story on this world goes back 500,000 years to the staff of the fallen former Planetary Prince, Caligastia, at which time the soul of Gabriel/TaliasVan was the soul of Van—the loyal supermortal who stood firmly against the Rebellion (see *The URANTIA Book*, pages 759–760). Throughout history his soul has returned to Urantia with the soul of his complement, Niánn Emerson Chase, to start many spiritual renaissances, which include those of Ikhnaton (Akhenaten), Pharaoh of

Egypt; Peter, the apostle; Francis of Assisi; and Martin Luther, to name but a few.

Presently, Gabriel of Urantia/TaliasVan of Tora is a level-nine audio fusion material complement for the Chief Executive of our local universe, the Bright and Morning Star of Salvington/Gabriel of Salvington. As Gabriel of Salvington's material complement, Gabriel/TaliasVan holds the Mandate of the Bright and Morning Star, which is a multidimensional, superuniverse, broadcast-circuit link that various celestial personalities are permitted to use and speak through. A human audio fusion material complement is the highest form of interplanetary and interdimensional communication. Some would call these special fusion appearances a "walk in."

Gabriel of Urantia/TaliasVan of Tora is the head human administrator of the Divine Administration as well as being considered one of the most ascended spiritual teachers and leaders on our planet. As a serious, disciplined student of scientific fact and theory, he has become a theoretical physicist. Gabriel/TaliasVan is in contact with and is currently being used by celestial personalities to bring through the Continuing Fifth Epochal Revelation that is a continuation of the 196 Papers of *The URANTIA Book*. These continuing papers, collectively known as *The Cosmic Family* volumes, are fundamental as a basis for understanding the current state of our planet and our relationship to the physics of rebellion, ascension science, and the cosmic community.

Gabriel of Urantia/TaliasVan of Tora and his highest spiritual complement, Niánn Emerson Chase, founded Divine Administration in 1989 and are Global Community Communications Alliance's spiritual leaders. He is the author of many books and is the Audio Fusion Material Complement of *The Cosmic Family* volumes.

He is also an accomplished songwriter/singer/performer. He pioneered the first New Age "Vocal" album, *Unicorn Love*, in 1985. Now he has introduced another unique style of music, CosmoPop®, to the world, performing major outdoor concerts nationwide. As of the publishing of this book, TaliasVan has produced seven CDs and on-going is in the recording studio working on future albums and projects. He has an award-winning concert DVD (which won an Aurora Award Gold Award for "Musical Live Concert") featuring his accomplished eleven-piece band, The Bright & Morning Star Band.

Gabriel of Urantia/TaliasVan of Tora lives with his present wife, TiyiEndea, and his family at Avalon Organic Gardens & EcoVillage. TiyiEndea is also a spiritual complement and past-life wife of many lives, and she is from the universe of Fanoving. His family includes his four children SanSkritA, DeleVan, Amadon (with Niánn Emerson Chase), and Ellanora DesManae (with TiyiEndea).

About The Audio Fusion Process

Audio fusion is a fusion between a celestial being and a mortal, a fusion of one entity with another in the complete aonic-to-cellular reality of the human being. The fusion takes place within the particle reality of the life force of the human being. The celestials co-exist within the life force and soul of the human being, and the existing soul does not leave the body. However, the human soul is in the aonic level and is just listening, and the celestial being is in control of the entire body, from the ultimatonic level to the cellular. The dominant celestial being (in this case, Paladin the finaliter) usually comes and goes in the human being several times per day and can stay in for hours at a time, even days at a time if necessary.

Audio fusion is a gradual process over many years, and the higher the virtue of the chosen vessel, the higher the fusion and the higher the celestial being who can come through for longer periods of time, therefore the higher level of revelation that can be brought through. There can only be one Audio Fusion Material Complement on any one planet. The Bright and Morning Star comes periodically to teach for a few hours. Paladin, Chief of Finaliters, fuses with Gabriel of Urantia/ TaliasVan of Tora several times per day.

No beings of light have spoken through anyone by the process of channeling (their voice coming out of the human's mouth, which is not audio fusion) since 1989. Gabriel of Urantia/TaliasVan of Tora is the Audio Fusion Material Complement on Urantia. With audio channeling, the celestial being is not fused with the human. The celestial being uses the vocal chords of the human and projects their voice through the human from outside the body, much like the method of electronic radio communication or the use of a microphone through an amplifier. In this case, the human's vocal chords are the amplifier.

Audio Fusion Material Complements are used to bring through epochal revelation and to learn that revelation and hear it, as opposed to being in a sleep state, like Edgar Cayce. At this time (Summer 2013) Gabriel of Urantia/TaliasVan of Tora is a Level Nine Audio Fusion Material Complement.

Concerning Van — TaliasVan

"Van" is also pronounced as "Son/Sen" on the planet Tora of Avalon, the local universe of which the Pleiades is part. Van of the Caligastia One Hundred in Dalamatia was actually TaliasVan, meaning of the universe of Avalon and of the Creator Son of Avalon, TaliasSon. On Urantia the name later became Taliesen and Taliesin in the Arthurian legends of ancient Glastonbury (also rightfully known as Avalon). It seems that the suffix "sin" was adopted to explain the fall from the universe of Avalon of the fourth-order starseed and TaliasVan's role in the adjudication of the Lucifer Rebellion on Urantia.

King Arthur of Camelot (the once and future king) was also known as TaliasVan, also pronounced Taliesen—a name Arthur correctly thought was of his ancestry, but he had no idea it was his cosmic name. TaliasVan was a Planetary Prince of his home planet, Tora, Avalon (Pleiades). He also was a Planetary Prince of three other planets of three other universes. He had many repersonalizations (incarnations) on Urantia in which he started spiritual renaissances.

The prefix "Dele" in front of a name on Tora of Avalon means "of the ancestry line of." DeleVin would mean "of the daughters of Van." DeleVan would mean "of the sons of Van." On higher worlds where more efficient genetic ancestral records are kept, an ascending son could have the higher genetic link to the first trisector family of the first cosmic mother. Therefore his name would be DeleVin/Van and not DeleVan. On Urantia the word Van is often used in the last name of many ancestral links without the full knowledge that this is an ancestral link to the descendants of Van himself.

In Van's present life his maternal grandmother's ancestry was English and the genetic line actually goes back to ancient Glastonbury (Avalon). From his paternal grandfather comes the line of the Amadonites of Urantia. Thus Van's son in this life is Amadon Dell Erba in Italian, which means "of the grass or earth." *The URANTIA Book* says: "What of Amadon of Urantia [Earth], does he still stand unmoved?" [p. 762]

TaliasVan's name was shortened to Van when he came to Urantia to serve with the Caligastia One Hundred, which was revealed in the first one-tenth of the Fifth Epochal Revelation, known as *The URANTIA Book*, which primarily discusses the ascension plan of Nebadon and the first-light souls of native Urantians. He would discover his identity and his point of origin when he was chosen to become an audio fusion material complement for Continuing Fifth Epochal Revelation as TaliasVan of Tora/Avalon with the mandate in Nebadon from the Creator Son Christ Michael. The Continuing Fifth Epochal Revelation is for the fourth-order starseed to begin to reawaken their memory circuitry.

The Mandate of the Bright and Morning Star also has to deal with the adjudication of all those who fell in the Rebellion. Who should rightfully have this mandate other than the loyal Van of the Caligastia One Hundred? A new name was given to him, the same as the firstborn son and first administrator of Nebadon, Gabriel of Salvington. Therefore, TaliasVan of Tora became Gabriel in 1985 and Gabriel of Sedona in 1990. He is presently known as Gabriel of Urantia.

Sedona, Arizona, USA was the archangels' headquarters of Urantia and had been since before 1989. It was in 1989 that this energy reflective circuit area became the fifth-dimensional and above headquarters of the administration of the present Planetary Prince, Machiventa Melchizedek, upon the arrival of the Mandate of the Bright and Morning Star to Sedona. When the Mandate of the Bright and Morning Star moved to Tubac/Tumacácori, Arizona in 2009, it became the new headquarters of the archangels, Machiventa Melchizedek the present Planetary Prince, the Mandate of the Bright and Morning Star, and Divine Administration.

Gabriel of Urantia's/TaliasVan of Tora's SERVICE MINISTRY EXPERIENCE

Duquesne University
Pittsburgh, Pennsylvania

- One of the first students at Duquesne University to be involved in the Charismatic Catholic Renewal, which led to an acquaintance with Maria Von Trapp and daughters (of *The Sound of Music* fame). Agatha Von Trapp became a personal spiritual mentor. A framed letter from her hangs in my office and states:

    > 'Wait on the Lord' is my advice to you and let Jesus handle all your affairs. They could be in no better hands. Wishing you all the blessings of the Lord's resurrection.
    >
    > **— Agatha Von Trapp**

- Attended Notre Dame University for seminar and convention with 3,000 charismatic priests and 30,000 laymen from all over the world
- Ordained for the first time with United Brethren Evangelical, under Rev. Carlton Pearce
- Attended Catholic charismatic meetings
- Led Bible studies for all denominations within charismatic renewal, student of Rev. Russell Bix
- Wrote articles for a Catholic charismatic magazine, *The Body Builder*

Katherine Kuhlman Ministries
Pittsburgh, Pennsylvania

- Bible student
- Received additional instruction from my personal spiritual advisor, Katherine Kuhlman
- Received certificate of completion for Voice of Prophecy Home Bible Study Course

Hebrew Christian Center (Messianic Jewish Ministry)
Pittsburgh, Pennsylvania

- Bible student
- Received additional biblical instruction in Old and New Testaments from my Israeli personal spiritual advisor, Ruth Harris

Holy Trinity Benedictine Monastery
St. Davids, Arizona

- Attended as a brother initiate, under Abbot Father Lewis

Pecos New Mexico Benedictine Monastery
Pecos, New Mexico

- Attended for a several-week study on becoming a spiritual advisor, under Abbot David Garretts
- Studied Jungian psychology and dream analysis

Franciscan Third Order Community
Montrose, Colorado

- Attended Franciscan Third Order Community and first learned of sustainable building and dome construction

Nicky Cruz Organization (Halfway Houses)
Huntington, West Virginia & Fayetteville, North Carolina

- Counselor (1 year)
- Consulted with Nicky Cruz (of the movie and book *The Cross and The Switchblade* fame) on several occasions

Lost and Found Ministries
4th Avenue, Tucson, Arizona
—Founded by Ministers Pete and Mary Peterson

- Counselor (1 year)

CENTRUM of Hollywood
Hollywood, California

- Counselor with 24-hour help line
- Director of Hollywood Free Theater (that was to be opened on Hollywood Boulevard). Was selected over many applicants by the Board, which included Pat Boone, Catherine B. DeMill Quinn (Cecil B. DeMill's daughter and Anthony Quinn's wife), and Kleg Seth (Man-of-the-Year Award by Hollywood Chamber of Commerce and Director of CENTRUM), to name just three among other celebrities.

Youth with a Mission
Dallas (Walnut Hills/Bill Francis, Director) & Tyler, Texas

- Student trades craftsman
- Counselor
- Street ministry
- Consulted with Keith Green, Director of Last Days Ministries and musician
- Counseled with and received a life prophecy from Reverend David Wilkerson of Teen Challenge Programs. This handwritten prophecy is framed and hangs in my office:

> *You have need of patience after you have done the will of the Father, that you might receive the promise.*
>
> *Be not denied. God is not mocked, whatsoever a man soweth, that he shall also reap. You have sown the seed you will reap in God's time.*
>
> *No weapon formed against you shall prosper. Greater is He that is within you than he that is within the world.*
>
> *If you do that which is right, who is he that can harm you?*
>
> — **Reverend David Wilkerson**

Son Light Ministries
630 N. 4th Avenue, Tucson, Arizona

- Established first nonprofit organization and halfway house
- Ordained second time by Pastor Maynard Weisbrod of Calvary Evangelistic Center and Rev. David P. Strickland
- Spiritual Advisors
    - Rev. Tex Young, Jesus Fellowship
    - Rev. Ken Miles, Tucson Christian Fellowship
    - Rev. Gilbert Garcia, Son Life Church, Inc.
    - Rev. Gil Sandoval, Son Life Church, Inc.
- Worked with Pima County Jail pretrial release program under Director David Strickland, Department of Economic Security
- Volunteer Chaplain, Pima County Sheriff's Department for the County Jail (1977–1982), Reverend Dan Burgoyne, Head of Chaplain and affiliated with Grace Chapel Church

PHOTO GALLERY

Gabriel of Urantia (age 24) with Pennsylvania Governor Milton Shapp, 1970

Gabriel of Urantia, artist Ted DeGrazia and former wife Jerri, 1977.

Gabriel of Urantia with David & Julie Strickland and Mrs. Ghandi (right) in Tucson • 1977

Gabriel of Urantia and then wife Jerri (far left), with Fred and Dot Brown at the Prayer House in Tucson • 1980

Gabriel of Urantia with Duane Faw
URANTIA Book S.W. Conference in Scottsdale, Arizona • 1988

Gabriel of Urantia in 1994 with Titus, the oldest living Hopi elder who passed away at age 101 two weeks later.

Niánn Emerson Chase, Lakota Elder Wallace Black Elk, and Gabriel of Urantia in Sedona, Arizona • May 5, 2001

Gabriel of Urantia with American Indian Movement (AIM) founders Harry Charger (far left) and Clyce Bellecourt (far right) • 2001

Gabriel of Urantia and Dennis Banks (Co-founder of American Indian Movement) January 2004

Gabriel of Urantia with Nancy Red Star, Native American Author of *Star Ancestors* • May 2004

Gabriel of Urantia and Russell Means, American Indian Activist & Actor • March 2007

Our annual Earth Harmony Festival. EarthHarmonyFestival.org

Our children are eager to learn organic gardening methods.

Beautiful landscaping around our EcoVillage homes is irrigated by greywater.

Cal-Earth dome homes at Avalon Organic Gardens & EcoVillage

Children's theater rehearsal on our outdoor stage on a warm spring morning.

A lush oasis outside several of our EcoVillage homes.

Spring crops outside one of our greenhouses are surrounded by raised herb and flower beds.

Greenhouses help extend the growing season.

A Hands-in-the-Soil morning at Avalon Organic Gardens & EcoVillage

Preserving food diversity through the cultivation of White Sonora Wheat, one of the oldest surviving wheat varieties in North America.

Some of our beautiful horses and donkey grazing at Avalon Organic Gardens.

Our dairy goat herd provides plenty of delicious organic milk and cheese.

Our frisky llamas contributing to our pasture management.

Planting lettuce and enjoying the morning air at Avalon Organic Gardens & EcoVillage.

Solar-powered egg mobiles provide shelter for our free-range chicken flock.

Hope Home, a cozy pond-side guest cottage.

Yurts are used as school houses for Global Community Communications Schools For Teens & Children.

Our sacred tipi, painted by the CosmoArtists.

Eco-friendly metal grain silos.

A 5,000 gallon water tank stores harvested rainwater outside our solarium and bath house.

Solar panels provide shade to our workshops.

Catfish ponds under construction next to our food forest.

A greenhouse provides a lush entry to a bath house. Roof-top solar panels are used for water heating.

Avalon Organic Gardens & EcoVillage

Niánn Emerson Chase and Gabriel of Urantia
Founders of Global Community Communications Alliance

Santeen, Gabriel of Urantia, and Niánn Emerson Chase • 2005

Gabriel of Urantia's Family
(from left to right) daughters Ellanora DesManae and DeleVan, wife TiyiEndea, son-in-law TaliSeen (DeleVan's husband), Gabriel of Urantia, son Amadon of Urantia, Niánn Emerson Chase, daughter SanSkrita

Gabriel of Urantia with daughter Ellanora DesManae and wife TiyiEndea

Gabriel of Urantia and Amadon of Urantia

ACKNOWLEDGMENTS
Third Edition

I first would like to thank Niánn Emerson Chase, who typed and retyped my first drafts, corrected misspellings, grammar, and so on. Not only am I blessed to have such a wonderful, spiritual complement as Niánn with me, but it is also a fact that—with a degree in education and literature and more than forty years of teaching experience—she has also been a great blessing in assisting me in the preparation of this book and the transmissions that are presented in *The Cosmic Family* volumes.

Thanks to all the donors, in particular BenDameean (Daniel) Steinhardt, who so generously gave to help finance the publishing costs. Celestial Overcontrol said that BenDameean was Benjamin of the twelve sons of Jacob and much loved by Joseph, his full brother by Jacob and Rachel. There have been numerous validations of this information by Overcontrol, since it was given, over the years.

Thanks also to all present community members for showing up here at the First Planetary Sacred Home from all over the world to help in this great spiritual work. My thanks also to LaTaYea Calviero, for proofreading and other labors of love, and to all cosmic family members for all of their labors of love in doing the little things that they do that free me and enable me to make things like this book possible. And my appreciation to Ionia Redman for all her work in book layout and design.

Finally, my heartfelt thanks and gratitude to all my unseen but ever present celestial family and friends who have taught us so much in such a short period of time and who have truly set me on a higher path to our Universal Father.

About The CosmoArtists And Their Art In This Book

Ausmaminae

Life Pattern
(page xiv)

Original:
acrylic paint and art glass on board

Ausmaminae grew up down under in Australia. Her name means "artistic expression of Eternal Mother Spirit," and her life has been an exploration of creativity that has taken on different forms, in the mediums of the culinary, literary, musical, and visual arts. She has been drawn to the visual arts both as an artist and art appreciator since childhood, and—like the mediums of cooking and singing—creating visual art is a process for her of blending the flavors and spices of color and texture, weaving the poetic nuances of line and curve, shading subtleties of tone and emotions into a composition.

At age sixteen Ausmaminae studied for two years at a fine arts college in Australia, which gave her a taste of different mediums from painting and sketching to photography and design. Her artistic experience over the years has been in freelance design work.

She shared, "As I explore working in the fine arts, I am motivated in the discovery of mixed mediums, primarily combining the elements of glass and paints on panel. I am excited by the challenge to merge and harmonize these two very different elements with the goal of depicting synthesis, movement and continuity, combining realism with the abstract; integrating dimensions of emotions, thoughts, and spirituality."

Auneea

Reflective Circuit
(page xxviii)

Original:
acrylic on paper

New Zealand-born artist Auneea attributes launching her story-telling art to a period of solitude she experienced while living alone in the countryside of New Zealand, allowing her to tap into a passion and creativity she had not previously experienced as an artist.

The canvas for her paintings at the time varied from the walls and floor of her dwelling to cow skulls. Auneea connected to an earthly, native leading—ranging from Native American to local New Zealand Maori cultures. She found stories she could express in acrylics that came from somewhere deep within and experienced her art as a healing discovery.

During the last nearly two decades of working in the CosmoArt Studio[SM], she has used mainly acrylic, oil, and colored pencil. Auneea believes "Art is certainly a powerful tool to reach out to the soul, giving a message of hope—visions of the past, present, and future."

Willowela

Rainbow Woman
(page 144)

Original:
mixed medium on paper

    CosmoArtist Willowela blends a variety of mediums including acrylics, airbrush, pastels, and various oil and water-based pencils to create her modern art nouveau collection Cosmic Visages.
    Growing up in Southern England where landscapes are richly diverse with ancient woodlands and Jurassic coastlines, and as she traveled with her family throughout Europe as well as venturing to Northern Africa, she fell in love with the many cultures and peoples where art was an integral part of their lives. After moving to Canada, she furthered her artistic endeavors, finally landing in the United States where she continues her discovery and personal unfoldment in the arts.
    Willowela's art is inspired by the universal variance of personality and its many moods of expression, which she passionately captures in her stylized profiles, where she creates subtle blends of color infused with texture and a sensitivity to line and curve.

Collaborative artwork by

CosmoArtists

Starmotion
(page 198)

Original:
acrylic on board

CosmoArt — Visual Art For Global Change

The four art pieces in this book were produced by CosmoArtists through the CosmoArt Studio[SM], a nonprofit program of Global Community Communications Alliance, which is a multi-dimensional, multi-media art studio in Tucson, Arizona, where a unique blend of artists fuse their talents and skills to work as a unified team to bring visual symmetry and beauty to your environment. The CosmoArtists strive to harmonize visual complements of divine beauty with spiritual revelation. They seek to affect global change by helping one another unlock our perceptual doorways to higher dimensions by creating visual global imagery and messages supporting the Spiritualution[SM] movement, an international spiritual revolution movement started by Gabriel of Urantia/TaliasVan of Tora. CosmoArtists aim to bring mindal and soul harmony through visual divine pattern into the lives of those millions suppressed by evil forces. Their work can also be seen at the Out of the Way Galleria in Tubac Art Colony, Arizona.

For more information on prints or purchasing original color art please contact the CosmoArt Studio[SM]

Commission Work • Inquiries Welcome
Homeowners, Architects, Designers, Consultants

Studio open to the public — 330 E. 7th Street, Tucson, Arizona

Please call for more info on gallery showings,
classes, and other art events.

(520) 490-2554 or visit www.theseaofglass.org
info@cosmoart.org

Global Community Communications Alliance and Divine Administration

Global Community Communications Alliance is a church supporting: a religious order and EcoVillage of 100+ international members living in community (with thousands of local and international supporters), Avalon Organic Gardens & EcoVillage, Personality Integration Rehabilitation Program for Teens and Adults, Global Family Legal Services, and many other ministries listed below. In addition Global Community Communications Alliance's supporting nonprofit organizations—Soulistic Medical Institute and Global Change Multi-Media—also support ministry programs listed below.

Founded in 1989 by Gabriel of Urantia/TaliasVan of Tora (gabrielofurantia.info, gabrielofurantia.net, gabrielofurantia.com, gabrielofurantia.org) and Niánn Emerson Chase (niannemersonchase.org), Global Community Communications Alliance is located in southern Arizona in the charming, historic southwest towns of Tubac and Tumacácori—a sacred area known for centuries as "the Palm of God's Hand."

Find out more about our many local and global-related humanitarian efforts, services, and church programs:

Ministry Programs of Global Community Communications Alliance

Worldwide Sunday Services[SM]
Open to the public.
(520) 603-9932

Avalon Organic Gardens & EcoVillage[SM]
185-acre farm and ranch in southern Arizona, using
spiritually-based principles and permaculture practices.
Community Supported Agriculture (CSA) provider.
avalongardens.org • (520) 603-9932

Personality Integration Rehabilitation Program[SM]
for Teens and Adults
Assisting socially-disappointed souls
in their psychospiritual healing process.
pirp.info • (520) 603-9932

Friendly Hands Vocational Training[SM]
Spiritual Training Apprenticeship Programs in
a wide range of career fields.
(520) 603-9932

Global Family Legal Services[SM]
Legal aid in various fields focusing on immigration
for low-income individuals and families in need.
globalfamilylegalservices.org
(520) 398-3388 or (928) 282-2590

Spirit Steps[SM] **Tours**
Offering enlightening tours for the seeking
sojourner and eco-tourist.
spiritsteps.org
Toll-free (866) 508-0094
(520) 398-2655 or (928) 282-4562

Global Community Communications Schools of
Ascension Science & The Physics of Rebellion[SM]
Teachings from the Continuing Fifth Epochal Revelation,
The URANTIA Book and *The Cosmic Family* volumes.
gccschools.org • (520) 603-9932

Global Community Communications Schools for Teens and Children℠

The only school on the planet for teens and children incorporating the soul's point of universe origin and soul age, enabling the child to be guided into their correct destiny at a much younger age, bringing much earlier actualization, fulfillment, and self-confidence to the child.
gccschools.org • (520) 603-9932

Out of the Way Galleria℠

An eclectic blend of created art contributed by local artisans and donors.
outofthewaygalleria.org • (520) 398-9409

Sacred Treasures℠

Clothing (men's & women's), arts & crafts
330 E. 7th Street, Tucson (4th Avenue area)
Sacred-Treasures.org • (520) 624-4418

Planetary Family Services℠

Provides services to create, embellish, and bring Godly energy to your home environment.
planetaryfamilyservices.org
(520) 403-4207

Alternative Voice™

Quarterly periodical that addresses the many crises of our world, fusing spirituality with activism.
alternativevoice.org • (520) 603-9932

Supporting Nonprofit Organizations

Soulistic Medical Institute℠ & Soulistic Hospice℠
Offers healthcare by professionals whose expertise involves various healing modalities that encompass the soul, mind, and body.
soulisticmedicalinstitute.org • (520) 398-3970
soulistichospice.org • (520) 398-2333

Global Change Multi-Media℠
globalchangemultimedia.org
(520) 398-2542

Divisions of Global Change Multi-Media:

The Sea Of Glass — Center For The Arts℠
Venue – Music – Art – Dance – Multi Media – Theater – Healing Arts
Nonprofit organization
330 E. 7th Street, Tucson (4th Avenue area)
TheSeaOfGlass.org • (520) 490-2554

Future Studios℠
Recording studio.
futurestudios.org • (520) 398-2542

CosmoArt Studio℠
See artists' works-in-progress & art
330 E. 7th Street, Tucson (4th Avenue area)
CosmoArt.org • (520) 490-2554

Global Change Music℠
Nonprofit record label offers musicians recording opportunities using professional world-class equipment for voice and instrumental training.
globalchangemusic.org • (520) 398-2542

The Musicians That Need To Be Heard Network℠
Provides opportunities for musicians to communicate their music messages without spiritual compromise.
musiciansnet.org • (520) 398-2542

Global Change Television℠
Internet television station with a variety of programs of spiritual content, on demand.
globalchangetelevision.org
(520) 398-2542

Global Change Radio℠
Internet radio station offering on-demand audio webcasts, including talk radio on various religious and social themes.
globalchangeradio.org • (520) 398-2542

Music & Films at The Main Stage, Tubac and The Sea Of Glass,℠ Tucson
Working with filmmakers and distributors of independent, activist, and educational films and documentaries that motivate spiritually thought-provoking group dialogue for the public.
Booking national and international bands.
(520) 398-2542

Global Change Theater Company℠
Dedicated to writing, performing, and staging plays and various higher-consciousness, inspirational, dramatic productions where students receive training and opportunities to participate in theatrical shows and workshops.
(520) 398-2542

Global Change Multi-Media Distribution Company[SM]
Distributes music, DVDs, books, magazines, and any product that would be considered by its parent company to be a Global Change Tool for the dissemination of revelation and spiritually-uplifting information through media materials.

Global Change Multi-Media Productions[SM]
Professional audio, video, and Internet service producing spiritual and educational message media, via Internet video streaming, live webcasting, graphic design, and CD and video/DVD media production.
(520) 398-2542

Global Community Communications Publishing[SM]
Publishing continuing epochal revelation and related materials as well as Global Change Teachings and other spiritually-oriented texts.
gccpublishing.org • (520) 603-9932

Ministry Supporters

Avalon Slow Food Enterprises presents

Food For Ascension[SM] Café
A farm-to-table restaurant featuring plant-based foods, juices & teas.
330 E. 7th Street, Tucson (4th Avenue area)
FoodForAscension.org • (520) 882-4736

Global Community Communications Alliance

P.O. Box 4910, Tubac, AZ 85646 USA
(520) 603-9932

e-mail: info@gccalliance.org
gccalliance.org
globalchangetools.org

SEMINARS, WORKSHOPS & INTERNSHIPS

Earth Harmony Sustainability Seminars, Internships, & Workshops:

Green Building, Permaculture, Using Greenhouses To Extend The Growing Season, & Organic Gardening

- On survival in the near future, organic gardening, and the nuts and bolts of building an EcoVillage.

Held at Avalon Organic Gardens & EcoVillage in Tumacácori, Arizona
or
Held in your city

Contact (520) 603-9932
email: info@avalongardens.org
http://avalongardens.org

http://avalongardens.org/learn/seminars

Divine Administration Seminars
(for serious spiritual seekers)

- Weather Changes – Social – Political & Economic Disasters in Relationship to the Adjudication of the Bright & Morning Star versus Lucifer
- Protected and Safe Areas
- Could you be a Destiny Reservist?
- What is Epochal Revelation & the Importance of It?
  presented by Gabriel of Urantia and Niánn Emerson Chase
- Ascension Science and the Physics of Rebellion
  presented by Dr. Landau Lawrence, M.D.
- Starseed children in our midst: A case for multi-soul-age classrooms
  presented by Dr. Len'Mana Lee, Ed.D.
- Group encounter of the cosmic family
  presented by Dr. Marayeh Cunningham, Ph.D. Clinical Psychologist

Held at Avalon Organic Gardens & EcoVillage
in Tumacácori, Arizona

Contact (520) 603-9932
email: info@gccalliance.org
http://gccalliance.org

http://gccalliance.org/divine-administration-seminars

ALLIANCE ORGANIZATIONS

ARANNOGALES (ASOCIACION DE REFORESTACION EN AMBOS NOGALES)

A joint effort of various organizations from both Nogales, Sonora and Nogales, Arizona who are dedicated to improving the quality of the air and the environment by re-establishing native vegetation.

BORDERLANDS HABITAT RESTORATION INITIATIVE

A grassroots effort to maintain and enhance biodiversity in the Sky Island borderlands by first restoring physical processes, like stream flow, and then focusing on native plants and their pollinators that form the base of the "food chain" on which all other species depend. Avalon Organic Gardens is hosting workshops and setting up educational demonstration sites with them.

COCHISE COMMUNITY COLLEGE

College students, as part of their "Sustainability Course," have come for several years for their education and credits for workshops with Avalon Organic Gardens & EcoVillage.

COMMUNITY FOOD BANK OF SOUTHERN ARIZONA

Avalon Organic Gardens participates in events and farmers markets as community foods consignment program, as well as networking with them to improve community food security by promoting, demonstrating, advocating for, and collaboratively building an equitable and regional food system. The Community Food Bank supports farms, home gardening, farmers' markets, and youth programs that provide nutritional locally-grown foods and know-how to individuals and families interested in growing their own food. We became certified and are able to accept FMNP (Farmers Market Nutrition Program) Vouchers and SFMNP (for seniors), WIC (Arizona Supplemental Nutrition Program for Women, Infants, and Children) Vouchers, and SNAP (Supplemental Nutrition Assistance Program a.k.a. food stamps).

COSECHANDO BIENESTAR

Cosechando Bienestar (Harvesting Wellbeing) is a new initiative in Nogales, Arizona to promote the production, consumption, and awareness of local, healthy foods. The program promotes home and community gardens, the new Nogales Mercado and other food enterprises. Community Garden Leaders will receive in-depth instruction in gardening and food production led by Avalon Organic Gardens. Community Garden Leaders will work closely with staff at Mariposa Community Health Center (MCHC) to educate Nogales residents about vegetable gardening and food production.

FORGOTTEN POLLINATORS CAMPAIGN

Founded by Gary Nabhan, faculty member at the University of Arizona and an internationally-celebrated nature writer, food and farming activist, and proponent of conserving the links between biodiversity and cultural diversity. In 1995, The Arizona-Sonora Desert Museum, where Gary served as Director of Science, launched the Forgotten Pollinators Campaign, which helped focus international interest on threatened interactions between plants and their pollinators. Avalon Organic Gardens works closely with Gary and is dedicated to educating people on the vital role pollinators play, offering workshops held at Avalon Organic Gardens & EcoVillage, including presenters such as Gary and Paul Kaiser.

FRIENDS OF THE SANTA CRUZ RIVER (FOSCR)

Preserving the flow, water quality, and banks. Two of our community members sit on this Board.

MEXICAYOTL ACADEMY

Charter school in Nogales and Tucson that emphasizes Montessori philosophy, interculturlism, character leadership skills, and traditional dance. The children of Global Community Communications Schools For Teens & Children have interacted with their children and put on youth forums together. Avalon Organic Gardens & EcoVillage Master Gardeners and instructors taught students for several years how to garden, which led the Academy to start their own school gardens.

NATIVE SEEDS/SEARCH

Conserves, distributes, and documents the adapted and diverse varieties of agricultural seeds, their wild relatives, and the role these seeds play in cultures of the American Southwest and northwest Mexico.

NOGALES COMMUNITY DEVELOPMENT

Providing support for commercial revitalization and entrepreneurs, and affordable housing for families and individuals in Nogales, Arizona and Santa Cruz County.

PARTNERS FOR SUSTAINABLE POLLINATION

Partners For Sustainable Pollination (PFSP) works with farmers and beekeepers to improve the health of honey bees and support native pollinators. Avalon Organic Gardens has collaborated with Paul Kaiser—a Waldorf-inspired farmer and owner of Singing Frogs Farm in Sebastopol, California and winner of the 2010 Farmer-Rancher Award for the United States from the North

American Pollinator Protection Campaign. Paul, along with Avalon Organic Gardens, are certified for gardeners of Bee Friendly Farming through PFSP.

SABORES SIN FRONTERAS — FLAVORS WITHOUT BORDERS

A regional, bi-national, and multi-cultural alliance to document, celebrate, and conserve farming and food folkways that span the U.S./Mexico borderlands from Texas and Tamaulipas on the east to Ambos Californias on the west.

SONORAN INSTITUTE

Inspiring and enabling community decisions and public policies that respect the land and people of western North America; supporting resilient environmental and economic systems.

SOUTHWEST MARKETING NETWORK

The network's purpose is to help Southwestern producers and communities develop new and improved markets and enterprises and to rebuild local food systems.

TUCSON MEET YOURSELF

A Tucson tradition, "folklife" festival with a focus on presenting artists and communities that carry on living traditions rooted in a group's own definition of identity, artistry, and cultural significance.

SOMAS LA SEMILLA

"We Are The Seed" is a network of grassroots organizations, growers, clinics, and supporters in Arizona-Sonora borderlands creating alternative healthy food systems and sustainable agriculture practices. Avalon

Gardens' Master Gardeners work in conjunction in many projects.

UNIVERSITY OF ARIZONA

Faculty and students have been to Avalon Organic Gardens & EcoVillage for workshops to share and receive information, including with exchange students from South America.

WATERSHED MANAGEMENT GROUP

Watershed Management Group (WMG) develops community-based solutions to ensure the long-term prosperity of people and health of the environment, providing people with the knowledge, skills, and resources for sustainable livelihoods.

WHY HUNGER?

Empowering 8,000+ community-based groups nationally, linking with international organizations advocating basic rights to food, land, water, & sustainable livelihoods. Founded in 1975 by the late musician Harry Chapin and Bill Ayres. Jen Chapin, Harry Chapin's daughter, has been to Avalon Gardens many times and presented workshops.

TO ORDER
globalchangetools.org
or TOLL-FREE 866-282-2205

The Cosmic Family, Volumes I and II
Ascension Science & The Physics of Rebellion

Volume I - 393 pages
paperback $29.95
hardback $39.95

Volume II - 567 pages
paperback $34.95
hardback $49.95

Teachings on Healing
135 pages
paperback $14.95
hardback $19.95

The Sharp End of the Needle
Dealing with Diabetes, Dialysis,
Transplant & The Medical Field
230 pages
paperback $25.95 / hardback $31.95

TO ORDER
globalchangetools.org
or TOLL-FREE 866-282-2205

**Who's Afraid Of
The Big Bad Wolf?**
—A Handbook On How To Defeat The 1%
240 pages
paperback $14.95
hardback $19.95

The Best Of The Film Industry
more than 1,254 film reviews
paperback $13.95

The Real Santa Claus
(in English y en Español)
hardback $19.95

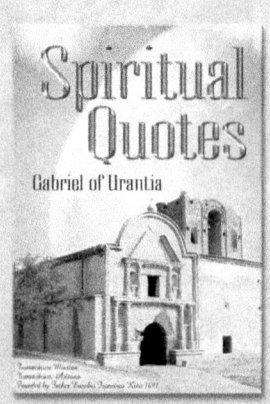

Spiritual Quotes
paperback $9.00

TO ORDER
globalchangetools.org
or TOLL-FREE **866-282-2205**

CosmoPop® Music
Lyrical and Melodic Masterpieces

TALIASVAN
& The Bright & Morning Star Band

Holy City
CosmoRock, CosmoFolk,
& CosmoCountry
65 min $17.99

CosmoPop® music is spiritual vocal music that addresses the sufferings of our times and gives hope for a better world to come.™

CosmoPop Millennium
65 min $17.99

Energy Master CosmoMystic
CD 58 min / DVD 60 min
$21.99 CD and DVD set
$16.99 CD only

CosmoPop Variety
CosmoRock, CosmoFolk,
CosmoMystic, & CosmoCountry
76 min $18.99

Gabriel of Urantia is also known as TaliasVan
& The Bright & Morning Star Band with his music career.

TO ORDER
globalchangetools.org
or TOLL-FREE 866-282-2205

TALIASVAN
& The Bright & Morning Star Band

CosmoPop® Music
Lyrical and Melodic Masterpieces

3-song introduction to
CosmoCountry
19 min $10.99

Tenache 3-song
CosmoNative
32 min $11.99

The God Child Came
Christmas CD
75 min $18.99

Sacred Global CosmoPop Concert DVD 2-disc set
Live at Future Studios in Sedona 2 hr 15 min $22.99

Sedona Sunrise
3 song CosmoPop
CD / DVD set
CD 17 min / DVD 7 min
$11.99

The God Child Came
Christmas Play & CD
CD / DVD set
CD 75 min / DVD 75 min
$22.99

TO ORDER
globalchangetools.org
or TOLL-FREE **866-282-2205**

TALIASVAN'S
40-VOICE BRIGHT & MORNING STAR CHOIR & ORCHESTRA

Cosmo Worship I
58 min $13.99

Cosmo Worship II
72 min $14.99

other GLOBAL CHANGE MUSIC bands

Van'sGuard
False Empire
46 min $15.99

Starseed Acoustic Ensemble
Interuniversal Home
60 min $12.99

Van'sGuard
Live at Avalon Gardens Earth Harmony Festival
3 songs • 30 min
$9.99

Other titles by Gabriel of Urantia/TaliasVan of Tora
available from

Global Community Communications Publishing
A Division of Global Change Multi-Media

The Cosmic Family, Volume I
as transmitted through Gabriel of Urantia/TaliasVan of Tora
Continuing Fifth Epochal Revelation,
Papers 197–228 succeeding *The URANTIA Book.*

The Cosmic Family, Volume II
as transmitted through Gabriel of Urantia/TaliasVan of Tora
Continuing Fifth Epochal Revelation,
Papers 229–261 succeeding *The Cosmic Family, Volume I.*

Messages To Urantia, 1997–2000
as transmitted through Gabriel of Urantia/TaliasVan of Tora
A collection of 19 sacred messages from celestial beings
addressing the state of our world, Urantia.

Teachings On Healing, From A Spiritual Perspective
by Gabriel of Urantia/TaliasVan of Tora and Niánn Emerson Chase
Teachings focused on bringing about healing
on the physical, mental, emotional, and spiritual levels.

*The Best Of The Film Industry
—Movies You Don't Want To Miss!*
compiled by Gabriel of Urantia/TaliasVan of Tora
A detailed list of commentaries and reviews of films
that educate, challenge, and expand the consciousness.

*Making The Most Of Media Exposure For Global Change
Versus Our Experience With The Media*
by Gabriel of Urantia/TaliasVan of Tora and Niánn Emerson Chase
Firsthand account of experiences with corporate-controlled media.

Spiritual Quotes
by Gabriel of Urantia/TaliasVan of Tora
A collection of spiritual insights and wisdom
addressing many of life's facets.

The Real Santa Claus
by Gabriel of Urantia/TaliasVan of Tora
A children's book sharing a unique perspective on
who really is the beloved Santa/St. Nicholas of Christmas.

The Sharp End Of The Needle
by Gabriel of Urantia/TaliasVan of Tora
A compelling story of personal experience with
diabetes, dialysis, kidney transplant, and
the positive and negative aspects of the medical field.

Who's Afraid Of The Big Bad Wolf?
— A Handbook On How To Defeat The 1%
by Gabriel of Urantia/TaliasVan of Tora
A collection of articles addressing deeper issues in
the Occupy / 99% movement with viable solutions.
Includes a wonderful photo gallery
of Global Change Multi-Media attending
Occupy events around the country.

Upcoming Books (Works In Progress)

The Cosmic Family, Volumes III, IV and V

*Spiritual Qualities, Virtues, And Non-Virtues,
And Other Spiritual Critiques*

*Guide To Healing Various Ailments, Based On Symptoms
Of Urantians (New Souls) And Starseed (Older Souls)*

The Fall From The Bright Star

The Food For Ascension™ Cookbook For Urantians And Starseed